Evocative Autoethnography

This comprehensive text is the first to introduce evocative autoethnography as a methodology and a way of life in the human sciences. Using numerous examples from their work and others', world-renowned scholars Arthur Bochner and Carolyn Ellis, originators of the method, emphasize how to connect intellectually and emotionally to the lives of readers throughout the challenging process of representing lived experiences. Written as the story of a fictional workshop, based on many similar sessions led by the authors, it incorporates group discussions, common questions, and workshop handouts. The book:

- describes the history, development, and purposes of evocative storytelling;
- provides detailed instruction on becoming a story-writer and living a writing life;
- examines fundamental ethical issues, dilemmas, and responsibilities;
- illustrates ways ethnography intersects with autoethnography;
- calls attention to how truth and memory figure into the works and lives of evocative autoethnographers.

WRITING LIVES
Ethnographic Narratives

Series Editors
Arthur P. Bochner & Carolyn Ellis
University of South Florida

Writing Lives: Ethnographic Narratives publishes narrative representations of qualitative research projects. The series editors seek manuscripts that blur the boundaries between humanities and social sciences. We encourage novel and evocative forms of expressing concrete lived experience, including autoethnographic, literary, poetic, artistic, visual, performative, critical, multi-voiced, conversational, and coconstructed representations. We are interested in ethnographic narratives that depict local stories; employ literary modes of scene setting, dialogue, character development, and unfolding action; and include the author's critical reflections on the research and writing process, such as research ethics, alternative modes of inquiry and representation, reflexivity, and evocative storytelling. Proposals and manuscripts should be directed to abochner@usf.edu or cellis@usf.edu.

Volumes in this series:

Evocative
Autoethnography

Writing Lives and Telling Stories

Arthur P. Bochner and Carolyn Ellis

Routledge
Taylor & Francis Group

NEW YORK AND LONDON

First published 2016
by Routledge
711 Third Avenue, New York, NY 10017

and by Routledge
2 Park Square, Milton Park, Abingdon, Oxon, OX14 4RN

Routledge is an imprint of the Taylor & Francis Group, an informa business

© 2016 Taylor & Francis

Library of Congress Cataloging in Publication Data
Names: Bochner, Arthur P., author. | Ellis, Carolyn, 1950- author.
Title: Evocative autoethnography : writing lives and telling stories / Arthur
  P. Bochner & Carolyn Ellis.
Description: Walnut Creek, California : Left Coast Press, 2016. | Series:
  Writing lives ; 17 | Includes bibliographical references and index.
Identifiers: LCCN 2015044196| ISBN 9781629582146 (hardback) | ISBN
  9781629582153 (paperback) | ISBN 9781629582160 (Institutional eBook) |
  ISBN 9781629582177 (consumer eBook)
Subjects: LCSH: Ethnology—Biographical methods. | Ethnology—Authorship. |
  BISAC: SOCIAL SCIENCE / General. | SOCIAL SCIENCE / Methodology.
Classification: LCC GN346.6 .B64 2016 | DDC 808.06/692—dc23
LC record available at http://lccn.loc.gov/2015044196

ISBN: 978-1-62958-214-6 (hbk)
ISBN: 978-1-62958-215-3 (pbk)
ISBN: 978-1-315-54541-7 (ebk)

Typeset in Minion Pro
by Hannah Jennings Design

Contents

For Mitch Allen,
who made a difference

Acknowledgments

Special thanks go to Mitch Allen, our publisher at three different presses over 20 years. Thank you, Mitch, for recognizing the promise of autoethnography and providing a publishing home where it could develop and thrive. Thanks go to Norman Denzin for his trust, belief, and steadfast intellectual and emotional support for our project. Thank you, Norman, for establishing a dwelling place for autoethnography and social justice research. Our work and our lives have been nourished and enriched by the friendships we have formed with many colleagues at the International Congress of Qualitative Inquiry, a community of scholars ceaselessly committed to social justice and the gifts of storytelling. We cherish the generosity of spirit and camaraderie we have found at the meetings of the Congress and are grateful for the invaluable learning they have provided. Thanks to Tony Adams, who provided a helpful prepublication review of our book and prepared our index. You have solidified your reputation as an indexer par excellence. We appreciate your passion for and identification with the academic life, in particular autoethnography, and the love and care that we share together.

Thanks to Stephanie Adams, Ryan Harris, and the entire staff at Left Coast Press, Inc., with whom this book was developed; what an amazing group! We appreciate Michael Jennings for his thorough, judicious copy editing, and Hannah Jennings for adding production features that augment and enhance the pedagogical mission of the book. Thanks to Lisa Spinazola for enthusiastically transcribing workshop tapes, and to Nate Hodges, whose ingenious classroom assignments provided valuable data for the chapters on truth and memory, and to Jerry Rawicki for his insights about and participation in our work on compassionate research. To our graduate students at the University of South Florida who have taken our courses on narrative inquiry and autoethnography over the past 25 years, we hope you recognize the many ways you have energized, inspired, and sustained us. We acknowledge, in particular, the individual graduate students we have had the honor of mentoring. Thank you for trusting us with your stories and your lives and keeping our dream going year after year. To the hundreds of participants in workshops we've led around the world, your passion, insight, and enthusiasm made this book possible.

We thank the University of South Florida for providing support, encouragement, and the resources that allowed us to develop an academic home for autoethnographic research and teaching in the human sciences. A sabbatical leave gave us the opportunity to complete this book in a timely fashion without the demands of daily university life.

We are grateful for our colleagues around the globe who are on this journey with us and for our friends and loved ones who fulfill our lives. We are deeply appreciative to have found each other as partners, to share our love and work, and to enjoy so many aspects of our lives together. We relish the companionship and love of Buddha and Zen. Though we often view our research, teaching, and writing as play, still the time has come to take more hikes, go to more parks and beaches, see more movies, read and discuss more novels, and play more fetch. Please, come join in!

Grateful acknowledgment is made to the following presses in which two of our included pieces first appeared: AltaMira Press—a Division of Rowman and Littlefield Publishers, Inc., for "Maternal Connections," and *Qualitative Inquiry*, published by Sage, for "Bird on the Wire: Freeing the Father within Me." We express our thanks for permission to reproduce published materials to: Sage, for "Nine Poems: Marriage and the Family," by Laurel Richardson, published in the *Journal of Contemporary Ethnography*, and to Rowman and Littlefield Publishers, Inc., for an excerpt from "The Same and Different" by Deborah Austin, published in *Composing Ethnography*. Complete citations are included in References.

Imagine a Workshop on Evocative Autoethnography

Imagine that you have an opportunity to take a workshop on autoethnography and personal narrative.

Imagine that the workshop is taught by two instructors who have devoted their academic lives to writing autoethnographic stories and teaching narrative inquiry.

Imagine the workshop invites you to think with the evocative stories you read, reacting and reflecting with all your senses.

Imagine that workshop participants, similar to you, want to learn to write vulnerably about crucial turning points that they've lived through.

Imagine that participants yearn to talk with each other about the goals, methodologies, and creativity of autoethnographic research and writing.

Imagine they want to write stories with raw and naked emotion that investigate life's messiness, including twists of fate and chance.

Imagine that the workshop will provide extended discussion of exemplars designed to teach you how to think with stories.

Imagine being in the presence of other academic researchers who think the human sciences should be relevant to real people leading actual lives, deal with social, ethical, and moral issues, and work on behalf of social justice.

Imagine that you could attend this workshop without leaving home.

~

In this book, we project what you imagine into an actual event at which we present an introduction to evocative autoethnography and narrative forms of representation in the human sciences. Though other useful books on autoethnography have been published, this one is uniquely designed as an introductory, instructor and student user-friendly text. It is suitable for stand-alone undergraduate, M.A., and Ph.D. courses in autoethnography, advanced undergraduate courses on personal storytelling and writing lives, and narrative and qualitative methods classes. Our goal is to provide a hands-on, concrete, and focused guide for instructors who teach and mentor students in autoethnography and for students seeking guidance and practice in writing autoethnography and interpretive ethnography. Although we envision the book as a classroom text, it also should be useful to new or experienced qualitative researchers who want to learn how to include the ethnographic "I" in their research (Ellis, 2004).

Evocative Autoethnography provides a straightforward and systematic treatment of the origins, goals, concepts, genres, methods, aesthetics, ethics, and truth conditions of evocative autoethnography and narrative inquiry. We work through these issues in two extended exemplars that show different ways of situating evocative autoethnography between the social sciences and humanities. Our focus is on the difficult questions students and other scholars confront in developing, writing, responding to, performing, evaluating, and publishing autoethnographic research.

We have been engaged in autoethnographic and narrative writing for more than 25 years. Art introduced a course called "Narrative Inquiry" into the graduate curriculum at the University of South Florida (USF) in 1990 and then a "Writing Workshop" a few years later. At the same time, Carolyn taught personal storytelling in courses such as "Communicating Emotions," "Writing Lives," and "Qualitative Methods," and then began teaching "Autoethnography," which worked in tandem with Art's "Narrative Inquiry."

In January 2001, the two of us were invited to speak at a symposium on "The Arts and Narrative Inquiry" at the University of Art and Design in Helsinki, Finland. The following year we returned to Finland, this time to The Research Centre for Contemporary Culture at the University of Jyväskylä, to present a four-day writing workshop for Ph.D. students from across Finland. The students in that workshop expressed a spirited enthusiasm for the ideals and strategies of "writing as method," using the "first-person voice," and "bringing emotion and subjectivity into the human sciences" that we emphasized in the workshop (see Bochner and Ellis, 2004). Their exuberant responses to the feedback we provided to their research proposals along with the responses we were getting in the courses we were teaching firmly planted the idea in our minds that students, mentors, and new Ph.D.s around the world were thirsting for an opportunity to learn about and practice autoethnographic and narrative inquiry. They inspired us to move forward.

At the first International Congress of Qualitative Inquiry in 2005, we offered a three-hour introductory workshop on autoethnography and narrative to a standing room only crowd. We have continued to offer this workshop at the Congress each year. Those who participate come from many disciplines and countries.[1] They often identify themselves as students in graduate programs with no courses covering autoethnography. Many find it necessary to work with mentors unfamiliar with or unsympathetic toward the creative genres of ethnographic and narrative expression and representation. On quite a few occasions, the mentors also have attended our workshops wanting to learn how they might do a better job of teaching autoethnography and working with students attracted to this genre of research. Young assistant professors make up the bulk of the remaining attendees, though some seasoned researchers also attend. In the last few years, we have started to get second generation students of former participants in the workshop, and participants from creative arts and other humanities programs. The range of countries, ethnicities, races, and sexual identities represented at our workshops continues to widen. We also have presented longer two-, three-, and even five-day versions of this workshop in other locations in the United States, Eastern and Western Europe, China, South Africa, Canada, Australia, New Zealand, and Malaysia.

Though fictional, the workshop we describe in this book is based on those we actually have conducted and on discussions we have held with participants, some of which we transcribed and followed closely while preparing this text. We write this book to meet the needs of the next generation of researchers and storytellers longing for instruction that provides a comprehensive introduction to evocative autoethnography. We bring together in this text what we've learned and tried to teach over the past quarter of a century. This time we include you, the reader, in the discussions we have with students and workshop participants. We hope that we have addressed many of the questions you've been wanting to ask.

Curious? Interested? Eager to enter the conversation? Then turn the page! It's time to begin.

Part One
Origins and History

Coming to Autoethnography

Preparing for the Workshop

"I can't stop thinking about the workshop," Carolyn says to Art. They have just settled into their Illini student union hotel room at the University of Illinois in Urbana, where they will give a workshop on 'Evocative Autoethnography' at the International Congress of Qualitative Inquiry.

Carolyn lies on the bed daydreaming, while Art sits in a chair near the window reading by the descending sunlight that streams through the window. With one hand, he turns the pages of the Congress program; with the other he jots notes, glancing occasionally at the printout resting on his lap that lists workshop participants. Periodically, he stares out the window, feasting on the beauty of the rhododendron, dogwoods, and peonies that dot the campus.

Suddenly Carolyn stands, picks up her workshop folder from the desk, and says, "Let's do a quick review of the outline. We haven't looked at it for several days."

"We've been doing this workshop for a dozen years. We ought to have our act together by now," replies Art, inserting his fingers between pages in the conference program to mark sessions.

"I know. But this one will demand more from us. Instead of three hours, it'll continue for three days."

"That means the pace can be more relaxed. We don't have to rush through topics, and participants will have more opportunities to raise questions. We can feel more at ease."

"That may be true," Carolyn acknowledges. "Though the extended length means we have to be prepared for deeper and more intense discussions of the topics. And we never know who is going to attend the workshop; each group is different."

"That's why I'm checking the program," Art says. Carolyn looks at him inquiringly. "I want to get a feel for the kinds of topics our participants are presenting, which may help us shape our workshop more to their interests."

"Hey, that's a good idea. What have you found?"

"More than a third of the participants are giving autoethnographic talks at the Congress. I saw their names listed on sessions on the professional self, memory, ethics, vulnerability, social justice, performance, and collaborative autoethnography. Some are telling personal stories dealing with race and ethnicity, loss and grief, home and homelessness, caregiving, the body, disability, mental illness, adoption, and divorce. In all, I counted about a hundred papers listed as autoethnographies."

"That's amazing," says Carolyn. "What a difference from when we first started giving these workshops. Remember how participants wanted us to help them justify using stories and the 'I' in their dissertation projects? Some had just stumbled onto autoethnography and wanted to know more about it. But not anymore."

"Now they come already engaged in ongoing autoethnographic research and familiar with the literature. I suspect this year's group will want to discuss how to do autoethnography better," says Art.

"So we can focus more on the ethical intricacies of their research…" offers Carolyn,

"…and how to become better writers and storytellers," Art adds.

"But let's make sure we also speak to those coming to auto-ethnography for the first time, seeking mentors, and asking basic questions."

Art nods. "Of course. We'll still get plenty of those. And they will find mentors here and learn from participants with more experience."

"We'll also get a glimpse from their projects about where autoethnography is headed," says Carolyn.

"Yes. The people in that room tomorrow will be the ones teaching other students and leading future workshops."

"So we better be on point," says Carolyn. "Now, can we get back to the issue of our outline?"

"Okay." Art smiles as he puts down his program and Carolyn hands him a copy of the workshop plan. He appreciates how organized Carolyn is; Carolyn appreciates that Art encourages her not to over-prepare, but instead to trust the interactive moment.

"First, we'll have the participants introduce themselves," Carolyn begins. "Assuming we have time for that with 40 people enrolled."

"The introductions are crucial," Art says. "Part of the value of the workshop is to acquaint autoethnographers with each other. They get to see themselves as a community."

Carolyn nods. "…and view autoethnography as an academic identity."

"I know it takes a lot of time upfront, but getting them to introduce themselves is a good way to start that community building process."

"I agree. Then we'll introduce autoethnography with our personal stories, first me, then you. After that, we'll perform the story of how we met and formulated our joint project,"

Carolyn continues. "Then you'll give your history of the rise of autoethnography. Do you have that part together?"

"Sure, I've composed a whole story on the origins of autoethnography. I think you'll like how I tell it."

"Okay, great," Carolyn nods. "That gets us through the first afternoon."

"Then the next morning, I'll talk about writing and telling evocative stories, with an emphasis on the 'graphy' and 'auto' parts of autoethnography," says Art, "similar to what I've presented before on storytelling, only expanded and more detailed."

"That afternoon participants will read 'Maternal Connections,' which always evokes strong emotions, stories, and questions about vulnerability, ethics, and literary storytelling," says Carolyn. "The experiences and insights participants share in the discussion of this story is one of my favorite parts of our workshops. I learn something new each time.

"The next morning is my session on the quandaries in doing evocative autoethnography ethically," Carolyn continues. "In addition to the usual concerns about our obligations to the other people in our stories, I've added new material on institutional review boards, a topic that always comes up. I'll also talk about how I arrived at the idea of a relational ethics of care and use it in my work with Holocaust survivors. I want participants to think about how to work ethically with research participants.

"In the afternoon, I'll turn to the 'ethno' in evocative autoethnography, ways to integrate ethnographic practices and principles into autoethnographic research, and how to bring autoethnography to ethnographic studies. I'll let participants direct the conversation. They'll break into smaller groups to formulate questions about the three areas of producing, analyzing, and telling stories."

"That sounds a lot like traditional social science—collecting data, analyzing it, and writing it up," Art ribs.

"Sometimes traditional schemes work," Carolyn teases back. "Besides they need to know how to use an autoethnographic perspective in conventional forms of analysis as well as creative analytic practices."

"On the final morning, they'll discuss my story, 'Bird on the Wire,'" Art says, following the outline. "I'll be curious to see how they respond to the conversation I imagine having with my deceased father. I'll give them an opportunity to talk and argue with each other as they think with my story. Afterward, I plan to talk about issues of memory and truth stimulated by that story. I envision that whole morning as a session on evaluating evocative autoethnography."

"Then we'll conclude with our surprise visitors. I can't wait for that."

"I'm excited too. We have a lot to cover in one workshop."

"We do, but it sounds like we're ready," Carolyn says, closing her folder. At that moment, a text comes over Carolyn's and Art's phones simultaneously. They read the message out loud together. "We're at Murphy's Pub. Where are you? We're all here. xxoo, Tony, Keith, Derek, and Mitch."

"Ready or not, looks like the Congress is about to begin, the social part anyway," Carolyn laughs. "Autoethnographers are gathering to socialize, and some of our workshop participants may be there as well. Happy hour at Murphy's! Let's go."

They smile, put on jackets, and rush out into the cool night air.

⁓

After staying out late, Carolyn and Art sleep in the next day and then go for lunch at the Illini Union Café. Deep in their thoughts about the workshop, they study their notes while they drink cappuccino and eat sandwiches. Soon they are greeting autoethnographers who have just arrived. Some are offering or taking other workshops during the next few days; others have arrived to hang out and interact socially with like-minded scholars before the Congress begins. After talking a while, Carolyn and Art excuse themselves from the gathering crowd to make sure they have enough time to find their classroom.

The Workshop Begins

Entering Union 314A, Carolyn and Art glance at the bare side walls of the long narrow room and realize they have forgotten to request an easel. They like to keep their workshop low-tech, with an emphasis on relating personally and spontaneously to participants, not be wedded to PowerPoint presentations. Without an easel, they will have to rely on the white board in the front of the narrow room, seemingly miles from the rows of desks. They put their books and papers on the large conference table in front of the desks and move two chairs behind the table. Then they greet participants as they enter the room.

As soon as most of the 40 registered attendees have arrived, Art begins, "Welcome. We are delighted to meet all of you and to be holding our twelfth Congress workshop on autoethnography. We have a large number of participants today, but this is a big room. We'd appreciate you filling the front rows so we can be closer together. Later, we will change the seating arrangements so that you can see and speak directly to each other."

The attendees slowly follow the directions, then Art continues, "Let's get started. We'd first like you to introduce yourselves briefly. Tell us about your research interests and concerns, particularly as they relate to autoethnography. This will give us a sense of the diversity of places and disciplines you're from, and the scope of the work you're doing. It also will help you get to know each other and identify people with common projects. If you can, relate your project to one that has been described by another participant. We'll take volunteers." Art points to the first hand he sees.

"Hi, everyone. I'm Jennifer, originally from Kenya, and now a postdoctoral research fellow at the Free State University in South Africa in a program on 'Trauma, Forgiveness, and Reconciliation.' I have done a study in Kenya about the importance of continuing bonds for family cancer caregivers. I'd like to write my results as stories and include my experience. Though I love oral storytelling, I have no clue how to write stories. That's why I'm here."

"I, too, am interested in trauma and forgiveness, particularly as they apply to Holocaust survivors," Carolyn replies. "Blake Paxton

(2015), one of my students, recently completed his dissertation on continuous bonds between survivors and the deceased. So we have much in common. Let's be sure to talk after the session."

Jennifer nods and says, "My therapist and I also plan to write a story on significant happenings in my life over the last seven years while I've been in South Africa."

"Interesting," says Art. "I once approached a therapist I was seeing to do the same, but he declined. Do you know the work of the narrative therapist, David Epston?" Jennifer shakes her head. "David lives in New Zealand and, with Michael White, was one of the originators of narrative therapy (White and Epston, 1990). Talk to me after the session and I'll put you in touch with him. He has written stories with some of his clients."

"There is also the work of the therapist and novelist Irvin Yalom," Carolyn says.

"*Everyday Gets a Little Closer,*" Art continues, "about his work with his patient, Ginny Elkin (Yalom and Elkin, 1991). They separately kept journals of each session."

And so it continues. Art and Carolyn walk down aisles and across rows to stand close to each speaking participant. One of them tries to respond briefly to each person before moving on, while the other takes notes so they can refer back to attendees' interests later in the workshop. The enthusiastic participants soon are responding to each other, and it's clear that most are familiar with autoethnography.

"I'm Toni from Penn State and a graduate student in Sociology. I'm interested in studying conflict in close relationships, particularly in couples who don't have children. I hope to include my own story with my interviews."

"I'm Erica, a graduate student from Ohio University, in communication. By the way, Bill Rawlins says hello. He's my mentor. My research relates to Toni's and Jennifer's in that I'm interested in relational conflict, particularly in studying forgiveness in families who don't accept their children identifying as gay. I've been keeping notes and writing stories about my experiences with my parents who are upset about my sexual orientation."

"Have you read Tony Adams's (2011) book on narrating the closet?" Carolyn asks. "He wrote about relational aspects of entering, being in, and coming out of the closet."

"Yes, that's why I'm here. I love that book, especially how he includes his own experiences. I've read everything he's published."

"Tony's also working on a project on forgiveness toward family members for some of their reactions to his being gay," Carolyn says, and Erica's eyes light up.

"I'm Regina, from Florida State, a graduate student in social work. I'm also interested in relational conflict. I'm writing about the divorce of my parents and my mother's mental illness. I have huge concerns about some of the ethical conundrums that have popped up, especially getting IRB approval to do this study."

"Institutional review board approval will be an important topic of conversation in the session tomorrow," says Carolyn, and nods to the next person with his hand raised.

"My name is Eric. I'm an assistant professor of music education at the University of Toronto. I'm interested in performance autoethnography and how embodied understanding relates to storytelling. Like Jennifer, Toni, Erica, and Regina, I'm intrigued with stories of loss."

"Impressive that you remembered everyone's name," says Art, and points to the woman beside Eric.

"My name is Karen. I live in Australia. I'm also interested in embodied learning. Eric, we need to talk. My area is creative arts, and I want to develop research practices that combine art-based approaches with the artistic process. I think that autoethnography is the perfect mode for doing that, and I hope to use it in my dissertation." Eric smiles and nods in Karen's direction.

"I'm also interested in embodied learning. My name is Inkeri, from Finland. I have a spinal cord injury and have been in a wheelchair for five years. I'm doing my dissertation on identity and sexuality for people who are differentially abled. I want to include my experiences as a woman with a disability, a counselor, and a researcher. My committee is not comfortable with the writing I've been doing about my own experiences. Still, I can't see doing this project without including my own experiences as a woman with a spinal cord injury."

"Certainly it would be richer to include your experiences," Carolyn says. "You should be the person to decide what you are and are not comfortable with, though you will have to think about your committee members too. I look forward to having this discussion with you."

"My name is Sadira. I'm a post doc in India. Inkeri, your project raises a lot of important issues about vulnerability. That's something that interests me too, as I study the meaning of home for my family, who now lives in the United States."

"Do you know Devika Chawla's book (2014) on *Home, Uprooted*?" asks Carolyn. "It's about what home means to people in India who have been displaced. I think it might be helpful for your project." Sadira writes a note about the reference.

"I'm Maria, a community health graduate student from Mexico, and I'm also interested in home. I'm studying the wellbeing of older adults in minority communities."

"My name is Kalisha. I'm an assistant professor at Georgetown University. Similar to Maria's research, mine looks at the role of women in African American communities and how they support the youth."

Marilyn goes next. She is an older graduate student in social work and aging studies who wants to be a writer and is studying her own bereavement as she interviews others who lost parents at an early age. Then comes Shing-Ling, an assistant professor in medical humanities from China, who is examining how families respond to the chronic illness of a child. Many participants are in education, such as Sophie from the UK, who wants to teach folks to become autoethnographers, and Silvia, who is getting a Ph.D. in English as a Second Language at Virginia Tech. She is writing about how language influences identity. "My professor took this workshop many years ago, and now I can't believe I'm here," she says.

The introductory discussion becomes livelier and livelier as the participants introduce themselves, find commonalities, and respond to each other. Carolyn and Art note that this group is similar in composition to other workshops they have given in the United States—mostly women; primarily graduate students and young professors; typically from social science, humanities, the arts, and education; predominantly from the United States, but still representing a wide variety of races, ethnicities, and other countries.

"What a fascinating and diverse group," says Art. "I wanted to stop and converse with each one of you. Hopefully, we'll have an opportunity for some of that during the next three days.

"Next on the agenda is Carolyn's personal story about coming to autoethnography. But first let's take a short break. Enjoy the refreshments in the back of the room."

Carolyn's Story

When everyone is seated, Carolyn stands and looks out at the eager faces, appreciating that these folks have expended much effort and expense to be with them. She finds it hard to believe that she and Art have been holding these workshops for almost 20 years. She hopes that she can convey the excitement that autoethnography and personal storytelling has for her, how much it has enriched her life, gotten her through hard times, and provided insights about her own motives, actions, and relationships with others. She wants to tell an engaging story, but express it efficiently so as not to overwhelm the workshop participants in the short time she has to share her history.

Carolyn takes a deep breath and says, "Hello, and again welcome to the workshop. This afternoon I want to introduce autoethnography autoethnographically by telling you about how I came to work as an autoethnographer and my earliest experiences writing personal narrative.

"For Art and me, an autoethnographic perspective merges our personal and scholarly lives. In this workshop, we connect these strands as well. I will begin by telling you the story of the events, personal and academic, that initially moved me toward autoethnography. Then Art will tell the background story of his engagement with autoethnography and the narrative turn. We will conclude this introduction by staging a brief dialogue about how we met and began to design our collaborative project. After a short break, Art will present his account of the rise of autoethnography in the human sciences, including the influence of the crisis of representation in the social sciences during the 1980s. Our four stories together will provide multiple windows into autoethnography from personal, relational, cultural, and historical perspectives.

Carolyn pauses. Then says, "Art and Carolyn fell in love in January 1990." She pauses again and chuckles along with attendees. "You might wonder," she continues, "what attracted us to each other and what experiences led us to the same scholarly place at this particular point in time. What was it in our histories that drew us to the kind of work we now call evocative autoethnography?

"Let me begin my story in childhood. I grew up on the outskirts of a small town in the mountains of Virginia. Telling local stories filled the days of the neighborhood kids as we rode our bikes on country roads, jumped from rope swings into rocky creeks, and rewarded ourselves with ice cream and candy at the corner store. There we would sit for hours every day talking and eavesdropping on the local men who, after working hard labor all day, relaxed and played cards in the evenings and chewed the fat about their daily lives.

"Though my parents had only elementary school educations, they supported my desire to attend the College of William and Mary—about three and a half hours away—for my B.A. and then to go to Stony Brook University on Long Island for my M.A. and Ph.D. I majored in sociology for all my degrees and took as many sociology classes as permitted. As soon as I learned how ethnographers did research, I knew that was what I wanted to do. For me, the ideal work was to be out in the world with people I wanted to learn about, experiencing their lives with them.

"My first ethnographic study at William and Mary focused on daily life in an isolated fishing community in the eastern United States. Living with the fisher folk—as I came to call them—I longed to feel what they felt—the wind at my back as we moved through the river in their tiny skiff, the quiet of the sun first peaking over the horizon, and the intense heat as it bore down on us when we tonged for oysters or fished the crab pots. I stayed in trailers that sometimes held a dozen people sleeping at night on couches and chairs and in available spaces in beds. I ate meals of boiled local fish and chunks of dry, heavy, white bread made with heaps of Crisco. I experienced floods, shootings, fights, and funerals. I piled into cars loaded with adults and children, with a baby on my lap, heading for a daily trip to neighborhood stores for pop and candy. I looked forward to the occasional trip to a nearby Walmart, when an unexpected tax return meant money to spend on clothes or a new TV, pleasures unattainable from government handouts that come with restrictions on what people could buy.

"For my dissertation at Stony Brook, I lived in a second isolated fishing village and compared social organization and change, work, and family structure in the two communities. In both places, I found myself examining my experience along with theirs. Rather than trying to be exclusively a neutral observer, I became attuned to how much I was learning about them through considering my thoughts, feelings, and actions as I participated in their daily lives. Being in these places with these folks reminded me of my own childhood in the mountainous rural south and often I compared my life to theirs—in my mind, though not in my writing. Occasionally, I sat back and watched, though mostly I participated and took in what we were doing together—what they told me, what I told them, how they treated me, our talk and bantering back and forth. When it was time to write, however, my focus stayed mainly on the people in the community.

"But I did sneak myself in as a minor character in a few of the short and lively vignettes I wrote. These action-filled and interactive vignettes captured the fisher folk better than the more abstract story of typicality I felt it necessary to tell in my role of 'sociologist.' The abstractions lumped the fisher folk together, separated them from the rest of us, and satisfied a need for coherent snapshots and patterns (Ellis, 1995b). Though I did not have a term for what I was doing, even then I was beginning to write narratively, appreciating a good concrete story over the more general and abstract one often prevalent in ethnography.

"In 1981, I received my Ph.D. and took my first academic position at the University of South Florida in Tampa. A few months later, my brother Rex died in an airplane crash on his way to visit me. At the same time, my romantic partner, Gene Weinstein, was in the final stages of emphysema. My life felt turned upside down and inside out as I struggled to cope with death and illness as a part of existence. Academically, I was deeply immersed in finishing a book on the fisher folk (Ellis, 1986), which would ensure my tenure, and making headway on a social psychology study of survey data on romantic jealousy. The research on jealousy was a way of examining my own experiences in romantic relationships during the open and experimental 1970s, though I did not say so at the time (Ellis and Weinstein, 1986).

"After my brother's death, and in the context of my partner's failing health, I moved passionately into the study of grief and loss. I wanted to use my sociological imagination and expertise in ethnography to figure out how to cope with illness and death for myself and provide new understanding of what grief and loss entailed. With my partner Gene's consent and participation, I kept notes on our experiences of coping with illness. Working in my study provided a time each day in which I felt I was living a 'normal' life, as I wrote notes about what had occurred, considered my life path, and organized my thoughts and feelings. Writing about my thoughts and feelings felt therapeutic, bringing me squarely into my experience but also providing distance and an escape from it. These 'field notes' helped me get through the crises and emergencies that occurred on almost a daily basis.

"When I am in the middle of a crisis, my mind tends to flit obsessively, chaotically, and emotionally from problem to problem—the insurance that needs to be settled, forms that must be filled out and submitted, visits to doctors, prescriptions to refill, the lift on the van needing repair, getting my writing and teaching done while taking care of Gene, and coping with his worsening condition. When I wrote down each day what was happening to us, I could relax, focus on what was most important to think about and do at that moment. That allowed me to put everything else in the background, knowing these events and feelings were recorded, and I could go back to them later.

"Though initially I wrote to help myself cope, quickly I came to see that these notes contained insightful sociology about illness processes, relational dynamics, and coping strategies. After Gene died in 1985, I spent nine years writing the sociological and experiential story of coping with the illness of a partner (Ellis, 1995a). Through living and writing about my experience, I learned directly about power dynamics and gender roles in relationships, and their potential reversal when one person is ill. I studied intimate communication and how complex interaction can be in a relationship struggling because of illness of one person and discrepancy in status and age between the two partners.

"I became a student of doctor-patient communication as I uncovered communication processes among the patient, doctor, and caregiver, and how a coalition can move from one dyad of patient and caregiver, to a second dyad of patient and doctor, to a triad of all three, and then finally to a third dyad of caregiver and doctor who make decisions about the patient's fate when near death. I also became immersed in the connections between hope and reality, and hope and truth telling in illness. As my partner's health deteriorated, I saw the need to live in multiple realities simultaneously. For example, both in the imagined reality of feeling hopeful *and* in the practical reality of dealing with the limitations and progression of the disease; both in the reality that there was something left to try *and* in the reality that my partner surely would die (Ellis, 2000b).

"I studied the intersection of intimate relationships and the illness process as we tried to cope with the plateau aspects of the disease. As soon as Gene and I figured out how to adapt to his condition, his health would drop to another level, never to return quite to where it had been, which meant our joint coping mechanisms had to be refigured. But mostly what I learned was experiential: how it felt to take care of an ill person I loved, the excruciating and confusing thoughts and emotions in accompanying Gene through deterioration, the pain of loss and death. Of course this experience was not without its joys—to be that close to someone in those intimate moments, to care that deeply, to feel the reality of existence, well, that's all a part of life.

"Which brings me to my brother's death," Carolyn says and sighs. She always finds it emotional to talk about Rex. Feeling from participants' rapt attention that they are with her, she continues, "This was another significant event that led me to writing personal narrative.

"Talk about excruciating. In the middle of Gene's illness, I lost my 29-year-old brother, who was two years younger. We were close friends and his death hit me hard. For a while after his passing, I was depressed, one of the only times in my life I would define myself as feeling that way. I wasn't clinically depressed, but I felt low, with thoughts occupying my mind, such as 'what's the use, we're all going to die' and the 'world is a frightening place where anything can happen, and does.' During this time, I discovered that writing in detail about getting the news of the plane crash, returning home to my little town in Virginia, the community of grief that awaited me there, and the emotions in coping with death of a loved one all helped bring me out of that low feeling (Ellis, 1993).

"These losses influenced me to focus in my studies on the lived experience of grief and loss in the context of relationships. This work made me feel I was doing something meaningful for myself and hopefully for others, and that feeling helped relieve my malaise too. In doing this writing, I no longer accepted that the words 'research' and 'therapeutic' were an anathema if said in the same sentence. I vowed then that I would only do work that had the potential to be helpful to my participants, readers, and me as a researcher.

"At first I hoped that sociologists would embrace my project of personal narrative as an extension of sociology. A few did, but others critiqued what I was doing as being literature, a single case, only my experience, not generalizable, and not research. Fortunately, I had received tenure in 1986 based on the fisher folk study, so I could afford to take some risks. Still, I could see that I needed to establish the credibility of the methods I was using. In 1987, I spent an entire sabbatical year doing a thorough review of introspection as a method (Ellis, 1991a). At first, I was committed to showing that my work was 'scientific.' I argued for systematic sociological introspection as a way to do social science research. The article I submitted got mixed reviews, but there was one response that significantly affected me. The reviewer called me schizophrenic. Imagine that. How would you feel if you got back a review that started by referring to your writing as schizophrenic?"

Carolyn pauses as the attendees gasp and laugh. "The reviewer was Norman Denzin." More gasps. "He said I was caught between two camps—hard social science and interpretive/imaginative/humanistic inquiry—and that I had made a case for the method and then turned hard science against it. 'You can't have it both ways,' he wrote."

"Didn't that upset you?" a woman in the back asks, when Carolyn nods toward her waving hand.

"Yes and no," Carolyn replies. "On the one hand, nobody wants to be labeled schizophrenic. On the other hand, the review opened me to considering the possibility that I didn't need to invest so much effort into being 'let in' to sociology. Instead, I might concentrate more on using my own lived experiences to write in ways that spoke to others about their human experiences. That review contributed to a transition I was undergoing: to trust that doing work that gave meaning to my life, and had the potential to offer meaning to and evoke meaning in others, was important no matter what academics called it or who rejected it. I felt passionate about describing and communicating the 'lived through' experience of life, with all its sorrows, joys, disappointments, satisfactions, and losses. I wanted to focus on speaking to people from all disciplines and walks of life who wanted to listen and respond with their stories, not concentrate on trying to persuade those who put up barriers before considering what the work had to offer.

"And then in January 1990, I met Art."

Art's Story

"Ah, yes," Art says, standing and approaching the workshop participants as Carolyn sits. "And before we tell that story, I'd like to give you a sense of what I had been doing prior to meeting Carolyn.

"How did I come to autoethnography and personal narrative? Now that's a long story," Art declares as he walks to the front and faces the classroom. "In fact, I could write a book about that journey."

He pauses momentarily, turning his back to the audience, then swiftly swings back around to face them, catching everyone's attention. "Wait a second, I did write a book about it," he says, a wide grin covering his face.

Art picks up a book from the table, and displays it prominently for the participants to see: "*Coming to Narrative: A Personal History of Paradigm Change in the Human Sciences* (Bochner, 2014)," he reads from the cover. "But don't worry. I'm not going to recite from it," he assures, placing the book back on the table.

"Whereas Carolyn grew up in a small rural town situated in the Shenandoah Valley, my childhood was spent in Squirrel Hill, a densely populated inner-city neighborhood in Pittsburgh, Pennsylvania. Like many once-poor Eastern European Jews whose immigrant parents or grandparents had originally settled in less safe and more ethnically and racially diverse areas of the city, my parents were attracted to the prospect of living in the city's center of Jewish culture. They loved its kosher butcher shops, delicatessens, Jewish restaurants, and bookstores, though they were among the poorest residents in the community. While my parents clung stubbornly to the traditions in which they had been raised, the majority of people in my neighborhood aligned with new secular forms of Jewish identity that made it easier for them to move freely and inconspicuously within the non-Jewish culture of the city.

"At school, I felt different from the other kids—poorer, less at ease with myself, more Jewish. At home I felt out of sync with my parents, who belonged to a different time and culture. I didn't want to be like the other kids at school, but I didn't want to be like my parents either.

"Perhaps some of you recall feeling that way," Art continues, and a number of participants nod. "In retrospect, I understand this feeling of being an outsider—of not fitting in—as a major reason that I decided to write my senior thesis in high school on the French philosopher and novelist Albert Camus. I felt alienated, yet I yearned to belong. But to what should I belong and with whom? What sort of life could be meaningful within a world in which it is impossible to know whether we exist for anything or any reason beyond ourselves?

"When I think about that now, I realize that I've come full circle over my lifetime. As a seventeen-year-old drawn to existential philosophy, I understood Camus as saying that the 'real' was what a person could feel in his heart or touch in the world. The English rock band Pink Floyd embraces a similar philosophy when they sing, 'All you touch and all you see is all your life will ever be' (Gilmour, Mason, Waters, and Wright, 1973)."

"Oh, I love that song," a woman with a British accent calls out from the back of the room.

"Then you have good taste," Art chuckles in reply. "And you probably know that the title of the song is 'Breathe,' which often is the first word a new-born baby hears. In harmony with Camus, Pink Floyd's song implies that human truth is personal. There is no truth beyond experience."

"Why do you say you've come full circle?" a man in the front row asks.

"Oh, you must be one of those people who read the last chapter of a novel before you've finished the first," Art grins. "What I mean is that I might have saved myself a lot of trouble if I had immediately followed the direction to which Camus was pointing me.

"'But what direction was that?' you may be wondering. In hindsight, I can see now that Camus was pointing me toward meaning, feeling, and empathy within the concrete human experiences of suffering and trauma. In *The Plague* (1947), which was awarded the Pulitzer Prize for literature, Camus exhorts readers to identify and feel solidarity with other people's suffering. But, hey, I'm skipping way ahead of my story. What I really want is for you to understand the circuitous, twisting route I took to get back to where I might have started.

"I was educated as a traditional empiricist and conducted a quantitative study for my dissertation. For more than a decade, I plied the trade I had been well trained to practice as a graduate student. My first appointment as a graduate professor was as the departmental methodologist in a communication department, which meant I taught graduate courses in statistics and experimental research design. I published quantitative research studies, directed quantitative dissertations, and was appointed to the editorial boards of top-tier quantitative journals. I felt proud of these achievements yet only marginally fulfilled by them.

"My research was skillfully developed, competently executed, rigorously defended, and capably interpreted. I experienced the satisfaction of achieving the stature of an expert technician. The work I published was statistically significant. But was it humanly significant? Deep down, I had serious doubts. My research seemed to lack imagination and liveliness. It was boring to read, and I knew that only a small number of statistically proficient empiricists in my field could understand it.

"Moreover, as a professor of communication, I found myself immersed in a troubling contradiction. The empirical methods I was applying were grounded largely in the premise that communication between humans could be described as an object. But human communication is not an object, nor is it a discipline studying objects. Communication is a process consisting of sequences of interaction and the dynamic human activity of studying them. As a communicating human being studying humans communicating, I was inside what I was studying. Gradually, I allowed myself to take this contradiction seriously. I began to question whether it was reasonable to 'bracket' the most important qualities of communication—its subjective and reflexive characteristics—'in the name of science' in order to produce 'objective' data.

"Besides, the social scientists I most admired—Erving Goffman (1963, 1967), Gregory Bateson (1972, 1979), Jules Henry (1971), Ernest Becker (1971, 1973), and Clifford Geertz (1973, 1980)—were cut from a different cloth than the dust bowl empiricists I had been trained to emulate. Their ideas and their writings were tantalizingly suggestive and generative. They had a respect for data, but the data that interested them were not statistical data. They shunned experimental studies of human behavior because these studies stripped context from life. Instead, they chose to study life in its natural settings, to think aesthetically, employ rich and expansive metaphors, give thick descriptions, and concentrate on meanings that can take readers into the heart of lived experience.

"In 1981, I published 'Forming Warm Ideas,' an essay that critiqued the imbalance between rigor and imagination in communication research and encouraged researchers to 'move closer to our subject matter' and into new, more catalytic, avenues of inquiry. But precisely what kind of inquiry would lead to warm ideas? I didn't know for sure. I only knew that I no longer wanted to do surveys and experiments. And my new research projects would need to connect deeply to issues I was dealing with in my personal life. Carolyn mentions how much she initially wanted to be let into sociology. I had already entered the room of communication studies, but I didn't feel at home there (Bochner, 2014). How could I make my academic house a place in which to dwell more comfortably?

"At about the same time—the late 1970s and early 1980s—I was preoccupied by a personal and professional crisis. I felt as if I were being held hostage to a professional identity I no longer wanted to claim and a marriage whose happiness had been eclipsed by my partner's severe bi-polar depression. At the university, I felt compelled to fulfill my obligations as 'the departmental methodologist,' thereby enacting a fraudulent self. At home, I found myself mourning the loss of a shared memory of the past and a rapidly diminishing expectation that my partner and I would grow older together (Bochner, 2014).

"I had been drawn to the field of communication studies by a desire to better understand the intricate interactional patterns of my family of origin, its immersion in angst, and my father's sudden and unpredictable bursts of violence. Now, more than ever, my personal and academic lives had merged. I yearned to understand the vulnerability of a person's structure of meanings, what sustains and threatens meanings, and how intimate partners can use communication to keep despair and dread at bay." The students wait expectantly as Art stares off into space. Art shakes his head, sighs, and continues.

"My confidence in orthodox social science methodology and my turn toward narrative also were provoked by my immersion in the history of the human sciences (Smith, 1997), postmodernism (Lyotard, 1984; Rosenau, 1991), and interpretive social sciences (Rabinow and Sullivan, 1987). I had read Thomas Kuhn's *The Structure of Scientific Revolutions* (1970) and was persuaded by his argument that there is no way to distinguish unequivocally what's in our minds from what's out there in the world. Kuhn placed human subjectivity at the center of scientific progress. And he was not the only one questioning the validity of the building-block model of scientific progress. In quite diverse ways, various postmodernist philosophers debunked and deconstructed the view that language could be a neutral or transparent medium of communication, which had been a crucial assumption in the positivist's ideas of representation and objectivity. Richard Rorty (1982), for example, showed that the foundations of epistemology on which the empiricist doctrine of 'truth through method' rested were fallible. If you couldn't eliminate the influence of the observer on the observed, then no theories or findings could ever be completely free of human values and subjectivity. The investigator would always be implicated in the product.

"I found Rorty's deconstruction of the correspondence theory of knowledge very exciting. I took his critique to mean that the observer needed to be observed. We needed to turn our observations back on ourselves and to write about what we observe in the empirical world from the source of our own experience. I no longer had any reason to believe that the human sciences were closer to physics than to literature or poetry. Also, I had come around to the idea that the practices of human communication—the ways in which human beings negotiate and perform meaning—ought to become the model for how we tell about the empirical world and how we deal with the human condition and make sense of our lived experience (Bochner and Waugh, 1995). These communication practices are central to how we create meaning in our own lives, and they should be how we put meanings into motion in our academic research as well. Communication should be *not only what we study* but *how we represent what we study*; that is, in stories that connect to readers.

"This was what I was thinking about at the time I met Carolyn. In my heart, I believed that social scientists needed to write from the source of their own experience. As the 1980s were coming to a close, I immersed myself in the theoretical and practical writings of scholars who had taken 'the narrative turn'—the philosophers, Alasdair MacIntyre (1984) and Charles Taylor (1989); the psychologist, Jerome Bruner (1986, 1987); the family therapists, Michael White and David Epston (1990); and the anthropologist, Barbara Myerhoff (1980, 2007). They helped me to appreciate the strong need in the human sciences to write or perform stories that put authors into conversation with themselves and their readers. I found myself drawn to stories that expose values and choices, and connect emotionally to readers' lives. We needed texts that bear witness to that which they communicate and which can deeply implicate the reader. I had a strong sense that things were moving in the direction of a new paradigm for the human sciences that would capture the minds and hearts of the next generation of students of communication and other social sciences. I had theorized some of these changes, but I had not yet put theory into practice. That would come after I met Carolyn."

Our Story: Carolyn and Art Come Together

Carolyn joins Art upfront, and they quickly push back chairs to create space for their performance. They stand near each other, each holding a script from which they will read and perform the birth of their relationship. They speak directly to the audience.

Carolyn: When Art and I met in 1990, I was in the Sociology Department.

Art: And I was in Communication.

Carolyn: Both of us had been at the University of South Florida for a while, I for nine years…

Art: …and I for six.

Carolyn and Art: Yet our paths had not crossed.

Art: That detail tells you something about how separate the humanities and social sciences were on our campus at that time—and elsewhere, I suspect, too.

Carolyn: Right away our personal and work lives intersected. We met when Art attended a talk I gave in the Business School on systematic sociological introspection, which focused largely on the book, *Final Negotiations* (1995a), I was writing about coping with my partner Gene's dying and death.

Art: Imagine that—Carolyn giving a talk on introspection in a college of business. I had never before heard the term "systematic sociological introspection." In my book (Bochner, 2014), I call that day "a simple twist of fate." By chance, I saw a notice about Carolyn's talk in the college newspaper. The title intrigued me, so I gathered a couple of graduate students, and we headed off to the business building.

Carolyn: I recall being a little nervous because I didn't recognize many people in the audience and I wasn't sure how interested folks in a business school would be in my talk. But I'd given a number of presentations on introspection before, so I took a deep breath and started talking.

Art: The first thing I noticed was Carolyn's magnetic energy, which made me feel as if I were being pulled across the room toward her. The talk felt more like a dance than a lecture. I was smitten.

[Carolyn and Art turn and speak directly to each other.]

Carolyn: But you didn't sound smitten when you started drilling me with questions during the Q&A. You started by praising me, but then you told me how defensive I sounded.

Art: I have to admit that some of my comments were devious. I wanted to get your attention. I loved how you were arguing for a social science that embodied emotionality and subjectivity. I even whispered to one of my students, "Hey, she's giving my lecture."

Carolyn: You got my attention alright, but your critique

caught me off guard. I didn't expect someone at a presentation in the Business School to suggest that I should stop worrying about whether my work was sufficiently scientific.

Art: I wanted to startle you, but when I look at it now, I can see there was a lot of self-criticism in that comment. I was talking to you, but I also was talking to myself. The stories you were telling were empirical. These were events that actually happened and you were staying close to the facts. But your stories drew on these facts artistically, as a novelist would. Whether it was science or not seemed trivial to me because you were dealing with messy and ambiguous, but real, dimensions of human experience. And your stories were moving people. Tears were flowing throughout the room, and people were on the edge of their seats. You were connecting to them in a visceral, sensual way.

Carolyn: I could feel that, and it felt good. In that context, your comments fascinated me. They dovetailed with the response I had gotten from Norman Denzin about being caught between hard social science and interpretive humanistic inquiry. But your comments also unsettled me because I was still caught up in defending my work to traditional social science audiences. It would take me a while and many conversations with you to process what it could mean to be freed from defending the scientific merit of my work. I do remember thinking at the time though, "wow, now that's an interesting take." Of course, I also noticed how handsome you were.

Art (grinning ear-to-ear): Oh. It never occurred to me to check out your appearance. Ahmmm (clears his throat to express the irony). I was taken only by your vitality and storytelling ability.

Carolyn: Right, Arthur. We walked out of the building together that day, and we both felt a spark, didn't we?

Art: Of course we did. But we didn't acknowledge it in any way.

Carolyn: No, we were all business. [Carolyn and Art smile at each other, then turn back to the audience.]

Carolyn: Within a couple weeks, we learned enough about each other to know we wanted something more. I was bold enough to arrange a "business meeting" at my house, which would give us an opportunity to explore some connections between the graduate programs in sociology and communication.

Art: Yes, a business meeting replete with wine and cheese, and dim lights.

Carolyn: Don't give the wrong impression. We talked non-stop for hours—all business.

Art and Carolyn: And we've kept talking for the last 26 years.

Carolyn: ...not all business. Art likes to say that "talk is the kiss of life."

Art: I lifted that line from Anatole Broyard (1992). What I remember about that night at Carolyn's home is how excited I got about what we could build together, though neither of us had any idea whether the disciplines of sociology or communication were ready for the kind of writing we wanted to do.

Carolyn: Academic disciplines don't tend to be brave, daring, or fearless, you know.

Art: But we were falling in love and anything seemed possible as we plotted our future together.

Carolyn: We felt this emotional and intellectual connection. I was the story-creator; he was the story-analyzer.

Art: Funny thing is that I also had entertained the notion of being a writer. I was happiest when I was writing, no matter what I was working on—quantitative articles, theoretical essays, or philosophical arguments. I liked arranging ideas, figuring out how to make a case, and putting the pieces together. I composed my scientific papers thinking of myself more as a writer than a scientist. I studied the conventions for writing scholarship and abided by them. I stayed within the boundaries but near the margins.

Carolyn: I had a hunch that Art had this evocative storyteller deep inside him trying to get out. Trouble was all those theories and concepts kept blocking the way. At the same time, in addition to writing short stories, I had branched out to more theoretical and methodological discussions of introspection, and when we met I was working on a conceptual article on emotional sociology that had spun off from my work on introspection (Ellis, 1991b). There I argued for passionate and evocative writing that examined emotions emotionally, told concrete and embodied stories about self and other, included the author's emotions, and opened up emotional conversations with readers. Given our mutual interests, just imagine the conversation Art and I had bouncing these ideas off each other.

Art: Ah, yes, on that first night at Carolyn's house, we dreamed up all sorts of fantasies about what we could do together. I suppose a part of me thought it was all delusional, but two people falling in love have to believe in their dreams, don't they?

Carolyn: Oh, Art's such a romantic. Don't let him fool you. He had already done a lot of the groundwork as chair of the communication department. He had led the development of a new Ph.D. program, one that would be exclusively qualitative and critical studies and was to begin the semester after we met. The foundation had been laid. Our dreams already had traction.

Art: When I left Carolyn's house that night, I couldn't sleep. I wanted to get started on our collaboration. I'd waited so long for someone who shared my vision of what was possible.

Carolyn: Actually, we began exchanging publications and work in progress virtually from the first day we met. We didn't immediately define it this way, but we were not only lovers, we also were writing buddies.

Art: As Carolyn's writing buddy, I agreed to read a draft of *Final Negotiations* (1995a). I was shocked when she sent me seven hundred pages, but I read every word.

Carolyn: Art was instrumental in discussing and editing that text with me, and helping me figure out what I wanted it to be.

Art: The manuscript was a story-reader's delight, stories within stories within stories. I was thrilled to see that Carolyn had refused to suppress her subjectivity or emotionality. She was making readers feel and encouraging them to enter her consciousness. She had lived through a demanding and difficult caregiving experience that many other people face over the course of their lives. She invited readers to share intimate moments of how life is lived in such situations. The main advice I gave her was to stay with the narrative arc and keep the main story moving.

Carolyn: Art insisted that I get rid of the excess, anything that slowed down the plot. In a way, he approached my text as if it were a song.

Art: That's music to my ears!

Carolyn: Art's feedback helped me immensely, as did his response to my ideas about "emotional sociology" (1991b) and his theoretical overview in his chapter on "theories and stories" (1994) that helped define the goals of our project.

Art: As we continued to share papers and talk about them, our joint project began to take shape.

Carolyn: We knew we wanted to emphasize how researchers could bring flesh and blood emotions and subjectivity into the human sciences, work interactively and reflexively with research participants, and present their work narratively in various genres of storytelling...

Art (interrupting): ...and we wanted to keep talking and talking and talking some more...

Carolyn: ...until we figured out what our project was going to be.

Art: First, it would provide an ethnographic alternative...

Carolyn: ...by focusing on the subjectivity of the researcher...

Art: ...and blurring the boundaries between social sciences and humanities.

Carolyn: Second, it would emphasize first-person accounts of concrete lived experiences...

Art: ...through narrative modes of writing local stories...

Carolyn: ...brimming with scenes, and dialogue, and unfolding action,...

Art: ...sensuous texts,...

Carolyn: ...often multi-voiced, conversational, critical, and performative texts,...

Art: ...and exemplifying strategies for practicing reflexive fieldwork.

Carolyn and Art: The rest is history.

Carolyn: We presented our first coconstructed first-person narrative at a conference in 1990 and published it in 1992 (Ellis and Bochner, 1992).

Art: The same year we moved in together.

Art and Carolyn: Three years later, in 1995, we married.

Art: We became partners in every sense of the word, creating a synergy and symbiosis in our work and life more powerful than either one of us could have achieved alone.

Carolyn: And now here we are decades later at this workshop with you, still excited about evocative autoethnography, thinking about its uses and possibilities for the future in our lives and in yours.

Carolyn and Art take a short bow. The participants applaud, and Art holds up a sign that says, "Ten minute break."

The Rise of Autoethnography

"We hope you enjoyed the snacks," Art says, cuing participants to return to their seats. "This afternoon, I'm going
to play the part of an historian. I'll also talk about autoethnography
as an idea, a kind of research, a mode of writing, and a way of life. In
between, we'll take a look at some precepts of qualitative research
associated with an autoethnographic mind-set.

"As you can see from the brief stories of our academic autobiographies, Carolyn and I encountered a few bumps on the road
to autoethnography—and one or two detours as well. Eventually,
autoethnography became our solution to the problem of staying
alive and lively as professors and researchers. But don't get the
wrong idea. When we were graduate students and young professors,

neither of us imagined that our academic lives would move in the direction of autoethnography. Nor did we foresee that one day qualitative research would achieve the standing around the world that it has today (Denzin and Lincoln, 2011; Leavy, 2014).

"Why couldn't we have anticipated these developments? Does this question pique your curiosity? Do you want to know the historical and cultural conditions that gave rise to autoethnography?"

Art pauses momentarily, then lifts his arms in unison, urging a response by which he can gauge the level of interest in these questions. "Come on now, don't you want to know something about the historical and cultural conditions that gave rise to autoethnography?"

Hearing no reaction, Art cups one of his hands behind his right ear, leans forward, and turns sideways.

"Yes, yes," several participants call out, finally getting the message.

"Thank you. That's more like it," Art smiles, turning back to face the participants. "I know history isn't the most fetching topic, but I think this one can help you see the human sciences in a new light. My goal is to help you comprehend research practices as cultural phenomena that evolve over time. Our autobiographies show how much Carolyn and I changed over the past 40 years. The same goes for the human sciences; they adjust, go through stages, develop, and transform.

"When you look closely at the history of the human sciences, you find that the forms of inquiry that gain acceptance usually are the ones that serve the needs of the culture at the time. As new research questions arise, older, more conventional methods of trying to address problems can prove unsatisfactory or inadequate. This can prompt an atmosphere of crisis in one's academic community, opening the flood gates to a wide range of new possibilities for transforming the values and convictions held by researchers. These kinds of profound turns have been called 'paradigm shifts,' a term Thomas Kuhn (1970) introduced to describe revolutionary changes in scientific fields.

"The crisis atmosphere that arose in the 1980s and its ensuing paradigm shift can help explain how and why autoethnography touched a nerve. I mean that in both a positive and a negative sense. Autoethnography brought heightened attention to human suffering, injustice, trauma, subjectivity, feeling, and loss; encouraged the development of reflexive and creative methodologies through which to navigate the landscape of lived experience; and legitimated unconventional forms of documenting and expressing personal experience in literary, lyrical, poetic, and performative ways. That's the positive.

"But the shift to an autoethnographic paradigm also unnerved those traditional, analytic social scientists who insisted on clinging to objectivity, detachment, theory-building, and generalization as terminal goals of scientific inquiry. They perceived autoethnography as a threat to the domination of their cultural practices, namely their insatiable appetite for analyses and abstractions grounded in objectivist empiricism, value neutrality, and the rationalist ideal of prediction and control. Feeling a need to defend themselves against a wave of pulsating energy, dissimilar values, and new practices of representation and performance, some early critics of autoethnography urged social scientists to stick to the older ideals of scientific knowledge as something to be possessed, analyzed, and organized into systems of mastery and control (Atkinson, 1997; Anderson, 2006). Their opposition to a human science that puts meanings in motion, embraces value-centered inquiry, and refuses to be owned by either the sciences or the humanities was heated and, ironically, quite emotional. But the desire for change was gaining momentum, and the old ways of doing things eventually would have to make room for the new.

"It may surprise some of you to learn that the origins of the social sciences can be traced to the moral philosophy of the eighteenth century, which focused not on *what is* but rather on *what ought to be* the case—what is good and right (Becker, 1968; Smith, 1997). The human sciences were conceived originally to be moral sciences that could guide human actions in the direction of the good. By the early twentieth century, however, the social sciences had become empirical sciences that were decidedly quantitative. This is not the place to go into the complicated reasons for this development. But do keep in mind that social science was initially inspired by questions of value and morality.

"In the aftermath of World War II, and under the influence of the rapid development of social survey methods, graduate programs in the social sciences gradually began to allow students to use a sequence of courses in statistics and quantitative research methods to fulfill the foreign language requirement for the Ph.D. degree. Once this quantitative orthodoxy took hold, students were able to complete their coursework with little or no exposure to the important role that ethnography, fieldwork, and interviewing had played in the social sciences prior to the 1940s.

"But as Leonard Cohen (1992) observes in his song, *Anthem*, 'there is a crack in everything.' In the mid-1970s the light began to creep in through openings in the fault lines of the objectivism, positivism, and value neutrality that had turned 'human sciences' into 'creature sciences' (Becker, 1968; Foucault, 1970). It would take another 20 years before a community of scholars open to bending, blending, and breaking through the conventional genres of research and writing practices in the social sciences would emerge (Clifford and Marcus, 1986; Denzin, 1997). Once the fissures opened, however, transformative change was inevitable.

"Before I convey the rest of my story about the history of auto-ethnography, I want to remind you that this is my version of these events. Other people might tell it differently. I lived through this period. Now I'm looking back, remembering, and trying to make sense of it. That's often what we autoethnographers do. We frame and cast our vision over experiences through which we've lived, and we invite others into conversation about the meanings of these events."

Origin of the Term 'Autoethnography'

"No comprehensive history of autoethnography has been written yet, though the origin of the term has been acknowledged in many publications (e.g., Ellis and Bochner, 2000; Ellis, 2004; Holman

Jones, Adams, and Ellis, 2013; Ellis and Adams, 2014). In 1975, Karl Heider asked 50 Grand Valley Dani school children, 'What do (your) people do?' and referred to their responses (collectively) as *auto-ethnography,* by which he meant 'the Dani's own understanding of their world' (p. 3).

"Four years later, David Hayano (1979) became the first anthropologist to refer in print to Heider's work. Following Heider's lead, Hayano equated auto-ethnography with *insider studies* in which the researcher was a native, or became a full insider, within the community or culture being studied—a genre of ethnography now routinely classified as *indigenous* or *aboriginal.* In his essay, 'Auto-Ethnography: Paradigms, Problems, and Prospects,' Hayano (1979, p. 103) pointedly 'disregard(ed) studies...which analyze one's own life through the procedures of ethnography,' and he made a clear distinction between auto-ethnography and self-ethnography.

"Although Heider (1975) and Hayano (1979) deserve credit for first putting the term 'auto-ethnography' into circulation, their definition and use of autoethnography was far different from what Carolyn and I had in mind when we developed our conceptualization and vision of autoethnography in the 1990s (Ellis and Bochner, 2000). Heider and Hayano did not think of auto-ethnography as a transgressive research practice that challenged, resisted, or extended the boundaries of conventional ethnographic writing practices. Nor did they conceive of auto-ethnography as a critical response to disquieting concerns about silent authorship, the need for researcher reflexivity, or as a humanizing, moral, aesthetic, emotion-centered, political, and personal form of representation.

"'Why not?' you might ask. Why didn't they see the potential of autoethnography to address these issues? The answer is uncomplicated. These issues simply weren't on their radar. In the 1970s, a few scholars were urging thicker descriptions, giving more attention to concrete details of everyday life, renouncing the ethics and artificiality of experimental studies, and complaining about the obscurity of jargon and technical language (Henry, 1971; Harré and Secord, 1972; Geertz, 1973; Gergen, 1973). But social scientists, for the most part, weren't all that concerned about the researcher's location in the text, the capacity of language to accurately represent reality, or the need for researcher reflexivity. Though anxieties simmered beneath the surface, they had not yet boiled over into the kind of widespread dissatisfaction that would shake confidence in post-World War II positivist paradigms of social science inquiry. As a new decade dawned, however, that was about to change."

"Can I interrupt?" a voice near the back of the room inquires.

"Of course," Art replies.

"Didn't some of the urban sociologists of the early twentieth century conduct research in the settings in which they worked, or in communities to which they were personally connected? I'm thinking of Robert Parks."

"You're right," Art says. "Robert Parks (1925) and Nels Anderson (1934/1961) were ahead of their time in that respect. A few of the symbolic interactionists in the Chicago school of sociology, such as Everett Hughes (1958) and Fred Davis (1959, 1994), come to mind as well. They advocated studying social worlds and subcultures in which the sociologist is immersed and has a personal stake. But you won't find a visible researcher self in their texts. Their books and articles adhered to the conventions of sociological reporting at the time. Observing oneself observing others—what we now call *reflexive self-observation*—was of little, if any, interest to them."

Crisis of Representation

Seeing no other participants eager to speak, Art continues, "By the mid-1980s, the social sciences had entered a period of crisis brimming with self-reflection. This turning point was prompted by a series of demoralizing critiques of the most revered premises of scientific truth and knowledge (Rorty, 1982; Lyotard, 1984; Clifford and Marcus, 1986; also see Denzin, 1997). Poststructuralists and postmodernists carried out an unrelenting attack on the authority of a humanly constructed text, casting serious doubt on the sanctified scientific doctrines of 'naturalism' and 'truth through method.' They showed that the traditional idea of an objectively accessible reality through which 'scientific method' could produce truth had turned out to be, in Rorty's (1982, p. 195) words, 'neither clear nor useful.'

"Think about that for a moment. Richard Rorty, one of the most famous philosophers of the time, was contesting the viability of the very foundations of social science methodology. What was needed, according to Rorty (1982, p. 195), was an approach to social science 'which emphasizes the utility of narratives and vocabularies rather than the objectivity of laws and theories.' Rorty recommended an 'experimental attitude' that would be open to the new rather than attached to the old, and in which 'we would have much less trouble thinking of the entire culture, from physics to poetry, as a single, continuous, seamless activity in which the divisions are merely institutional and pedagogical' (1990, p. 76). Boundaries dividing the social sciences from the humanities would be blurred and, in some cases, dissolved entirely.

"The seeds for change eventually blossomed into a desire for something new—something qualitatively different and useful. Philosophers continued to emphasize the manner in which the social world is *meaningful* in ways the natural world is not (Taylor, 1977). Their critiques showed how empiricism's value neutrality masks domination, conserves the interest of the status quo, and reinforces oppressive social practices (Bernstein, 1983; Giroux, 1984; Habermas, 1985). As a result, an increasing number of social scientists began seeing the age they were living through as 'an experimental moment,' one that invited risk and innovation (Marcus and Fisher, 1986; Geertz, 1988; Rosaldo, 1989; Tedlock, 1991).

"Rorty seemed to be endorsing an approach to expressing lived experience that could move seamlessly between social sciences and humanities. What sort of inquiry could do that? What do you folks think I have in mind?" Art stops and cups his ear again. When he raises his arms slowly, palms up, acting as if he's conducting a symphony, the workshop participants cry out in unison—well, sort of unison—'autoethnography!'

"Yes! That's right. And Carolyn and I seized the moment. We had been waiting for just this kind of opportunity to express the longing in our hearts for something new and different, *an abnormal kind of inquiry*—the term *queer* had not yet made it into our vocabulary—that would breach the borders of convention, muddling the boundaries between humanities and social sciences (Bochner, 2014). We had a hunch this would be a risky endeavor, but a door had opened. Carpe Diem, this was our chance."

"That reminds me of a line from *Queen to Play*, a movie we watched recently," Carolyn interrupts from her seat. "Kevin Kline tells the woman he is teaching to play chess, 'If you risk, you may lose. But if you don't risk, you *will* lose.'" Many of the participants nod, affirming Carolyn's point.

Art continues, "In 1991, we collaborated on a project that we called *ethnographic alternatives*, drafted the first exemplars of the kind of writing we had in mind, and presented a live performance of one of the stories at an academic conference (Ellis and Bochner, 1992). Initially, we conceived our project as *an experimental form of narrating personal experience* that embodied the anthropologist Michael Jackson's (1989) idea of *radical empiricism*, a call to 'make ourselves [as researchers] experimental subjects and treat our experiences as primary data' (p. 4).

"In retrospect, the change we wanted to make doesn't seem that radical. We simply were acknowledging that researchers live in the world too. The problems of being alive and facing serious existential and moral questions related to mortality, loss, belonging, loneliness, love, adversity, violence, racism, discrimination, and complicated feelings affect all people—researchers as well as non-researchers. Many of us were drawn to a life of research by our lived experiences of emotional epiphanies that changed or deeply affected us. We believe these experiences are worthy of observation, examination, and reflection. We also believe that these experiences strongly influence our perceptions and interpretations of other people's lives.

"As social scientists, we have learned how to be systematic, methodical, and analytic. Our expertise places us in an ideal position to bring to light the meanings of emotionally draining, difficult, and demanding epiphanies on which human lives turn, including our own as researchers. Our project emphasized and underscored subjectivity, self-reflexivity, emotionality, and the goal of connecting social sciences to humanities through first-person, ethnographic storytelling. As you will see, we placed storytelling at the center of our project, which meant that some of the conventions of academic reporting would have to change. We wanted readers of our stories to be forced to deal with the concrete—particular people in particular places facing particular, often traumatic, circumstances of lived experience (Conquergood, 1990). We planned to speak to these readers in an intimate, introspective, and self-reflexive storytelling voice. Our project would be a theatre for investigating some of the most serious questions of existence as a living being, and promoting social justice as a societal imperative."

Naming Our Project

"In those early days, we weren't sure what to name the kind of work we were embracing. We could have called it personal essay, socioautobiography, confessional tale, ethnographic autobiography, self-ethnography, or personal ethnography. Though a myriad of possibilities existed, we landed initially on 'first-person accounts' and 'evocative narratives' as our covering terms (Ellis and Bochner, 2000)."

Art hesitates momentarily. Turning toward Carolyn, he asks, "Do you recall when you first used the term 'autoethnography'?"

Carolyn stands and replies. "I can't be exact—sometime in the late 1980s or early 90s. At first, I was wedded to terms such as 'sociological introspection' and 'emotional sociology' and, after we met, 'personal narrative.' I recall that when I was writing *Final Negotiations*, I thought of the story I was telling at various times as autoethnography, but I used that term only once in the book."

"And you didn't list it as a keyword in the index," Art says.

"Good observation," Carolyn replies. "I opted instead to use 'self-ethnography,' 'autobiographical sociology,' and 'ethnographic novel' as key terms."

Art nods and continues as Carolyn sits down, "Beginning in the mid-1990s, we situated what we were doing in *the narrative turn* (see Mitchell, 1981; Polkinghorne, 1988; Bruner, 1990), which we considered a viable option to the mechanistic 'creature science'

(Becker, 1968) from which we were trying to break away. Human beings are storytelling animals, we reasoned, and thus a human science ought to understand persons as 'self-interpreting animals' (Taylor, 1985). The narrative turn pointed inquiry toward *acts of meaning* (Bruner, 1990), focusing on the *functions* of stories and storytelling in creating and managing identity; the *forms* of story-telling that individuals use to make sense of lived experience and communicate it to others; the *relational* entanglements that permeate how life is lived and told to others; and *reflexive* dimensions of the relationship between storytellers and story listeners.

"In 1995, we decided to arrange a collection of original essays and stories that would extend and explore the use of the first person voice, the appropriation of literary modes of writing to express lived experiences, and the complications of being positioned within the events and experiences a researcher studies. We settled on the terms *autoethnography, sociopoetics,* and *reflexivity* as subheadings to represent these three goals in the text that became *Composing Ethnography* (Ellis and Bochner, 1996a). Shortly after that book was completed, we collaborated with Lisa Tillmann-Healy on a chapter that endorsed the use of first-person accounts in research on personal relationships (Bochner, Ellis, and Tillmann-Healy, 1997); Carolyn wrote her first chapter on 'evocative autoethnography' (Ellis, 1997) and another on the use of autoethnography to explore loss (Ellis, 1998a); and Deborah Reed-Danahay (1997) published a collection of essays, *Auto/Ethnography: Rewriting the Self and the Social.*

"As the end of the twentieth century approached, we understood the goal of our project as one in which readers would not only know but also *feel the truth* of first-person accounts, and thus be more fully immersed and engaged—morally, aesthetically, emotionally, politically, and intellectually (Bochner and Ellis, 1996). In the process of editing a special issue of *Contemporary Ethnography* (Ellis and Bochner, 1996b) and planning the millennium meeting of *The Society for the Study of Symbolic Interaction (SSSI),* we witnessed a wave of passionate enthusiasm and keen interest in experimenting with hybrid forms of ethnographic representation that blended various combinations of short stories, performances, photography, poetry, painting, dance, and music. *Composing Ethnography*, in particular, prompted numerous young scholars to write to us expressing both their exhilaration about telling the stories that haunted them and the many roadblocks they had faced when proposing the use of first-person writing in their dissertations or in submissions for publication.

"Perhaps some of you have experienced a similar reaction," Art says. Several participants nod in acknowledgement, and Art continues, "Their responses inspired us to dedicate the conference to knocking down barriers to this kind of work, displaying its value, and increasing the excitement (Bochner and Ellis, 2002).

"In 1997, Norman Denzin published *Interpretive Ethnography: Ethnographic Practices for the 21st Century* in which he praised efforts like ours to make social science texts 'a means for the reader's own moral experience' (p. 202), and called special attention to *narratives of the self* that 'show us how to feel the sufferings of others' (p. 201), privilege emotions and emotionality, and 'humanize the ethnographic disciplines' (p. 215). Denzin had portrayed the goals of our project concisely. Still, the term *autoethnography* was passed over quickly in Denzin's text, and discussed only as a footnote to Carolyn's chapter on evocative autoethnography. But Denzin must have intuited the enormous potential of autoethnography, because he invited Carolyn and me to author the first handbook chapter that would explicitly highlight autoethnography and personal narrative (Ellis and Bochner, 2000).

"Although we recognized that autoethnography was a blurred genre that covered many different forms of first person accounts and narratives of personal experience, we decided to use our handbook chapter to treat autoethnography as a *genus* or *genre* of writing or performing research stories under which many species of autobiographical narrative and self-ethnography could fall. In effect, we were engaging in a rhetorical process of forming a narrative identity for a loosely aligned community of scholars."

"You have to realize that Art's one of those language people," Carolyn interrupts with a smile. "His antenna is constantly tuned into how language is used and/or abused and for what purposes."

"Carolyn's right about that. I worry about how language reveals and conceals; how we do things with words; and the things words do to, and evoke in, us. As a communication professor, I appreciate how naming can produce symbolic power. Naming brings things and ideas into existence, making them real and lasting.

"Carolyn and I were convinced that a rapidly expanding population of scholars across the globe identified with our project but lacked the feelings of solidarity and community that a unifying narrative identity could provide. The *Handbook* chapter provided a rare opportunity to name something still in the process of evolving. Of course, it was not so much about naming as it was about specifying and attaching meanings to a term, 'autoethnography,' which had yet to realize its vast symbolic potential. We were taking an active approach to grasping, naming, and defining an emerging reality by attaching new meanings to an existing term. We adapted, extended, and offered a vision for autoethnographic research that could serve the needs and goals of those who wanted to write in ways that express the living body, consciousness, and subjectivity of the author/researcher through a personal, vulnerable, reflective, self-conscious, self-reflexive, and narrative voice (Berry, 2013). By bestowing new meanings onto the term, 'autoethnography,' we were laying a symbolic foundation for a unifying cognitive structure, a narrative identity that could bring together scholars drawn to this kind of work.

"Through proposing a rubric of autoethnography that encompassed various genres of first-person writing within its fluid and expansive boundaries, we were actively encouraging others to see themselves as one of us and attach themselves to the ideals of an autoethnographic way of life and work. We knew we were not the only social scientists attracted to the fertile new ground being broken by writers, artists, and performers experimenting with genre-bending and messy-text forms of representation that move away from third-person, silent authorship.

"Still, we did not anticipate what would take place over the next fifteen years (see Sikes, 2013; Adams, Holman Jones, and Ellis, 2015; Marak, 2015). In 1999, when we were writing that first handbook chapter, we identified fewer than 40 scholarly articles or chapters focusing explicitly on autoethnography. Preparing for this workshop, we did a search on Google Scholar and found more than 21,000! How did this happen?"

Touching Readers' Hearts

"We believe that the meteoric rise of autoethnography was stirred by the ways in which it touched people where they live. Autoethnography struck a chord in students and seasoned scholars whose personal and caring connection to research (and the people they studied) had been stifled and inhibited—if not crushed—by discredited methodological directives and inhibiting writing conventions. These people—some in this room today—wanted to tell stories that invited others to think *and* to feel. Eager to depart the safe and comfortable space of conventional academic writing in order to engage in non-alienating research practices, the new breed of qualitative researchers wanted to read, write, and/or perform texts that would make the hearts of their readers skip a beat (Hyde, 2010; Bochner, 2012a). They also understood that doing research focused on human longing, pleasure, pain, loss, grief, suffering, or joy ought to require holding authors to a higher standard of vulnerability, which we will be discussing and exemplifying over the course of this workshop."

Precepts of Autoethnography

"Okay, time for a break," says Art. "During the short break, please take a few moments to look at the document labeled 'Handout #1, Research Precepts for Interpretive Qualitative Research,' which is in your Workshop Packet. This handout outlines ten precepts associated with the turn away from realist, positivist, and modernist social science and toward the ideal of a reflexive, relational, dialogic, and collaborative research process grounded in a distinctively interpretive social science. These precepts are foundational to the autoethnographic paradigm. When you return, we will talk about them. Bring your comments and questions. Let's reconvene in fifteen minutes."

HANDOUT # 1

Research Precepts for
Interpretive Qualitative Research

(1) The researcher is part of the research data;

(2) A social science text always is composed by a particular somebody someplace;

(3) The writing process is part of the inquiry;

(4) Research involves the emotionality and subjectivity of both researchers and participants;

(5) The relationship between researchers and research participants should be democratic; the researcher's voice should not dominate the voices of participants;

(6) Researchers should accept an ethical obligation to give something important back to the people and communities they study and write about;

(7) What researchers write should be "for" participants as much as "about" them;

(8) Researchers and participants should be accountable to each other;

(9) Research should be about what could be (not just about what has been);

(10) The reader should be conceived as a co-participant, not a spectator, and given opportunities to think with (not just about) the research story (or findings).

When participants return, Art says, "Everybody, stand for a moment and take a big stretch. Shake your arms. Touch your ankles. Bend backwards. Try to get the blood circulating through your veins! That's great! Is everybody ready to go?" The participants give a big shout out and Art shows his appreciation, pointing two thumbs up as the participants take their seats.

"Let's start with some comments or questions about the precepts…"

A woman in the first row, Jan, raises her hand, and Art signals for her to speak.

"Would you tell us what you mean by a precept?" Jan asks. "I'm aware of the need to make the research process more democratic and dialogic, but I've never seen the points on your handout arranged like this. I need some guidance about how to use them."

"That's a good place to start. I think of precepts as teachings or assumptions. Taken together, they constitute a way of thinking about the research process as a whole—from start to finish. These particular precepts grew out of the response to 'the crisis of representation' in the human sciences that I mentioned yesterday. They are relevant to all forms of qualitative research construed as interpretive. That includes not only autoethnography but also arts-based inquiry, narrative analysis, and performance or interpretive ethnography.

"For example, look at Precept #1. Instead of thinking of the researcher as a neutral bystander, an objective spectator standing apart from the people being studied, we encourage you to think of the researcher as part of your data, a flesh and blood person who is alive, active, and feeling. This means that as a researcher you are obliged to acknowledge the self-interests, values, political ideals, and emotions that you bring to your research project. Why? Because your own lived experiences, beliefs, and values influence your observations and interpretations. Anthropologist Michael Jackson (1989, p. 17) insists that the knower cannot be separated from what the knower claims to know, because 'our understanding of others can only proceed from within our own experience. And this experience includes our personalities and histories as much as our field research.'

"I treat these precepts as *ethical obligations.* We are obliged to give something back to the people or communities we study and write about; we should democratize the research process; we should be accountable to our research participants, and so on. But these are not absolutes. Context counts and local circumstances matter. Still, as a researcher you are responsible for making humane decisions throughout the research process.

"I advise my students to go through the list of precepts systematically and ask themselves whether and how they've addressed these issues in their research projects. Carolyn will be taking up the question of how you can represent the voices and actions of other people in your autoethnographic stories—and other ethical conundrums— when she discusses relational ethics tomorrow. And we're both going to dwell on the ways in which the writing process poses dilemmas, challenges, and opportunities for you.

"I want you to start thinking of yourself as a composer; that is, as a writer. In the past, very few social scientists looked upon their writing as 'compositions.' They thought of themselves as reporters, not as writers. In autoethnography, as in many forms of qualitative research, writing is a crucial part of the research process. At this point, it seems odd to us that we ever thought the author was somehow not part of the story, essay, or book that was written. But that's ancient history now. There's no going back. To subscribe to the view of interpretive qualitative research as reflexive, dialogic, relational, and collaborative is to value writing as a means of communicating with readers in a way that gets to them. As an autoethnographer, you want your readers to feel something and/or to do something. That's where the artistry and creativity of autoethnography enters. But now I'm getting ahead of myself. Forgive me if I'm going beyond your question, Jan. As you likely can tell, I'm eager to get us into the whole issue of composing autoethnographies."

The Genre of Evocative Autoethnography

"I can't see everyone's badge, so you'll have to help me with names," Art says, pointing to a man in the second row who has raised his hand.

"My name is Tom," the man says, turning first to those behind him, then back towards Art. "My question is about categories of evocative autoethnography. The word *evocative* keeps coming up. It appeared in each of your autobiographies. You and Carolyn both talked about wanting to publish 'evocative' stories. Last year, I took a course at my university that covered autoethnography. Evocative autoethnography was the headliner, but other kinds of autoethnography also were covered."

"I'm curious. What other types were dealt with in that course?" Carolyn asks from her seat.

"Let me see. The ones I recall off the top of my head were *critical autoethnography, analytic autoethnography, queer autoethnography,* and *performance autoethnography*. But that is just my point. I learned a great deal in that course, but I left feeling as if I had a malady that might be called 'category confusion.' Are these equivalent kinds of autoethnography or are they different types of evocative autoethnography?"

"Do you want to take the question or do you want me to respond?" Art directs at Carolyn.

"You go ahead," Carolyn says.

"Well, I'm not a psychiatrist so I can't prescribe a pill to make you feel better," Art jokes. "But let me try to give you a framework for thinking about types and categories that can reduce the confusion you're experiencing.

"Typologies in social science research need to be looked at differently than those in sciences such as biology, where they describe mutually exclusive classifications in the natural world. For instance, a dolphin is a mammal and not a fish even though dolphins live their entire lives in the water. Why? Because dolphins are warm-blooded and breathe air using their lungs. A mammal can't be a fish. But critical autoethnographies can be evocative, and evocative autoethnographies can be critical; and queer autoethnographies can be critical and evocative, as can performance autoethnographies (see Adams and Holman Jones, 2011; Gergen and Gergen, 2012; Alexander, 2014; Boylorn and Orbe, 2014). No wonder you got confused, Tom. This is why I believe it's important to take an historical perspective.

"When Carolyn and I started calling what we were doing evocative autoethnography, we considered our work both *transgressive* and *critical*. We were breaking bad, misbehaving, and defying the rules. You know what 'breaking bad' means?"

Nobody responds, so Art continues. "It's an old Southern expression for raising hell. Think for a minute about what the two of us had advocated. We sanctioned writing in the first person; we approved of research in which the researcher became a principal object of research; we summoned stories that give voice to groups of people traditionally left out of social science inquiry; we gave permission to concentrate on a single case; we encouraged researchers to think of themselves as writers and to tell stories the way novelists do; we promoted emotional, vulnerable, and heartful writing; we discouraged jargon and celebrated erotic and close to the bone prose in which knowledge is delivered through emotional arousal, identification, and self-examination rather than abstraction and explanation. 'Let the story do the work,' we insisted. 'Be evocative. Make your readers feel stuff; activate their subjectivity; compel them to respond viscerally.' What mattered most to us was intimate detail, not abstracted facts. We were prepared to be scorned, ridiculed, and dismissed as off our rockers. But we believed in what we were doing, and thought others would too, if given permission.

"Initially, we didn't identify types of autoethnography. As I said earlier, we hadn't anticipated that an autoethnographic paradigm would take hold across the globe. We knew about critical theory, had read Foucault (1970, 1982) and Butler (1990), and were strongly aligned with the cause of social justice for LGBT people. You could say that we were 'queering' social science, but we didn't think of expressing ourselves that way. That's not the kind of voice either of us typically uses. We think Stacy Holman Jones and Tony Adams

(Adams and Holman Jones, 2008, 2011; Holman Jones and Adams, 2010) are on target to consider autoethnography as a political, 'queer' methodology useful for opening more ways of being in the world, but we don't believe that's all it is or should be, and we doubt they do either. We understand autoethnography not only as a method but as a way of life, a point we will highlight later in the workshop.

"From the beginning, even before we settled on the term 'autoethnography,' we saw evocation as a goal. So do many writers who use queer, critical, and performative autoethnography to move audiences emotionally in order to engage questions of identity, diversity, racism, sexism, injustice, and human suffering. We never believed, and still don't, that seeking to evoke, turning away from the presumptions of mimetic representation, and bringing the 'auto' self-consciously into ethnographic writing meant that we were shunning criticism. We agree with David Shields (2013, p. 3)—'all criticism is a form of autobiography,' and we wish more critics were as open about their autobiographical influences as he is. We conceive all autoethnography as potentially a form of criticism as well and, in the future, autoethnographers may need to be less subtle about the critical nature of their work."

Analytic Autoethnography

"What you're saying," Tom follows up, "is that there's a lot of overlap among the different kinds or autoethnography, but virtually all of them seek to evoke and arouse audiences or readers."

"I'll accept that way of expressing it. Yes," Art replies.

"I'm not trying to put you on the spot," Tom continues, "but I'm curious to know why you haven't included analytic autoethnography in your remarks."

"You're a good listener, Tom. I was hoping to sidestep the question of where or whether analytic autoethnography fits into the autoethnographic paradigm," Art kids.

Art pauses momentarily, thinking about how much he wants to say about this topic. He looks away from Tom and directs his comment to the participants as a whole. "Tom is referring to an article on analytic autoethnography that sociologist Leon Anderson (2006) published. In that article, he sketched the case for autoethnographies that emphasize analysis and theoretical abstraction in the tradition of the Chicago school realist ethnographers. When I initially read the article, I interpreted analytic autoethnography as an attempt to appropriate autoethnography into the mainstream and poach on its growing appeal across the human sciences.

"At the time Carolyn and I had a definite image in mind for what we wanted autoethnography to be and do. We conceived autoethnographic writing as intimate and vulnerable. It would seek to make people care, feel, empathize and do something on behalf of social justice. These goals were instigated by a desire to move ethnography away from disengaged reason and distanced analysis. But Anderson's (2006) analytic orientation reverses that course. He wants to take what is unruly, vulnerable, rebellious, and creative about autoethnography and bring it back under the control of reason and analysis. Is it any wonder I felt suspicious and defensive?

"Was I overreacting? Perhaps I was. Actually, Carolyn didn't react to Leon's paper as guardedly as I did, and she'll likely want to pick up this topic later." Art looks toward Carolyn, who nods.

"But I had good reasons to feel suspicious given some of the exaggerated and unsupported criticisms introduced by opponents of autoethnography: that autoethnography was nothing more than an author's quest for personal fulfillment; that autoethnography offered nothing new or different; that autoethnography made the ethnographer more important than the ethnography; and that all social science must, by its very nature, be theory-driven and committed to analysis. Though Carolyn thought I was acting overly suspicious, I read analytical autoethnography as yet another attempt to serve the interests of one class of academics over another—story analysts over storytellers (see Bochner, 2010; Bochner and Riggs, 2014). But of course, it can be treacherous to try to discern other people's motives.

"By and large, analytic autoethnographers highlight their obligations as 'story analysts.' They eschew both the 'art' of 'he(art)-ful' autoethnography and its value-centeredness. Instead, they cling to the traditional goals of generalization, distanced analysis, and theory-building, directing their work mainly to other scholars. They show little interest in the kind of understanding aroused by evoking emotional reactions that inspire readers to reflect critically on their own lives and turn those reflections into actions. That's why it didn't occur to me to include analytic autoethnography among the genres of evocative autoethnography.

"We have no desire to police the use of the term 'autoethnography.' We are thrilled that interest in autoethnography has escalated and expanded in many different directions. From the beginning, Carolyn and I hoped that other scholars would build on what we had started, opening options for the use of autoethnography that we could not have imagined.

"In this workshop, though, we concentrate on evocative forms of autoethnography that seek to make people feel deep in their guts and in their bones, using various forms of literary artfulness and storytelling to place the reader in the action. The 'story-likeness' of evocative autoethnography is what produces its lifelikeness, making it feel true and real. The reader feels it is true largely because of the story's striking sensory detail.

"I see Carolyn motioning to me that it's time for a break," Art says. "When we come back, I'll talk about how to take your actual lived-through experiences and make them into lifelike stories that feel real and true. There is no formula to follow in order to achieve this. But there is a craft to storytelling that can be practiced and nurtured over time.

"Stephen King (2002) refers to the craft of storytelling as a writer's toolbox. You carry it with you and use the appropriate tools to achieve the goals of evocative autoethnography. We've been talking around and about autoethnography as storytelling and about writing as method. Now we need to get down to specific details. What happens when you begin thinking of yourself as a writer? How is writing a method? How does storytelling work to make readers feel truth?

"But first, let's take a break and come back sharp. We'll resume in fifteen minutes."

Defining Evocative Autoethnography

Art and Carolyn huddle near the front table as the workshop participants trickle back into the room. They express their pleasure with how the workshop has started, though both acknowledge a desire for more interaction with participants. Art says he thinks this will happen more quickly once they get through the material on definitions and goals of autoethnography.

Carolyn takes a seat behind the table. Art continues to stand and begins speaking as a few lingering participants re-enter the room.

"The first thing my college debate coach taught me was to define my terms. Quoting Voltaire, he insisted, 'If you want to converse with me, define your terms.' Fair enough! I'm here to converse with you, so let me define my terms.

"Please turn to 'Handout #2.'" Art pauses as the participants locate the handout in their packets.

"This definition of autoethnography is adapted from the chapter Carolyn and I published in *The Handbook of Qualitative Research* (Ellis and Bochner, 2000). Take a minute or two to read over the definition. Then, we'll discuss it.

"Keep in mind that this was our first attempt to introduce our conception and vision of autoethnography to a broad audience of social scientists. We knew that autoethnography would be new to many of them. But a number of readers of the *Handbook* likely would come to our chapter with an ethnographic sensibility. They would see themselves as researchers and be looking to thicken and expand their knowledge of methodologies for studying cultural, institutional, and relational life. We wanted to speak to readers in a way that would encourage openness to the otherness of autoethnography. They might perceive autoethnography as strange and different, but we didn't want the abnormality of autoethnography to pose a threat to researchers' ingrained beliefs about, and orientations toward, qualitative research. As readers got deeper into our approach to autoethnography, we hoped they would begin to appreciate its benefits, the ways in which autoethnography expands the scope and depth of the human sciences, bringing human subjectivity, reflexivity, emotionality, gender,

HANDOUT # 2

Autoethnography: Definition and Key Terms

Autoethnography is an *autobiographical genre of writing and research* that *displays multiple layers of consciousness, connecting the personal to the cultural.* Back and forth, autoethnographers gaze, first, through an *ethnographic* wide-angle lens, *focusing outward on social and cultural* aspects of their *personal experience*; then, they *look Inward*, exposing a *vulnerable self* that is *moved* by and *may move through, refract, and resist cultural interpretations.* As they zoom backward and forward, inward and outward, distinctions between the personal and cultural become blurred, sometimes beyond recognition. Usually *written in the first-person voice*, autoethnographic texts appear in *a variety of forms*—short stories, poetry, fiction, novels, photographic essays, personal essays, journals, fragmented and layered writing, and social science prose. In these texts, *concrete action, dialogue , emotion, embodiment, spirituality, and self-consciousness* are featured in *relational, family, institutional, and community stories* affected by *history, social structure, and culture*, which themselves are *revealed through action, feeling, thought, and language* (Ellis & Bochner, 2000, p. 739).

Key Terms:

Autobiographical *and* ethnographic; writing *and* research; personal *and* cultural; outward *and* inward focus; relational *and* institutional; multiple levels of consciousness; vulnerable self; first-person voice; variety of forms; concrete action; dialogue; feeling; embodiment; self-consciousness; stories.

race, sexual identity, and the body more centrally into the vocation of the human sciences.

"If you examine our definition and key terms closely, you should be able to unveil how we went about joining rather than alienating our readers, while at the same time bending the customary 'rigorous' ways of doing things—neutral tone, fact-based exposition, third-person voice—toward a fresh approach to re-presenting realities of lived experiences.

"First, we depict autoethnography as *an orientation to research,* but we also call attention to *writing as central* to the autoethnographic paradigm.

"Second, we emphasize both the *ethnographic, outward lens (toward culture)* and the *autobiographical, inward scrutiny (toward the self),* however blurred, of *a vulnerable observer.*

"Third, we normalize, but qualify, *the first-person voice* as usual but not imperative, emphasizing the *variety of forms* autoethnography can take, as well as the numerous and *diverse stylistic features* by which its concrete action is expressed.

"Finally, we underscore the necessity of casting a wide net of *multiple layers of consciousness, self-consciousness, and reflection* that embody autoethnography's desire to cope with dilemmas and contradictions of being alive and to deal with blows of fate and *epiphanies of circumstance.*

"Although we aspired to make autoethnography attractive and unintimidating to newcomers and outsiders, we also wanted to trouble, unsettle, and transgress boundaries. Autoethnography inhabits a space between science and art; between epistemology and ontology; between facts and meanings; between experience and language; between the highly stylized conventions of fact-based reporting and the unfixed alternatives of literary, poetic, and dramatic exposition; between a cold and rational objectivity and a hot and visceral emotionality; between a commitment to document the reality of what actually happened and a desire to make readers feel that truth coursing through their blood and guts."

Art pauses and Tom says, "That's a lot of information. Would you summarize the goals of autoethnography for us?" Art looks at

Carolyn, who takes his cue and says, "In short, autoethnographers would compose stories that fused social science and literature by merging the methods of the interpretive human sciences with the aesthetics of the arts and humanities (Benson, 1993). In autoethnography, we combine the systematic, 'scientific' methodologies of ethnography with the evocative, creative, and artistic elements and forms of storytelling."

"Thanks, Carolyn," Art says, "for that crisp synthesis."

"Now that terms have been defined and I've sketched our perspective on evocative autoethnography, we should be ready to get down to the nitty gritty of writing autoethnography. I'm going to use the rest of my time today to focus on autoethnography's storytelling dimensions. Tomorrow, Carolyn will take up the 'ethno' in autoethnography, as well as the ethical dilemmas and methodological choices one encounters in autoethnographic research.

"But first I want to give you an opportunity to make comments or ask questions. Oh, by the way, I want to express my thanks to the Congress staff who were able to make those large name tags. Now I can call you by name.

"Andrew, you're up."

"I was fascinated by your depiction of autoethnography's liminality—it's between-ness," Andrew begins. "I love how autoethnography sits in the middle of things—you know, between art and science, between rationality and emotionality, and so on. I am especially attracted to the ways in which autoethnography moves between epistemology and ontology. So thank you for that. I did hear some hesitation in your voice, though, when you were talking about autoethnography as method. Do you consider autoethnography a method?"

"I'm glad you brought up liminality," Art replies. "Twenty years ago, autoethnography had no status or ranking whatsoever. It existed in the liminality that anthropologist Victor Turner (1967, p. 97) calls 'a realm of pure possibility.' Actually, that can be a good place to occupy, because that's where novel and creative ideas arise. Ultimately, liminality ends in recognition. Of course, we weren't exactly outsiders trying to get inside. As autoethnographers, we sat comfortably on the margins, but we imagined that others like us existed; we just didn't know how many. We didn't see autoethnography as a passage to something else, except perhaps the development of *communitas* (Turner, 1974), a style of life that others would want to embrace and join, akin to what hippies did in the 1960s and 70s in the United States.

"By saying this, I'm alluding to autoethnography's ontological status. I think this may be where your question about autoethnography as method arises. Sooner or later, life brings each of us unanticipated and/or unwanted darkness, sadness, frustration, and loss. These moments leave their mark on us. You could say that our bodies are tattooed by them, though not by choice. Heidegger (1962/2008) referred to such moments as 'simplifying' insofar as they make us aware of what is extraneous and peripheral and the possibilities that exist to dedicate one's life to what is definitively important. But neither Heidegger nor anyone else can tell *you* what is truly important for *your* life. That's why epiphanies often bring us to a decisive moment in which we may feel as if we're standing on a sheer existential cliff. How do we survive the chaos and confusion? What can we do to shine a ray of hope through the boundless darkness to find positive meanings in even our gloomiest experiences? These lives we live, they have to mean something, don't they? But what do they mean and how can our pursuit of their meanings help us decide what to do to recover our lost innocence, our faith in ourselves, our friends and lovers, and the future?

"My answer to these questions, the autoethnographic answer, is to return to the scenes that tarnished us, the ones hovering in our memories awaiting an opportunity for us to take pen in hand and write ourselves into a moment of transcendence, however fleeting. That's what I have tried to achieve between the lines of the stories in my book, *Coming to Narrative* (Bochner, 2014). I have tried to place the contingencies of life on the page—its unknowability, uncertainty, and mystery—in a form that bends and blends—as it must—fictions, fantasies, meditations, ethnographies, confessions, and self-consciousness about what it means to be alive.

"What do you think, Andrew? Does my description make auto-ethnography sound like a way of life or a research method; or am I saying that the autoethnographic way of life is a continuous process of research into one's being and meaning and thus methodological as well as ontological?"

"I think I get what you're saying," says Andrew.

"What's that? Tell me."

"You're saying that a way of being can be thought of as a meth-od of living. Autoethnographers are perpetually researching their own lives, delving into, thinking about, and reflecting on them."

"Not only their own lives, but others' lives too," Art replies. "Carolyn will have much more to say about this tomorrow when she talks about interactive and compassionate interviewing."

"As a method?" Andrew asks, winking at Art.

"Yes, as a method." Art winks back. "This is the ethnographic part of autoethnography."

"But ethnography can also be thought of as a way of life, can't it?" a woman named Jane interrupts from the back of the room.

"Yes, of course. The anthropologist Dan Rose wrote a stunning little book, *Living the Ethnographic Life* (1990), in which he made precisely that point."

Autoethnography's Ethics of Sympathy

"Before we move on to storytelling, I'll take one more question," Art says.

"I have one," Jack calls out. "Why aren't autoethnographies hap-pier? They always seem to focus on tragedies or personal traumas?"

"Oh yes, that's a question that comes up often in our work-shops. Many people do read autoethnographies as overly tragic or sad, which suggests to me that we need a deeper grasp of the connection between suffering and happiness (Bochner, 2012c). We know that suffering is an inevitable part of every life. Sooner or later each of us has to deal with suffering. Autoethnographic sto-ries attempt to bring vivid and resonant frames of understanding to one's anguish and pain. Unfortunately, the way some stories get told (or read) creates the impression that tragedy and happiness are opposites. But happiness is at stake in every autoethnographic story of suffering. Indeed, the possibility of happiness in the presence of suffering is central to the whole project of autoethnography. Is there love without suffering? Is there happiness devoid of conflict, anxiety, or trouble?"

The room grows silent. When nobody moves to reply to Art's questions, he speaks into the silence. "If a story frightens or terrifies the listener, then the story has failed to evoke the kind of sympathy autoethnography seeks. Tragedy is supposed to evoke the listener's capacity to be concerned for the well-being of the other. I call this phenomenon autoethnography's *ethics of sympathy*. You could also think of it as an *ethics of happiness* (Bochner, 2012c). In this respect, every autoethnographic narrative of suffering refuses to be an end in itself; it anticipates and seeks something beyond suffering. Often the call of autoethnography is an appeal for social justice."

On Reading Autoethnography

"But is that how readers approach autoethnography? Not often enough in my opinion. People need to be taught how to listen to autoethnography. I don't think we've concentrated near enough attention on the question of how autoethnography should be read. We need informed readers and audiences.

"We autoethnographers want our audiences to see that there was meaning and value in our suffering and that we are affirming life, ours and that of the other people who are characters in our stories. When you read autoethnography, you become a *witness* to the narrative context of another person's suffering. Autoethnographers expect their readers to become deeply involved and drawn into the predicaments of their stories. The reader's life is implicated in and by the text and the life it depicts. Reflexivity is a charge not only to the writer, but also to the reader, who is not just a consumer of the story but also by implication a character in it. When autoethnography works, it evokes not only a sympathetic response and a reflexive questioning of the connection of one's own life to the story, but also a desire to correct the injustice(s) depicted (Berry and Patti, 2015).

"I recall telling students in one of my graduate seminars that the whole project of autoethnography can be understood as a search for better conversation in the face of all the barriers and boundaries that make good and evocative conversation increasingly difficult to find. I suppose that's the communication professor in me speaking.

"But that conversation is not only with others; it's also with one's self. The autoethnographies we write put us into dialogue with ourselves as we expose our vulnerabilities, conflicts, choices, and values. We take the measure of our uncertainties, our mixed and amalgamated emotions, and the multiple layers of our consciousness of what happened to us. Our accounts seek to express the complexities and difficulties of coping and trying to feel resolved, showing how we changed over time as we struggled to make sense of our experience. Our accounts of ourselves are unflattering and imperfect, but human and believable. In this sense, we use the autoethnographic text as an agent of self-understanding and ethical dialogue.

"In autoethnography, this dialogue extends outward to our readers as well. We use storytelling as a method for inviting readers to put themselves in our place. The dialogue centers on moral choices—decisions having more to do with how to live than with how to know (Jackson, 1995)."

Art points toward Erica, who is waving her arm feverishly to gain his attention. "I have a good example here of the kind of moral choices you're speaking about. Listen to how Tony Adams (2006, p. 721) agonizes over the moral choices presented to him as he reflects on the aftermath of coming out as a gay man to his father:

> I'm stuck between two canonical stories: one that says my father and I must always try to work things out to fulfill my responsibilities as son and another that tells me to let go, to realize that I "can't choose my relatives," and to view the relationship as a waste of time. Such thoughts provide me with an all-or-nothing scenario, not allowing for a middle on which to rest. I have thought of terminating the relationship, but in a few, recent interactions, I've noticed a spark of love I've tried to grab. Maybe that spark only developed out of hope for what I consider a more reciprocal exchange of love.

"Thank you, Erica. That's a terrific example of the moral workings of autoethnography and the ways in which a writer's consciousness gets placed on the page.

"I want to bring this part of the workshop to a close by reminding you that we want readers to enter autoethnographic stories from the perspective of their own lives. The story's usefulness rests on its capacity to provoke readers to broaden their horizons, reflect critically on their own experience, enter empathically into worlds of experience different from their own, and actively engage in dialogue regarding the social and moral implications of the perspective and standpoints they've encountered in the story. Invited to take the story in and use it for themselves, readers become co-performers—you can think of them as additional characters in the story—examining themselves through the evocative power of the text.

"Our time is up for today. Tomorrow we'll turn to the topic of autoethnographic storytelling. Carolyn and I live what we sometimes call 'a writing life.' Overnight, think about what that could mean. Do you live a writing life? What kind of life is a writing life? That would be a good topic for dinner conversation.

"The material you received when you registered for the Congress included a list of good restaurants in town. You might want to go together in small groups. Have fun, and we'll see you bright and early tomorrow."

Part Two

Composing Evocative Stories

Crafting Evocative Autoethnography

"**G**ood morning," Art says. "We have a packed day, so I'm eager to get started.

"We're ready now to turn to storytelling, my favorite topic. When I offer my narrative seminar, I start by reminding students that a story is always told by someone to someone at some place. Yesterday, I talked about the importance of the people to whom we tell our autoethnographic stories—the story readers. Now, I'm going to reverse course and focus on the storyteller.

"As human beings, we live our lives as storytelling animals. We are born into a world of stories and storytellers, ready to be shaped and fashioned by the narratives to which we will be exposed. The stories we hear and the stories we tell are not only about our lives;

they are part of them. Our lives are rooted in narratives and narrative practices. We depend on stories almost as much as we depend on the air we breathe. Air keeps us alive; stories give meaning to our existence. One of the main goals of autoethnography is to put meanings into motion, and the best way to do that is to tell stories.

"At breakfast this morning, Carolyn and I got to thinking about the stories many of you told yesterday when we asked you to introduce yourselves. During our conversation, I was reminded that Michael Bamberg (2006), a psychologist at Clark University, calls the kind of narratives you were sharing 'small stories.' He studies how people establish and/or negotiate an identity using small stories in relatively brief interactions with other people. Most of you told how you identify yourselves as academics. You expressed what brought you to this workshop and the kind of research you want to do to make your academic life meaningful. The way you described yourself showed that you were mindful of being in an academic setting talking to other researchers.

"You may have observed—I know I did—that none of you referred to yourself as 'a storyteller.' That's not surprising. Few researchers think of themselves primarily as storytellers. In the social sciences, we don't normally offer methods classes under the heading 'storytelling.' But we do offer courses that give instruction in how to conduct research. Most of you have taken several classes focusing on measurement theory, statistics, and research design, as well as on developing interview, survey, and data analysis skills. These courses constitute your basic training as a researcher. In some of them, you've had to carry out a research project and 'write up' the results. These assignments have been an integral part of your socialization as a social scientist. Through the process, you learned to think and act like a researcher. Eventually you took on that identity, and began to think of yourself as a researcher." Art pauses momentarily, noting the large number of participants nodding their heads.

"But hold on for a second. Did you ever wonder if anything had been left out of your training as a social scientist?" Art pauses momentarily to allow participants to ponder his question.

"Let's go back to that class in which you were asked to 'write up' your research study. Did you know how to do that? If you are, or were, like graduate students in most social science programs, you didn't have any formal instruction in writing. Certainly, you heard a lot about how you would need to publish, but you weren't offered any formal instruction on the 'writing part' of publishing. Like most of us, you were left on your own.

"Lacking formal instruction, what did you do? I assume you did what most of us did. You read the research articles, monographs, and books of other researchers in your field. Perhaps you detected similarities among them and tried to model or copy the pattern. For example, most empirical research reports follow a standardized format. They start with some justification and a literature review; they describe methods and procedures; they detail the results; and they discuss and interpret findings. Witnessing this uniformity, you may have reasoned that your written document should conform to this structure: *'If I deviate from this pattern, I'll be risking the scorn of my advisors or rejection from journal referees. I better master and follow the conventions.'*

"When you write an empirical research paper for the first time—even the first few times—you may feel unprepared, even intimidated. I know I did, because I hadn't received any specific instruction on how to write a research article. Why not? Why did I have to fly by the seat of my pants? Because I was being trained as a *researcher*, not educated as a *writer*. After all, researchers in the social sciences don't have to be storytellers." Art walks toward the whiteboard, stops suddenly, then turns back quickly. "Or do they?" he asks.

Writing in the Social Sciences

"We'll get to that question later. But first, I want to ask you what you think of social science writing. Not autoethnography, but other kinds of social science writing. Are published social science articles a good read? Do you look forward to reading empirical research monographs? Do you keep social science journals and research papers by your bedside to browse at night?"

"Only if I'm looking for something to put to me to sleep!" a male voice calls out from the back, and the participants erupt in laughter.

"Tell me why so many of you reacted that way," Art invites.

"The jargon, oh, I hate all that technical language," a woman named Betty responds. "It's incomprehensible to most people and hideous to me. I find myself constantly consulting a dictionary. Why do social scientists insist on talking that way? I think they do it to impress other scholars, to show that they're smart and they belong in the field. I just wish they'd talk like ordinary people."

"BORING," sings out another participant. "I am hardly ever able to get through a traditional research article in one reading."

"Not worth the time and effort," someone else offers.

"Too abstract," says another.

"Okay, okay, stop!" Art says. "We don't need to belabor the point. Reading social science research is not a lot of fun. 'Torturous' is the word some undergraduates use to describe their reading assignments in social science courses. I have compassion for them. Most of them are not lazy or indifferent students. When I talk with them in class, I am impressed with how hard most are trying to understand what they read. It pains me to see their confidence shattered by the poor writing to which they are subjected.

"Laurel Richardson (1994a) has complained bitterly about the way social science monographs are written. She claims that seasoned scholars don't finish half of the research studies that they start out to read because the writing is dry, uninviting, and drenched in jargon. After a while most give up reading the journals they should be reading, many of which they've published in themselves. As Carolyn sometimes quips..." he turns to Carolyn.

"Life's too short," she says on cue, and the participants laugh.

"I'm not saying that these articles are unimportant or fail to contribute to knowledge of the social world," Art continues. "Many of them do. But they aren't widely read or appreciated by the public or by students majoring in the social sciences.

"Why isn't traditional social science more read and appreciated? Michael Billig (2013) blames this condition on what he calls 'the academic dialect.' According to Billig, if you want to succeed in the social sciences, you have to learn to write badly and to make the topics about which you are writing difficult to grasp. You learn to cloak ideas in jargon, using long and obscure words. As Betty suggested, you think you need to sound smart in order to gain respect, so you stop speaking like an ordinary person and start talking like an academic, that is, in the academic dialect. Not many people have mastered the academic jargon you use, but you needn't worry. You sound as if you know what you're talking about. Besides, the readers' insecurities will assure that you will be respected. Like a bully, the obscure writer humiliates the reader into submission by centering the action on theoretical 'things' rather than on actual people who, of course, would never talk in an 'academic dialect' unless they were seeking to be admired as academics (Billig, 2013).

"By comparison, evocative autoethnographers focus attention on people. We want to connect with our readers. Unimpressed by jargon, we prefer to talk the way most human beings talk. Communication is the pleasure and burden of our work. Since we live in much the same world as our readers, we believe our readers should not have to struggle endlessly to understand and relate to us. Our challenge is to artfully arrange life in ways that enable readers to enter into dialogue with our lives as well as with their understanding of their own.

"How did writing in the social sciences become so deplorable? The answer is not complicated. On the whole, social scientists seek to gain respect as researchers, and writing has not been considered part of the research process. Since the researcher is considered a carrier—someone who delivers results without affecting them—realist models of inquiry attach little importance to writing. This neglect tacitly communicates that competence as a writer has little to do with getting one's work published. As a result, one's identity as a researcher does not incorporate the idea that a research paper, article, or monograph ultimately is something made, something constructed and crafted. Is it any wonder, then, that most social scientists never get around to asking, 'How can I write this in such a way that people will want to read it?'

"As a professor of communication, I study communication. But communication is not only *what* I study; communication also is *how* I study and *how I represent* what I study. That's one of the main things I'm trying to impress upon you today—that you should think of yourself as a writer, a communicator, and especially as a storyteller. When this happens, you will by necessity begin to attend not only to *what* you are trying to communicate, but also to *how*.

"In autoethnography, writing is not an activity that stands apart from the rest of the research process. Autoethnographers want to twist and turn readers' heads and make their hearts skip a beat now and then. We want to evoke feeling and induce readers to make a personal connection to the stories we are telling. Our writing is not simply academic; it's personal and artistic too.

"To evoke the kind of personal connection that I'm talking about, autoethnographers usually resist the temptation to surrender to orthodox conventions of social science writing. Our goal is to extend the borders of legitimate scholarship to matters of practical, moral, aesthetic, and emotional importance to human well-being. Since we are frequently focusing on issues of human fulfillment, survival, and justice, we are responsive to a different call of conscience than orthodox social scientists."

The Autoethnographic Call of Conscience: Vulnerable Writing

"Carolyn and I propose a reflexive ideal of conscience applicable to authors as well as readers, one in which the researcher/writer answers the call by saying, 'Here I am.' Audre Lorde (1984) provides an evocative example of what I have in mind when she writes, 'Because I am a woman, because I am Black, because I am Lesbian, because I am myself a Black woman warrior poet, doing my work, I come to ask you, are you doing yours?' (pp. 41–42).

"Lorde is issuing a call to conscience as a vulnerable writer. She's asking, 'Are you doing your part? Where art thou?' She goes on to say that she is afraid, because hers is an act of self-revelation fraught with the danger of vulnerability introduced when what has been silenced is put into language.

"Her daughter answers the call, acknowledging the gift of Audre's revelation. 'Tell them about how you're never really a whole person if you remain silent,' she insists, 'because there's always that one little piece inside you that wants to be spoken out, and if you keep ignoring it, it gets madder and madder and hotter and hotter, and if you don't speak it out one day it will just up and punch you in the mouth from the inside' (p. 42).

"Lorde's question and her daughter's evocative response tell us who they are and how they propose to meet the challenge to which they are called. They are vulnerable observers and vulnerable writers. They make their work *personally* important, exalting difference, responsibility, and openness to otherness by showing their faces. You don't need to be black, a lesbian, or a poet to appreciate the force of the question, 'Who am I and what work am I doing here?' Audre Lorde and her daughter show the kind of openness to otherness that vulnerable writing implies, attempting to form a personal connection between author and audience, which is rare in academic prose.

"Often, the work of autoethnographers expresses a personal and cultural urgency with a critical edge. Ruth Behar (1996, p. 177) states this point succinctly when she speaks about the often heartbreaking work of anthropologists who become vulnerable observers: 'Call it sentimental, call it Victorian and nineteenth century, but I say that anthropology that doesn't break your heart just isn't worth doing anymore.'

"Carolyn and I talk often about how much we appreciate authors who write vulnerably about their own personal experiences (Tompkins, 1987). This is how an author's face is shown to readers in the constrained medium of academic writing. How can I, as a reader, answer the call to respond to an author's otherness, as one beating heart to another, if I am denied access to what makes the author distinctively other?

"Though autoethnographers sometimes fall short of this goal, what we are seeking is communion with the writer's 'circle of existence' (Tompkins, 1987, p. 170). This kind of communion is unlikely to take place when writers abide strictly by the conventions of

third-person academic prose, which denies readers an opportunity to enter into dialogue with the writer's existence as well
as their own. That's why autoethnography as a writing project
diverges radically from the analytic, third-person spectator voice
of traditional social science prose. Ursula Le Guin (1986) refers to
the third-person voice as 'the father tongue,' a high-minded mode
of expression that seeks and embraces objectivity. Spoken from
above, the father tongue distances the writer from the reader,
creating a gap between self and other. Autoethnographic writing
resists this kind of emotional distancing.

"What is missing from social science is 'the mother tongue'
(Le Guin, 1986), a binding form of subjective and conversational
expression that seeks and covets 'a turning together' of writer and
reader. Communicated in a language of emotions and personal
experience, the mother tongue exposes rather than protects the
speaker through a medium that can bring author and reader closer
together. The absence of a mother tongue reflects the conventions
of disembodied writing that extol the virtue of objectivity. As Le
Guin (p. 151) notes, 'People crave objectivity because to be subjective is to be embodied, to be a body, vulnerable, violable.' The real
discourse of reason, she claims, is a wedding of the father to mother
tongue, which produces 'a native tongue.'

"When this fusion of voices occurs, which is rare, it's a beautiful
thing (Eastman, 2007). Tomorrow Carolyn will show and discuss
exemplars of layered accounts, seamless narration, and other
modes of writing autoethnography that seek this fusion. But now is
the time to be practical. Let's talk more directly about writing lives
and telling stories."

Features of Stories

"If you're going to be a storyteller, you need to know something
about the structure of stories and principles of storytelling. The
story is what gives artistic shape to autoethnography. I'm going to
say much more about the 'artistry' of autoethnography, but let's
start by identifying basic ingredients of a story."

Carolyn walks to the whiteboard, marker in hand. "I'll be your 'spontaneous PowerPoint,'" she says playfully.

"Alright, so what are the features of a story?" Art asks.

"*Character, setting, time,*" a voice proclaims from the middle of the room.

"Character, setting, time," Art repeats, and Carolyn scribbles these words on the white board under *Story Features*. "Good, good, thank you very much. That's a mouthful. You're easing my work-load," Art kids. "In a few moments, we'll dig into these features a little deeper. But I don't think we've yet exhausted the elements of stories. What are we missing?" Art nods toward Bill, who has his hand raised.

"*Plot.*"

"Yes, of course. A story is expected to have a plot. You can think of plot as the basic idea, the point of the story. Plot is the answer to the 'why' question. Why are you writing this story? What does the story mean? You may remember reading Aesop's fables in elementary school. Does anyone recall how each fable ended?"

story features:
-character
-setting
-time

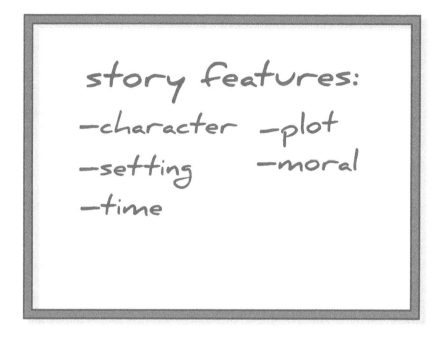

story features:
—character —plot
—setting   —moral
—time

"With a *moral*," Bill replies.

"That's right. The moral of the story could be 'one person's pleasure is another person's pain,' or 'necessity is the mother of invention,' or 'try to please all and you end up pleasing none,' and so on. I bring this up to make the point that stories are arranged around events that lead somewhere. The action of a story moves toward some larger significance or meaning. But I don't want you to think of plot as some neat, Hollywood-type ending that ties up all loose ends.

"Actually, quite a few postmodern writers tell stories that destabilize or play around with 'realist' storytelling conventions. They use unfinished scenes, question whether people can confidently determine the reasons things happen the way they do, and compose nonlinear, discontinuous collages or fragments of story that end up not being story-like at all. They want writers to take more risks, to convey the fractured character of contemporary life, and to bend and blend genres. Their stories pay homage to ambiguity and the messiness and incompleteness of life in forms that reveal lived experiences as both tragic and laughable."

"What do you think of this kind of writing?" asks Andrew.

"In general, I approve of these goals. But once you acknowledge that the world doesn't tell you what it means, what then? Most of us desire to live a meaningful life, and to live that life in a world that is moving toward greater justice, love, and mercy. After we acknowledge that human existence is riddled with inconsistencies and contradictions, we still have to deal with the predicaments we find or make for ourselves. Besides, even the most complicated and bizarre (to read and follow) postmodern literature is targeted at a larger meaning. It has a purpose. The writer is selecting and arranging materials to make a point. Even if the point is that life is pointless or that every perception can be made to contest itself—which many people don't concede—the writer still must compose sentences that negate or contradict themselves to make that argument.

"But now I fear I'm getting us off track. We're not here to interrogate the purpose of postmodern literature. I draw on the example of that genre to highlight the caution that we should exercise as we draw our autoethnographic stories to a close.

"Most autoethnographic stories situate people in predicaments in which they must deal with and/or solve problems in order to find and/or create some emotional truth out of experiences they've lived through. Autoethnographers want to make knowledge that others can use. Inevitably our stories arrive at a place in which actions are required. What to do becomes severed from what to think. There we confront an important difference between *theorizing* and *dealing with* a predicament. As Karl Knausgaard (2013, p. 129) observed about his own life, 'I thought in abstract reality in order to understand it. I thought in concrete reality in order to deal with it.'

"I have one other question that can direct our attention to plot. Are you still with me?"

"Yes!" several participants shout before Art can cup his ear.

"Good. Then here's the question: How do you feel when you sit through a movie for two or three hours and, as it ends, you're left scratching your head because you feel lost?"

"Dissatisfied and stupid," Amy interrupts.

"You didn't get it. 'What's the point?' you ask yourself," Art continues.

"I know just what you mean," Bill says. "That's frustrating. I feel as if I flunked the test."

"I do too," Art says. "That's the challenge you sometimes face as a writer. You don't want to boil everything down to an overly simplistic meaning, but you also need to accept the burden of the storyteller, which is to address the most fundamental question of storytelling for the reader: *what does all this mean*? What's the point? And this is not as easy as it may sound.

"Laurel Richardson (1994a, 2000) refers to writing as 'a method of inquiry.' She conceives of the writing process as a way of discovering the story in your experience and what it means. In concert with Richardson, Vivian Gornick (2008, p. 8) acknowledges that 'what actually happened is only raw material; what the writer makes of what happened is all that matters.'

"I usually find myself digging and digging for the deeper meanings of the situations I'm working through as I construct the story. I don't start out with a ready-made plot. I trust that the story is going to lead somewhere and eventually I'm going to find myself there. As I make my way through drafts of scenes, dialogue, emotions, and conflicts, I gradually arrive, however tentatively, at the place the story wants to rest. Often, that's not where I expected it to go. Once I've landed, though, I realize I have a lot more work to do. If I want to hold the reader in a state of page-turning excitement, I need to go back to the beginning and fulfill my obligation as a trustworthy guide, steering the reader through the journey by means of character, dialogue, action, and exposition. Many options exist. We'll be taking up exemplars of this process over the next two days.

"Okay, then, we have several elements—character, setting, time, plot, moral," Art reads from the board, then turns back to face the class. "Is that it?"

"*Drama.* You need some sort of dramatic element," says Ruth.

"That's excellent, Ruth. Drama is essential. As I suggested a moment ago, you want readers to keep turning the pages and to get

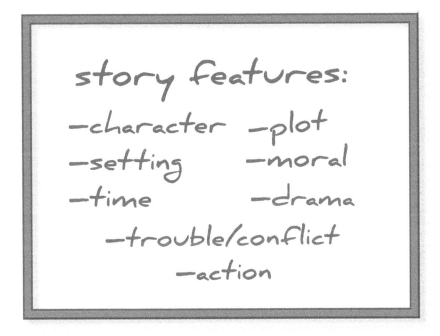

story features:
—character   —plot
—setting   —moral
—time   —drama
—trouble/conflict
—action

lost (and found) in the story. I prefer the word *trouble* or *conflict*, some difficulty around which the *action* of the story revolves and the character(s) struggle. So, I would add 'action' to our list too. *Trouble* is the complication that motivates the story's action. The reader is pulled into the story by the hurdles and obstacles with which characters are wrestling. Injustice, pain, puzzlement, contradiction—whatever you end up labeling them—these troubles are what drive narrative and make it possible for others to find their own plights in the quandaries with which these characters are struggling. We want our readers to see themselves in us. In this way, perhaps they can feel momentarily relieved of some of their loneliness. Performing these lived-through dramas, we transform private troubles into public plight, making evocative autoethnography powerful, comforting, dangerous, and culturally essential.

"Actually, the main features of storytelling haven't changed since Aristotle discussed them in *The Poetics*. Since you've been listening to and telling stories nearly all your life, they're already wired into your nervous system. You already know them. Now you know that you know them. I've summarized the features Carolyn's been writing on the board in Handout #3.

"Now, let's add a little flesh to the bones of these features by considering five activities in which you're engaged when you're composing an autoethnographic story: characterizing, dramatizing, timing, structuring, and revising. I start with *characterizing.*"

HANDOUT # 3

Features of Storytelling

Normally, the stories people tell follow certain conventions of storytelling. Most stories contain similar features and follow similar patterns of development. These include:

(1) People depicted as *characters* in the story;

(2) A *setting, scene, place,* or *context* in which the story occurs;

(3) A *temporal ordering* of events;

(4) An *epiphany* or *crisis* of some sort that provides *trouble* and *dramatic tension,* around which the *plot or action* depicted in the story revolve and towards which a resolution and/or explanation is pointed;

(5) A point or *moral to the story* that provides an explanation and gives meaning and value to the experiences depicted.

Characterizing

"Storytellers portray the people in their stories, including themselves, as characters: protagonist, antagonist, hero, victim, or survivor. Every character has unique traits. People talk, move, and do things a certain way. No two people look or act exactly alike. They differ emotionally and physically. Most people have a light side as well as a dark side. As an autoethnographer, you're not so much creating character as you are investigating and discovering it, then putting what you observed on the page. For example, here is a brief excerpt from my book in which I introduce a former professor, Dr. David Levine, to readers:

> Short and slim, Dr. Levine wore the same brown tweed sports coat every day with an open collar shirt, khaki slacks, and brown loafers; and he brought a pipe to class, which he chewed on constantly, but never smoked. The hacking, chronic cough that sometimes interrupted his lectures suggested he found ample time to smoke outside of class. His thick-rimmed eye glasses, pale complexion, and short, cropped hair reminded me of Wally Cox, who played Mr. Peepers, a shy and mild-mannered science teacher, on one of my favorite TV series of the early fifties. Often prone to long and deliberate pauses, Levine spoke softly and deliberately in a monotone, often staring off into space and rarely making eye contact with students. His calm and quiet manner eventually made me feel more comfortable in his presence than with any professor I'd known. (Bochner, 2014, p. 40)

"I can picture him," Beverly calls out.

"Good, that's what I'm seeking. I want you to visualize him, get an impression of his mannerisms and what he sounds like when he talks."

"He reminds me of my major professor," says Blaine. "Very laid back. I imagine other people in this room made similar connections," he says, pointing to other participants nodding or raising their hands.

"You may be interested in why I highlighted these particular features of Levine. The answer is uncomplicated: *Character animates story*. In the book, a relationship evolves between Levine and me, one that profoundly affects me as time passes. Readers don't know this yet, but I've established how relaxed and at ease I feel in Levine's presence, which later on will help make his influence on me believable.

"Following this introduction, I develop several scenes both inside and outside the classroom in which readers observe Levine in action. In these scenes, Levine's persona speaks for itself in the way he talks, moves, and relates to other characters in the scenes.

"Toni, you've been trying to get into the conversation."

"When I read your book last summer, I really connected with Levine. I thought of him as your ethical guide, someone whose wisdom had been passed to you more or less unconsciously. Some of the tough decisions you made were a direct result of the way he resided in your consciousness even though you had only one face-to-face talk with him. That made me think about the awesome influence I can have on students and how enduring my hold on them can be."

"What a lovely observation," Art replies. "We do, indeed, have a powerful effect on students. And I very much like how you were reading with my story. As you suggest, character and plot are closely connected. We understand or identify with characters through a plot that ties together what happens and invites readers or listeners to evaluate the meanings of the actors' actions and decisions. Here is the place where readers enter an ethical dimension in which stories invite evaluations of 'goodness' and 'character,' evoking reflections, evaluations, and reactions to human qualities such as faithfulness, thoughtfulness, and responsiveness (Ricoeur, 1992). Often, we find ourselves evaluating or coming to terms with the degree to which characters have participated *with* and *for* others (Ricoeur, 1992). Levine may never have known it, but in my mind he had very much participated with and for me.

"Next, let's look at *dramatizing*."

Dramatizing

"Stories revolve around an epiphany or dramatic event. The event take place somewhere, sometime—in *scenes* that provide context and give setting, framing, and texturing to the story. The point or goal of the story is to come to terms with, explain, or understand the event(s): Why did this happen to me? How can I understand what these experiences mean? What lessons have I learned? How have I been changed? Often, an autoethnographer's story is a tale of two selves, a journey from 'who I was' (before my epiphany) to 'who I am' (now), after living through these events. The story bears witness to what it can mean to live with shame, abuse, addiction, stigma, discrimination, or bodily dysfunction, and to gain agency through testimony (Couser, 1997).

"Autoethnography responds to the call to question what is important, good, just and/or meaningful. The autoethnographer is compelled to ask what kind of a life is worth living and to measure the meaningfulness of a particular life against some acceptable version of the good, which requires a narrative understanding, 'a sense,' as Charles Taylor (1989, p. 48) observes, 'of what I have become which can only be given in a story.' The story's drama brings the character along a journey from then to now. In a good story, we often witness a main character transformed by a crisis. Through dramatic action we see the person move from the 'self I was' to the 'self I am' now."

Timing

"All living beings exist in time. Everyday experience has a temporal character. As we become conscious of our existence, we gain aware-ness that our lives are finite and that we have a past, a present, and a future. We are historical creatures who find ourselves thrown into the chaos of a mortal life lived in deep temporality—between birth and death, between history and destiny, between what we have inherited and experienced from the past and what we anticipate and can become in the future (Ricoeur, 1980). In short, human life is saturated with 'an autobiographical imperative' (Eakin, 1985, pp. 275–278), a longing to make sense of and to reckon with the plural unity of time—past, present, and future. As long as we can remember, and can remember remembering, we are likely to remain steadfast in our determination to recover the past and stretch what we make of it across the temporal trajectory of our lives. Though we live only in the present, we also 'sojourn in the land of memory' (Hampl, 1999).

"Our only view of the past is in the present—in hindsight (Freeman, 2010). Since the present is itself a passing moment, vanishing swiftly into the infinite past of memory, every look back is a gaze from a different moment, a different perspective, and a different remembering self. We live in-between, perpetually moving forward into experience and backward into memory. Still, our stories keep the past alive. What we don't or can't remember can be considered dead. To have a memory of something or someone is a kind of resurrection of the dead (Ricoeur, 1980). In important respects, *every autoethnographic story is a reckoning in and with time*. Narrativity and temporality are inextricably connected. In the final session of our workshop, we will focus considerable attention on the importance of memory work in autoethnography.

"The events depicted in a story occur over time as well. Most—though by no means all—personal stories are told in an order that follows linear, chronological time, giving the sense of a beginning, middle, and ending. The endpoint is particularly important, not only because it represents the goal toward which the events or actions are pointed and thus gives the story its capacity for drama and closure, but also because it is imbued with value. Like Aesop's fables, there is a moral to the story we tell. 'Could we ever narrativize without moralizing?' asks historian Hayden White (1980, p. 27), a question answered by Alasdair MacIntyre's (1984, p. 456) insistence that: 'Narrative requires an evaluative framework in which good and bad character helps to produce unfortunate or happy outcomes.'"

Structuring

"As the storyteller you have a distinct advantage. You eventually know how your story is going to end. The reader does not. Once you know where the trouble in the story is leading, and how it is going to be dealt with, you have an opportunity to direct the action and the meanings you put in motion.

"Every story has a *narrative arc* that moves the action along from one event to another, one complication to another, building to a climax where bad fortune turns to good, or good to bad, and finally to the falling action that Aristotle referred to as *the denouement*. Reading drafts of autoethnographic stories—my own as well as those of other writers—I find myself pointing to places where the story is stalled, jotting in the margins, 'move the story along' or 'is this detail necessary.' I advise the writer to 'let the story breathe.'

"As I mentioned before, the story's plot often doesn't take shape until the writing begins. The idea of 'writing as inquiry' calls attention to the new discoveries and meanings we make as we translate observed experiences into language by putting words on a page. In the storytelling dimension of autoethnography, what matters most are the dramatized events and actions and the insights drawn by and through the story. The storyteller is the architect and engineer who takes the raw material of experience and builds a structure to contain it that puts the parts in their right places."

Revising

"When evocative autoethnographers write or perform stories, they interpret and give meaning to experiences that they've lived through. The act of telling is a performance, a process of interpretation and communication in which the teller and listener collaborate in sense-making. The burden of the academic storyteller is to *find the story in the experience* (Stone, 1997) and tell it in a fashion that brings the reader into the story, activating the reader's subjectivity, emotionality, and available frames of narrative intelligibility. Once told, the storied experiences become constitutive of the storyteller's life. By this I mean that *the story not only depicts life, it also shapes it reflexively.* Thus, the stories we make and tell exist in a continual process of production, open to editing, revision, and transformation (Ellis, 2009). As Rosenwald (1992, p. 275) observed, 'Not only does the past live in the present, but it also appears different at every new turn we take.'

"As you may know, Carolyn wrote a book on revision (Ellis, 2009)," Art says, turning toward Carolyn and motioning her to join in.

"In my book," Carolyn begins, "I showed the ways in which my autoethnographic stories had evolved over time, how the meanings I attributed to the stories had changed, and how significantly this altered how I think about and do autoethnographic storytelling. This is one of the reasons that Art refers to autoethnography as *a genre of doubt and uncertainty* (see also Gannon, 2013, pp. 230–231). The stories people tell should not be regarded as 'maps,' 'mirrors,' or 'reflections' of the experiences they depict. Instead, stories should be recognized as fluid, coconstructed, meaning-centered performances achieved in the context of relationships and subject to negotiable frames of intelligibility that change over time. Over the course of our lives, we reframe, revise, remake, retell, and relive our stories (Ellis, 2009). That's all I want to say about revision right now. I'll have a chance to add more later on."

Art takes a deep breath, sighs, and points toward the clock on the wall. Carolyn signals for him to wrap up. He stands and says, "I think we've had a good overview of the building-blocks of storytelling. Thanks to Carolyn, we have a whiteboard covered with key terms for the features of storytelling. We'll leave these intact in case some of you want to refer to them during the next part of the session. After the break, I want to hear from you. I'll treat this next part of the workshop as an open-mike. Anything goes!

"Get up and stretch, kibitz, and grab a snack off the table in the back of the room. Return with your questions and comments in fifteen minutes."

Living a Writing Life

"I'm psyched about the energy in this room," Art says to Carolyn, as participants engage loudly in conversation around the conference table. He pauses while they take their seats, then begins. "We're sorry we didn't get to everyone who came up to talk with us during the break. But we can take up your comments and questions now. Barbara, I appreciated the points you raised with me during the break. Would you start us off?"

Sitting in the first row, Barbara turns to face the other participants. "I was just saying to Art how validated I feel here. It's been my dream to do work that touches people, makes a difference, and feels meaningful to me. The whole idea of thinking like a storyteller is new to me, and I know I have a lot to learn. I have to admit I've never thought of myself as a writer, so I'm trying to process how I might need to reorganize my life. My question is: How do I prepare myself to be a writer? They don't offer courses or workshops on writing in my department, which is sociology. I've been working on my writing, but I question whether I'm doing the right things. I don't think I've found my voice. Some days I feel so frustrated I could scream; other days I feel weary and want to give up because I don't feel I'm making progress. Can you help?"

Writing Regiments

"I like how you phrased the question and your comments, Barbara. Your desire *and* your exasperation—both come through. I've inhabited the cave of despair many times when my writing wasn't going well. At those times, I try to loosen the rope by not taking myself too seriously. I ask, 'what is a writer anyway'? Then I remind myself of Thomas Mann's (1947) mocking portrayal of a writer as 'someone for whom writing is more difficult than it is for other people.'

"Seriously, do you know anybody who finds writing easy?" Art asks. Barbara shakes her head.

"I don't either. Yet many of us imagine that real writers sail smoothly across the pages of their manuscripts. They don't have bad days; get bored, impatient, or testy; and don't experience periods of deep insecurity. But that's not what the writers themselves say.

"I read a recent interview with Philip Roth published in the *New York Times* (Sandstrom, March 2014). Asked why he quit writing, Roth said he could no longer take the frustration, feelings of failure, and isolation. For him, the writing life meant no calls, no e-mail, and no distractions. Roth called his writing life 'a fanatical habit' that needed to be broken. Alice Munro gave a similar account in an interview in the *Guardian*, saying that she wanted to quit writing because she didn't want to be alone so often (Allardice, 2013). She had grown tired of chasing people away so she could write.

"Stephen King (2002) says that all a writer needs is a room, a door, the determination to shut the door, and a concrete goal. Ideally, there should be no TV, no social media, and no video games to preoccupy or distract you. When you're writing, you want to separate yourself from the outside world because you're in the process of entering the writing zone." Several participants moan and groan in response to King's advice.

"I can see from the reactions I'm getting that some of you don't agree. Is it that you hate the idea of spending so much time alone?"

"I get anxious when I'm alone in a silent room," Andrew volunteers. "I can take it for maybe ten or fifteen minutes. Then I need something to break up the monotony. I get on social media or check my twitter. That calms me."

"Starbucks is my writing home," Monica chimes in. "I like feeling in the middle of things. In a coffee shop, there's background noise and people walking by, but I've learned to tune them out. And when I want conversation, I can find it immediately. I actually feel less distracted there than at home."

Art calls on Alex, who seems eager to enter the conversation. "I don't know, Monica. I see a lot of students in Starbucks who look busy from a distance, but when you get up close you find out they're surfing the web or checking Facebook. I rarely see any of them surrounded by or immersed in books or articles."

Kalisha interjects, "The thing is, no matter where you choose to write these days, you're looking at a computer screen. So what's the big deal, write wherever you're comfortable. I've got kids distracting me when I'm at home, so I have to write late at night. I can't choose an ideal or appealing workspace."

Art sticks out his right arm, giving the group a stop sign. "You've given me something to think about. Some of my students have raised these same points. I get it. I understand that the world is different

3. Crafting Evocative Autoethnography

now, and many people take comfort in the availability of public places to write. All Virginia Woolf (1929) wanted was 'a room of her own.' She didn't have all these choices. Neither does Kalisha.

"If writing in a café or at a lunch counter works for you, go for it. But I have my doubts. I understand the angst that Andrew feels when he's alone in a quiet space; I feel that too at times. Some mornings, I think to myself, 'oh how nice it would be to go back to bed and end the frustration I'm feeling.' But I resist the temptation. I try to concentrate on what's making me drift away from the task at hand. I think all of us gain from looking carefully at the choices we're making.

"Quite a few students have admitted to me that they overestimate their ability to resist distractions. Some people think that social media have rewired our nervous systems so that we now require constant arousal (Zimbardo and Duncan, 2012). If that's the case, more and more people are likely to have more and more difficulty staying focused. Of course, you can get distracted anywhere these days. So the questions become: Can you resist? What is your level of discipline and determination? These are questions only you can answer.

"Annie Dillard (1989) advises against appealing workplaces. A writer wants a room without a view, she insists, 'so imagination can meet memory in the dark' (p. 26). She considers the life of a writer 'colorless to the point of sensory deprivation' (p. 44). It's a mentally and physically demanding life. Your heart will break, your back will ache, and your mind may numb as you struggle to turn life into language. Dillard depicts writing as a form of alligator wrestling. 'Half-naked with your two bare hands, you hold and fight a sentence's head while its tail tries to knock you over' (p. 75).

"That image is a knockout," says Andrew, laughing.

"Yes, it is," Art replies falling backwards as if he's taken a punch. "Dillard wants us to understand that a writer must adore the sight and sound of sentences as much as a painter loves the smell of paint." Reading from his notes, Art continues, "'You find and finger a phrase at a time; you lay it down cautiously, as if with tongs, and wait suspended until the next one finds you: Ah yes, then this; and yes, praise be, then this' (p. 76).

"I hope I'm not sounding too downbeat. I can see from the expressions on some of your faces that you're wondering why anybody would choose a writing life."

"That's just what I was thinking," Betty replies.

"Well, we know that plenty of people do choose this life, including Carolyn and me. People write for many different reasons. Some write because they're angry, or sad, or restless. Others write to heal or find peace. Some write to get tenure and promotion or qualify for academic positions. Still others find the commitment and dedication rewarding in itself. Some of us get a thrill out of the writing, reading, and corresponding we do more or less on a daily basis. This is the way we continue to learn and stay passionate about work and life. I imagine that many of you are sitting here in this room today because you have a strong desire to give voice to stories that have been neglected, forgotten, or left out of social science inquiry. You want to make the world a better place, and you feel contributing to a just cause will improve your life and make it more meaningful. Getting stories that have been silenced into circulation is one of the ways to do this. That's as good a reason as any to want to dedicate a sizeable portion of your life to writing regardless of the demands it may pose.

"But let me go back to Barbara's concerns. Barbara isn't asking why she should aspire to a writing life; she's asking how to live that life. She's already decided to take up a writing life. You want some practical advice, right Barbara?"

"Yes, I do."

"If you want to be a writer, you need to do two things, *read a lot and write a lot*. That's easy enough. Most of you are students or professors, so you're already situated in a reading and writing world. Don't stop. If anything, increase and expand your reading and writing. The more you write, the more you'll begin to read with a writer's eye. You'll pick up tips every time you come across artfully constructed scenes, flowing and believable dialogue, and captivating characters. You'll need to be selective, of course. Read more short stories, novels, poems, and narrative ethnographies; and continue to read autoethnographies and memoirs.

"*Determination*, that's another key. That word and the other 'd' word, *discipline*, come up over and over again in these workshops. How badly do you want to be a writer? Will you give it everything you've got? Nearly every day? For the rest of your life? Maybe that's asking too much. But when you make that kind of a commitment, you may find that you can't live the life you want without it. The discipline of a writing life is not captivity. You choose it freely, or you don't. You decide 'I'm going to keep my butt in this chair,' as I've heard Carolyn say, or you don't. Anne Lamott (1994, p. 233) says that 'discipline brings liberation,' and she goes on to tell how 'there are moments when I am writing when I think that if other people knew how I felt right now, they'd burn me at the stake for feeling so good, so much intense pleasure.'

"But now you may be thinking that I'm painting too rosy of a picture. Lamott (1994) also points to the days of torture, self-loathing, and tedium. Through it all, though—the highs and the lows—at the end of the day she usually has something to show for it. And so will you.

"'So why does our writing matter again?' Lamott's students ask her (1994, p. 237). 'Because of the spirit,' she responds. 'Because of the heart. Writing and reading decrease our sense of isolation. They deepen and widen our sense of life. They feed the soul.'"

Finding Your Voice

Art pauses to take a drink of water.

"What about finding her voice?" Bill interrupts. "Can you give Barbara, all of us that is, some practical tips?"

"I can certainly try. I apologize for taking a circuitous route in responding to Barbara's desire for practical guidance. Sometimes in these workshops I feel like a football coach giving a half-time pep talk. I want you to come away inspired and motivated. But I'm not beseeching you to do it for me. Do it for you!

"Here's the best advice I can give you on that elusive topic of finding your voice. Write fast! Write free! Don't censor yourself, at least not until you've begun the editing process.

"Everyone has a particular and somewhat idiosyncratic voice. Your voice is the verbal or prose equivalent of your signature. Of course, we all know people who have manufactured a signature for whatever reason. Some people seem to think that the more illegible their name, the more important they will seem to others. As a writer you get into trouble when you try to sound a certain way— more academic, more scholarly, more like one of the intellectual elite. I've already mentioned the bad writing that populates social science journals. That's why writing fast works. You aren't stopping to obey all the 'shoulds' in your mind. You're moving at a fast, free pace."

"Could you say more about writing fast? How do you teach people to write fast?" asks Bill.

"In my writing workshops for graduate students, I often use the last hour for a free writing exercise. I start with a prompt such as the following: 'This is yours now,' your mom says handing you _____,' and each of us starts writing. I instruct my companion writers to keep moving forward. Do not reread anything you've written while you are engaged in the exercise. And off we go.

"We write for ten or fifteen minutes until I call a halt. Some people find this kind of writing difficult at first because they're used to monitoring themselves, but they get the hang of it quickly. Initially some participants are reluctant to read their free writing to other participants, but as they gain trust in the process they become eager to share. They begin to hear the 'natural voice' that free writing evokes, and members of the group comment openly on each other's ways of expressing themselves.

"Free writing works because writing fast relaxes the tension and stress in your body. You're not clenching your teeth, stiffening your back, or tightening your shoulders. The more easygoing, the more informal, and the more unwound you become, the freer you are to sound like yourself. When you quit agonizing over every word and worrying about the correctness of your speech, you are more likely to have fun and express yourself naturally. You are not so much 'finding your voice' as you are 'freeing' and 'exposing' it."

"Are there any other exercises that you assign routinely in your writing workshop seminars?" Barbara asks. "I plan to try the fast writing one as soon as I get to my room tonight."

"Yes, the whole course is built around exercises, activities, and confidence-building writing and editing assignments. One of my favorites is assigned the first day: 'Autobiography of a Writer: My Writing Life.' This assignment is designed to increase students' awareness of their own writing routines and practices, the origins of those practices, the emotions that writing stirs in them, the aesthetic and psychological dimensions of their practices, and their level of dedication to writing. As I said earlier, writers need to be aware of their hopes, fears, motivations, and goals. A copy of this assignment can be found in your packet as Handout #4."

Second-Person Voice

"Does anyone else want to jump in here?" Art asks. Carolyn points to a man sitting at the side window, and Art nods for him to speak.

"My name is Jim. Thanks for calling on me. You and Carolyn have emphasized first-person writing. Are you opposed to writing in the second- or third-person?"

"Not at all. Some stories are told effectively in the second-person. Take a look at Handout #5, which contains two examples, one taken from Nathan Hodges's (2015) article on 'The Chemical Life,' and a second from my book on *Coming to Narrative* (Bochner, 2014)."

Art waits for participants to read the excerpts. Then he says, "Hodges's use of second-person plunks you right into the scene. Second-person enables Hodges to draw you into his point of view as he goes through daily rituals of bodily hygiene, while carrying you along into your own routines. You become the character in his story, placing yourself immediately into the setting and imagining yourself being there.

"Second-person can also be used to move between the particular and the general. In the second example in Handout #5, titled 'Lost,' I use second-person not only to reflect how I am feeling but also how others would likely feel when confronted with an unexpected blow of fate."

HANDOUT # 4

Autobiography of a Writer: My Writing Life

<u>Directions:</u> Write the story of your life as a writer. Write creatively, focusing on as many concrete events as you can within the space limitations of this assignment. Give your story a beginning, middle, and ending. Make your autobiography an interesting story that others will want to read. Do this by showing some of what happened in dialogue and scenes, rather than telling about it in a "this happened, then this" fashion.

Include memories of childhood and adolescent writing experiences. Do you remember being taught how to write? What principles were you taught? By whom? Where did you write? What feelings do you remember associating with writing? Do you recall any of the products of these early writing experiences? What made you like or dislike writing?

When you write now, how do you feel? What emotions circulate through your body? Do you feel as if you are a subjectively or emotionally different person when you are writing? Characterize these differences.

Is writing a rational, emotional, or spiritual experience for you? Explain or specify. Do you feel compelled to write or do you avoid writing as much as possible? Describe the best and worst writing experiences of your life. What made each memorable?

How do you write? Where do you write these days? Is writing integrated into your daily routines? Do you write every day or only when you must? What are your work habits as a writer? How do you get started? From what sources do you draw your inspiration to write? How many drafts do you typically write? Do you write with the door open or closed? In restaurants, bars, or coffee shops? What is your ideal writing environment? How do you organize your space for writing? With whom do you share what you write?

What are your revising or rewriting habits or patterns? How do you evaluate your own work? Do you have someone you rely on as an editor, critic, or writing buddy?

How do you know when you've finished writing a particular piece? Do you act "professional" as a writer? What does "acting professional as a writer" mean to you? What forms of writing have you engaged in other than scholarly writing, e.g., poetry, journalism, short stories, memoir? Which do you enjoy most? Why?

What are your hopes and aspirations as a writer? What are your fears and apprehensions? What kind of a future do you envision as a writer? What would you like to accomplish? What will you need to do to achieve this goal?

What obstacles get in the way of your writing? To what extent do you get distracted by social media, e-mail, text messaging, and phone calls? How can these distractions be overcome? Do your family members and/or friends understand the importance of writing to you? Are you able to keep them from disturbing you while you are working?

(Note: Please do your best to write an honest account of your life as a writer. Try to make this a story from which you and others can learn. Approximate length should be 10–15 double-spaced pages.)

2.

HANDOUT # 5
Writing in the Second-Person

Excerpt from "The Chemical Life"

You take the cap off your deodorant and smell the musky scent before giving both your armpits a thorough rub. As you put the lid on the deodorant, you read that aluminum zirconium tricholorhydrex is an active ingredient. You contrast that with the long list of inactive ingredients. You wonder what it means to have something active in your armpit hair. Images of gerbils running on wheels go through your head. You are happy they smell good. You grab a bottle of cologne off the counter and spray the diethyl phthalate on your neck. (Hodges, 2015, p. 628)

Excerpt from *Coming to Narrative*

Your life rolls along smoothly. It makes sense. You are moving ahead. The forward momentum feels good. You don't question it. The paradigm is working. It gives you the illusion of predictability and permanence. One chapter foretells the next. The story is sufficiently familiar to feel secure; sufficiently puzzling to hold interest. You think you know the plot and have a notion where it's leading. Some days you feel as if you've been here before; other days you feel as if you're making it up as you go along. Neither feeling threatens you. There has to be a little mystery in every story, you tell yourself. Go with the flow. There, far off in the distance, you catch a glimpse of an ending toward which your story is pointing. But you're in no hurry to finish. The ride is more important than the destination. You don't want to miss anything on the way. You expect a few bumps along the road, but you've done your homework. You have a map; you're prepared.

Then one day, an anomaly appears—out of the blue. You come to a place that isn't on your map. You can turn left or right, or continue straight ahead. You don't know which way to turn. You look behind you and all you see Is thIck, dense fog. The road back home disappears from view. Vanished, gone—it's nowhere to be found. You turn back and gaze ahead. Which path do I take? You hesitate, unsure.

Each path is a different story, leading you in a different direction. But there are no signposts. There is nobody to guide you, no book or map to show the way. Fear and doubt engulf you. You feel lost and scared. Darkness moves in. You hear the sounds of nocturnal creatures approaching. You can't stay put. You must decide. (Bochner, 2014, p. 164)

2.

Third-Person Voice

"The use of third-person is relatively rare in evocative autoethnography because the third-person voice positions the reader as an onlooker standing outside the action, while the writer elevates himself above the action in the position of an objective and all-knowing observer. When executed with style and grace, however, third-person can be highly effective.

"A good example is Dan Franck's *Separation* (1994), a daily chronicle of a man's obsessive attempt to understand and prevent the dissolution of his marriage. Using a third-person narrative style, the main character—presumably Franck himself—keeps detailed notes of his conversations with friends. He also records micro-detailed observations of his wife's behavior during a period when she enters into a relationship with another man. Written 'to purge himself, to give some direction to his excavation of his own feelings, and perhaps to win her back' (pp. 58–59), *Separation* is not only about the demise of a relationship but part of it: 'his children and his wife were like characters getting ready to walk out of his book' (p. 52).

"*Separation* begs the question of the power of blending and bending literary and social science genres of representation. Occasionally, the first-person leaks into Franck's narration. Was this accidental or purposeful? Is *Separation* a novel, a memoir, or an autoethnography? Is it fiction or nonfiction? Does it matter what we call it?"

Action

"Debra, you've been trying to get into the conversation. What's on your mind?" Art asks.

"My question is about putting *meanings into motion*. I assume that phrase refers to autoethnography's capacity to provoke dialogue and social action? Do I have that right? Also, how can we learn to do this? What skills are involved?"

"I'm glad you picked up on that phrase, 'putting meanings into motion.' The psychologist Jerome Bruner (1990) considers stories 'acts of meaning.' Over the course of our lives, we are shaped and fashioned by the stories to which we are exposed. When we, as evocative

HANDOUT # 6

Third-Person Voice

Excerpt from *Separation*

She sits beside him stiff and distant, wrapped in her black shawl, molten glass earrings dangling. Normally she would lean her head against his shoulder, glance up at his profile, and gently mock his intense concentration. But not tonight.

He takes her hand, a palm lying lifeless in his. Not the merest movement of fingers, nor the barest responsive pressure. Dead skin. He squeezes her fingers and turns to look at her. She stares at the stage impassive. He takes his hand away and drifts into an austere silence of his own, his mind casting about for reasons for her uncharacteristic stolidity. He finds none....

He moves his thumb along her fingers and waits. Nothing. He presses. Still nothing....

"Let me watch the play, will you?" she hisses in exasperation, pulling her hand away and moving it to the opposite side of her body. (Franck, 1994, pp. 3–5)

autoethnographers, put meanings into motion, we are engaging in a material intervention into people's lives. The stories we tell not only express and represent experiences through which we've lived, they also shape and create them anew. We're putting meanings into play. Ideally, autoethnographic research doesn't end with a monograph, an article, a chapter, or a performance. It moves beyond a product into a dialogue.

"The received view of knowledge into which I was socialized did not take this process and flow view of research. The receiver of knowledge was treated as a passive receiver, not an active participant in the creation and negotiation of meaning.

"In autoethnography, however, we want the reader to be in the action with us. We're creating an experience of the experience, inviting others to join in. As I mentioned earlier, the usefulness of autoethnographic stories rests on their capacity to inspire dialogue and conversation from the point of view of readers, who enter from the perspective of their own lives. Readers become co-performers, examining their own lives by engaging with the story. Arthur Frank (1995) refers to the encounter between a story listener and a story as 'thinking with a story.'

"During this workshop, we're going to use two stories: 'Maternal Connections' by Carolyn and 'Bird on the Wire' by me. They will illustrate what can happen when meanings are put into motion, extending research beyond publication. We'll be asking you to enter into dialogue with each of these stories.

"Thus far I've emphasized what happens after the autoethnographic story is put into circulation. But Debra also wants to know what skills a writer needs to learn to evoke readers' emotions and open a space for dialogue. Her question takes us back to life as a writer.

"I'll start with the basics. Writers must master certain skills and keep them nearby in their toolbox. I'm referring to some of the things you were supposed to learn in high school but may have forgotten, neglected, or slept through. I'm talking about correct grammar, punctuation, and usage, removing clutter from your writing, deleting unnecessary words, treating adverbs as enemies, and not overusing adjectives. You know how to do these things, don't you?" Art chuckles.

"You can review, refine, or renew your skills in these areas by consulting books such as Zinsser's *On Writing Well* (2001) and Strunk and White's *The Elements of Style* (1979). You should be able to find numerous exercises on grammar and punctuation online. We don't have sufficient time to go through these drills in this workshop. But I do want to take a few moments to provide an overview of optional writing strategies that can be of help when you're trying to turn 'true' lived-through experiences into stories.

"Action is crucial to the kind of movement I've been describing as putting 'meanings in motion.' Usually I recommend that autoethnographers write their stories in the present tense. But the past tense is acceptable as well. I try not to be too categorical about these things.

"What I like most about the present tense is its immediacy. The reader is placed directly into scenes that are happening now. The brief excerpt we looked at from Hodges's 'The Chemical Life' (2015) achieves that goal. Readers feel as if they are in the scene. They see themselves rubbing deodorant under their arm pits.

"Good autoethnographic writing avoids complicated tenses like past perfect or present progressive (see Hart, 2012). Rather than saying 'Lightning had struck the tree,' or 'Lightning is striking the tree,' you gain more effect by saying 'Lightning strikes the tree' or 'Lightning struck the tree.'

"When people act, they do things rather than have things done to them. This distinction highlights the important difference, often emphasized in creative nonfiction, between active and passive voice. A sentence written in active voice usually follows the pattern subject-verb-object. For example, 'Art explained the difference between active and passive voice.' A sentence written in passive voice usually reverses the pattern to object-verb-subject. For example, 'The difference between active and passive voice was explained by Art.' When Carolyn says, 'Art wrote a book on storytelling in the human sciences' she is using the active voice. If she says, 'A book on storytelling in the human sciences was written by Art,' she is using the passive voice. In the first sentence, Art performs the action; he wrote the book. In the second sentence, the direction of action is changed and Art becomes the object of the preposition 'by.' Art's authorship becomes indirectly (or passively) noted as the focus shifts activity away from Art's work as a writer. The target or object of Art's writing—the book on storytelling—becomes the subject, but the book is not doing anything. Passive voice constructions slow down the action. They are not so much 'wrong' as they are inactive, thus the term 'passive voice.'

"In Handout #7, we present a worksheet that focuses on differences between active and passive voice. Take about twenty minutes to rewrite the sentences that sound better in active voice and discuss them with two or three people sitting near you. When you've completed your discussion, take a break and enjoy the refreshments in the back of the room. If there were disagreements among you, continue to talk about them during the break."

Showing and Telling

"I'm glad you had fun with that exercise," Art says. "Jake told me during the break that he had started re-reading the paper he's presenting at the Congress on Saturday and found three sentences on the first page that needed to be changed to active voice. I suspect more of you will want to check that tonight.

"'Show the readers everything; tell them nothing,'" Art says suddenly. "With some moderation, this is the advice given to most young writers and to aspiring evocative autoethnographers. Why do we give that advice?

"Barry," Art says, responding to a waving hand.

"Because showing evokes, whereas telling tends to inform or analyze. Also, showing arouses the senses. You've been emphasizing action and movement. Showing moves, draws attention, and speeds up the story. The characters are doing and saying things, which enables readers to enter the scene as if it's happening now."

"Nicely expressed, Barry! On the whole, we prefer writing that is physical and emotional. Some people call this kind of writing 'embodied' or 'performative' (Pelias, 1999, 2004; Denzin, 2003). Performative writing can be likened to a cinematic portrayal. Readers' senses are activated by scenic details, active verbs, and a passionate and vulnerable writing voice. They can smell, hear, taste, touch, and feel.

"Annie Dillard (1989, p. 78) tells us that one of the few things she knows about writing is that you have to give it all you've got. 'Spend it all, shoot it, play it, lose it, right away, every time...give it, give it

HANDOUT # 7

Exercise on Active and Passive Voice

Directions: Rewrite the following sentences changing passive constructions to active verbs. *WARNING!* Some of these sentences do not use passive verbs or are better off left in the passive, so this exercise also will engage your attention in recognizing passive constructions and using them when appropriate.

1. The new doctoral program in sociology has been approved by the Board of Trustees.

2. With three seconds left in the game, a time-out was called by one of the players.

3. The employees were informed of their impending dismissal by the boss herself.

4. The necessity of emphasizing the active voice was taught by Stephen King himself, but quickly forgotten by the students.

5. Melvin was raised by his grandmother.

6. An unexpected storm destroyed several homes in the area and uprooted trees in a suburb of Tampa.

7. I was shocked to receive a rejection by the journal editors.

8. *Final Negotiations* was written by Carolyn Ellis.

9. Participants in our study were asked to write a story about their worst experience as students.

10. The dangerous mountain roads were avoided by Elizabeth because of her fear of getting close to cliffs.

all, give it now' she urges. Laurie Stone (1997, p. xvii) echoes Dillard. 'Perhaps every story worth telling,' she writes, 'is a dare, a kind of pornography, composed of whatever we think we're not supposed to say, for fear of being drummed out, found out, pointed out.'"

"Easy for her to say," comes a male voice from the back of the room.

"Point well-taken, whoever said it," Art affirms. "People are unlikely to go that far if they think they have something really threatening to lose. Stone recognizes that. She says that the daring truths she admires tend to be told in layers and laced with ambivalences and mixed feelings, which is what being alive often personifies.

"But let's get back to the goal of arousing readers through sensory detail. We want readers to live for a while in the scenes we write. Telling slows down the action; it tends to take you out of the scene, creating distance by providing analysis, information, and explanation. Showing is experience-near, while telling is experience-distant.

"Handout #8 asks you to practice converting telling to showing. Do this one at home tonight. Carolyn and I will be available at breakfast and during the breaks tomorrow to go over your rewrites with you.

"Carolyn, would you talk about composing dialogue?" Art turns and asks. "I call Carolyn 'the queen of dialogue,'" he kids, as Carolyn stands and moves forward.

"Of course, you know this is one of my favorite topics," Carolyn begins. "Dialogue moves the action of a story forward and brings characters to life. As Art indicated, 'don't tell us if you can show us' is one of the cardinal rules of writing stories. Dialogue that is a joy to read provides a resonance and realism that is difficult to duplicate in exposition. Two good lines of dialogue can stand in for one or two pages of expository telling.

"Is there a secret to writing good dialogue? It's no secret that you need to be a good ethnographer, though not all good ethnographers write dialogue well. Becoming a good ethnographer requires that you pay attention and are mindful of what's going on around and through you. Those who write true-to-life dialogue are

HANDOUT # 8

Showing and Telling Exercise

This exercise asks you to practice turning still life into moving pictures. Try to make the reader see, feel, and recognize what you are trying to communicate. Work for sensory details, be specific, use strong and active verbs, and write dialogue where appropriate. Be prepared to share your work with a writing buddy (or group member).

PART 1. Practice showing:

1. Show an emotion without telling what it is.

2. Show a place without naming it. Your description should allow us to recognize it.

3. Show someone doing something but don't tell us what the person is doing.

4. Show a short conversation that sets the scene and advances action.

PART 2. Convert the following telling sentences by providing vivid description and dialogue that show rather than tell:

1. She had a secret crush on her hairdresser.

2. Manny was crushed when he learned his article had been rejected.

3. The kitchen was a mess.

4. He was nervous.

5. The dog was smelly.

HANDOUT # 9

Writing Dialogue

Every person has a style of speaking. Try to capture some of what makes a person's manner of speaking idiosyncratic.

- Edit dialogue carefully. Long and continuous dialogues can become boring. Cut, trim, and make the dialogue do the work of moving the story forward.

- Break up the dialogue with action and description.

- Make dialogue sound like real speech but without filler words and conversations that don't contribute to the plot.

- Let the dialogue itself show how the character is speaking.

- Make the emotions come through the words. If the character speaks with animosity, make this come through in what is said. It should not be necessary to add a tag such as, 'she said, loathing the sight of him.' The same is true if a character is shouting, crying, or laughing. Keep the reader's attention on the dialogue, not your explanation of it.

- The best ways of making attributions in dialogue are the simplest ones: he said; she replied.

- Remember the goal. You're breathing life into your characters through the words they speak.

- Punctuate dialogue correctly.

careful, vigilant listeners and note-takers. They have a good ear for conversation and pick up nuances and manners of speaking that other people miss or overlook."

"But it's hard to remember exactly what each person said and how it was said," notes Betty.

"Is that what we try to do when we're writing dialogue?" Carolyn asks. When no one speaks, she says, "Think about dialogue in the movies. It moves the action forward. It's crisp and sounds realistic. Good screenwriters realize that actual conversations between people tend to be humdrum and monotonous when precisely reproduced. So they eliminate the vocal pauses (ums and ahs), repetitions, and incomplete expressions of actual speech. They've mastered the fine art of writing evocative, meaningful, and realistic dialogue that is believable and holds the attention of readers." Carolyn turns toward Art, indicating she is finished.

"Thanks, Carolyn," Art says. "Over the next few sessions of the workshop, we'll be focusing on two stories brimming with dialogue. I'll be anxious to hear your impressions of whether, when, and how these conversations work effectively. For now, though, take five minutes to look over the bullet points about writing dialogue included in Handout #9. You'll want to keep these points in your toolbox."

Exposition

"I've been highlighting ways of moving the story ahead, keeping the action going through vivid description, revealing detail, and believable dialogue. Still, I am not advocating that we shun the telling voice entirely. The writer's job is to communicate. Showing is one way of communicating, and telling is another means. Novelists combine dramatic showing with long sections of narration expressed in a telling voice. If we rail against telling, we may do a disservice, leading aspiring writers to think that everything should be acted out.

"Don't tell us a character is angry, show us how he screams, inveighs, and condemns in fury is the advice usually given. But not so fast. As a writer you need to have many tools in your toolbox. You must learn to recognize when a story calls for showing and when it calls for telling, and to appreciate the difference between the two as well as the appropriate uses of each. The telling voice allows you to convey a lot of details succinctly. Nearly every story has background, context, and details of character and place that readers need to know. The objective is to tell what must be known and no more. You should ask yourself, do my readers need this exposition to understand what's happening? Too much exposition delays and slows down the storyline that draws in and holds readers.

"Then again, let's not forget that most evocative autoethnography gets published in academic journals or scholarly books where the telling voice is appreciated and embraced. Academic writing in the social sciences—and the humanities as well—has tended to center on analyzing a problem, explaining human behaviors, and demonstrating command of an area of research. Explaining experience has taken priority over rendering it. To some extent, autoethnography attempts to restore some balance, insisting that something crucially important has been omitted from research in the human sciences. But there are ways of layering telling and showing, and moving seamlessly between the showing voice of the storyteller and the telling voice of the story-analyst. Tomorrow, Carolyn will be offering examples from the stories of autoethnographers who specialize in these forms."

"I recall reading one of your essays in which you were arguing that the distinction between theories and stories was untenable, that a good story theorizes. Am I mistaken about that?" Vicki asks.

"No, you're not. But I'm afraid the argument I made in those essays has not gotten through to the wide audience for which I intended it. The point actually is uncomplicated. Good stories provide rich detail and analysis, but they do it in a storied form. Stories explain, theorize, and moralize. It's not an accident or an oversight that what we say we're doing is story-telling. We don't call it story-showing. To me this implies that stories tell—they analyze, abstract, and even theorize. They just do those things differently, in the genre of story rather than exposition. Useful theories often take the form of a good story, providing explanations and moral points of view. Evocative autoethnographers carry the burden of making meaning out of all the stuff of memory and experience. We theorize by telling stories that put meanings in motion where they can be used, discussed, debated, and prolonged."

Art takes a quick peek at the clock. Before he can speak, Andrew interrupts, trying to get in one last question. "One of the things I most admire about good autoethnographies is the way they take you into the consciousness of a person faced with complicated circumstances, trying to get through a difficult experience and move on. Is this a reasonable interpretation of what autoethnography does?"

"I love that point, Andrew. It's more than reasonable. I consider it necessary. Autoethnography attempts to cast a wide net of consciousness—personal, political, spiritual, and moral. Evocative autoethnographers can't hide from their consciousness. One of the joys of reading and learning from autoethnography is the pleasure of following the consciousness of a thoughtful, introspective, flawed human being struggling to disentangle from some knotty experience and in the process tossing his or her voice into the confusion. As Lopate (2013, p. 6) observed, 'the great adventure in reading nonfiction is to follow, as I say, a really interesting, unpredictable mind struggling to entangle and disentangle itself in a thorny problem, or even a frivolous problem that is made complex through engagement with a sophisticated mind.'"

Art notices Carolyn tapping her watch, signaling that he should draw the session to a close. "Thanks so much for your energetic and rapt attention. Your comments and questions inspire me, reminding me why we do these workshops. We covered a lot of territory this morning and time does not permit a detailed summary. One of the main points I was trying to get across was how important it is to build your confidence and enhance your productivity as a writer. To close this session, I want to share what I do to stay focused on these goals." Art nods to Carolyn, who turns on the monitor, which projects a document titled 'Living the Writing Life' onto the screen.

"Let's go through these one by one," Art says. "Repeat after me:

Living the Writing Life

→ I organize my time, space, and energy to accommodate my writing life.

→ I tell other people I am a writer. I let them know how much that means to me.

→ I interact and surround myself with people who support, respect, and contribute to my writing life.

→ I do not allow my writing to get tangled in terminology.

→ I write to be read and to converse with my readers.

→ I share my work with writing buddies. I count on them to convey their reactions to my writing openly and with sensitivity.

→ I read what I write out loud—over and over again. I listen to the words and the sounds. I attempt to be respectful and mindful of my readers.

→ I write what I care about. I write to learn what I care about and to feel it. I write to make connections with other people who may care about these topics and help me understand better the implications of how what I care about matters, and what it means.

→ I accept the necessity of revising what I write. I am mindful of the patience required to improve my writing by rewriting. Commitment to revision makes me a better writer.

→ I question, I doubt, and I live with uncertainty. I live an auto-ethnographic life. I bend, I blend, and I blur, hungering to experience a slice of reality, evading dogma, breaching rules, trying to cast a wider net of consciousness and social justice.

"On that note, we end this session. Carolyn and I will hang out in the coffee shop over lunch. Join us if you want to continue the conversation informally.

"During the lunch break, we want you to read Carolyn's story, 'Maternal Connections,' which is in Appendix A of your workshop packets. We will begin the afternoon session by discussing this story. I'll begin by asking how you responded to it. What did you feel? What aspects of your life came to mind? What did the story make you want to do?

"Have a nourishing lunch."

Thinking with "Maternal Connections"

"Welcome back," Art begins. "In this session we're going to concentrate on Carolyn's story, 'Maternal Connections.' I assume you had a chance to read it during lunch. Does everyone have a copy?" The students nod and take out their printed version. "Good. For the next few minutes, address your responses to me. Carolyn will listen for a while and then join the conversation. She'll provide some context and background about how she composed the story and answer some questions."

Thinking with a Story

"First, let's focus on what was evoked for you. What did you think and feel as you read? Did Carolyn's story arouse any stories or issues of your own? How did it affect you?"

For a moment, there is silence. Then, suddenly, hands go up. Art moves around the room, calling on different students. "I thought of my mother," says Jan, "and how she took care of my grandmother. I was fortunate to be able to be there to help her. The experience was almost identical to what Carolyn describes. I caught my breath a couple of times as I read through tears, laughter, and memories of how fond I was of her."

"It took me right into my life," says Marilyn, who Art remembers is from aging studies. "I had a similar experience with my mother. I cared for her and washed her as she was dying. This story brought me back to that time."

"I appreciated the description of the relationship between mother and daughter. My mother is well now, but she is approaching her later years," says Debra. "Carolyn's story gave me a glimpse of my future. Reading it makes me think I want to improve my relationship with my mother, which hasn't been the best."

"My relationship with my mother also had not been the best prior to this experience," Carolyn says, unable to hold back any longer. "This was a turning point for us." From the silence and inquisitive looks, Carolyn intuits the participants want to hear more. "Once I left home and had experiences in college and as a professor, I didn't think my mother could understand me. I also didn't want to discuss my changing values with her, so I didn't share much about my life. I called her every week and visited two or three times a year, but I kept myself emotionally removed. My guess is that she wondered whether she could count on me—whether I'd be there when she needed me. Frankly, I hadn't spent much time thinking about how I would respond if she should become ill. Young adults can be pretty self-absorbed, rarely thinking about what their parents might need." Carolyn purses her lips and sighs.

"That all began to change after my brother died in 1982—and then my father in 1987. Family took on a new importance, and I began to be more appreciative of how much Mom meant to me. So when she became sick in 1993, I came home to help take care of her, and I found a lot of meaning in the experience. I think she did too."

"Do you wish Carolyn had included this back story in 'Maternal Connections'?" Art asks.

"I do," says Debra. "Then maybe I would have felt more hopeful that I could improve my relationship with my mother. I found myself envying her intimate connection with her mother and thinking, 'I could never have that.' But hearing her history, now I don't feel that way."

"I don't," says Jane, and others nod their heads in agreement. "I liked being cast right into the middle of this emotional scene with no warning or back story. Then I could put myself and my own relationship with my mother into the scene. That's part of what makes this story so effective—the immediacy that Art stressed this morning. Telling the back story would have let readers off the emotional hook, let them distance themselves from the experience. This way the scene pulls readers right into the emotion."

"These are decisions you have to make when you write," Art says. "How much to tell and how much to leave out. The leaving out is the hard part."

Art points to the next person who raises her hand, "More stories?"

"I'm thinking about myself as not a mother," says Toni, who Carolyn remembers is studying couples who decide not to have children. "So the scene with the babies resonates with me. I'm feeling the mixed emotions associated with being childless and wondering whether I will ever be a mother. I feel selfish, thinking about myself, and ignoring the rest of the story."

"So you're all thinking out of your own histories and current circumstances," Art says, and participants nod.

"I am too," says Andrew. "But my feelings are different. I feel envy and guilt."

"Can you elaborate?" asks Art.

"Sure; I envied Carolyn's mother. It's a panic of mine, a fear that I won't have anyone to do that for me…"

"We hear that quite a bit in reaction to this story," says Art.

"And guilt in that I recently left my partner, who is 62. I wonder how he is now and who will take care of him." Andrew speaks in a low voice and hangs his head.

"Wow, that is powerful. Thanks for making that comment," Art says.

"This is the second time I've read this story," says Jan. "The first time I thought about my husband, who almost died soon after I started dating him. He coughed holes in his esophagus, and bacteria from his mouth went to his heart. He was a young guy with tubes coming out of him. But reading it this time, I thought of my grandmother. I just visited her two days ago on her 90th birthday. She said to me…" Jan pauses, then, "I might cry…"

"We'll cry with you," Carolyn says.

"…she said she didn't want to see 91."

"That's hard," says Carolyn. She and Art pause as several students near Jan turn to her, put their hands on her back, and speak softly.

In a moment, Jan continues. "Just watching my grandmother need someone to take her to the bathroom… Well, now Carolyn's story is even more powerful and meaningful to me."

"It's interesting to see how you all are relating to this story in a personal way, which is what autoethnography often evokes," says Art, and participants nod. "You're thinking *with* the story, which means to take on the story, live in it, and experience it affecting your life (Frank, 1995)."

Concrete Sensory Details

"Reading this story doesn't remind me of anything that has happened to me," says Jane. "But still I was right there in Carolyn's experience."

"Why is that?" asks Art. "What drew you in?"

"The details. Definitely the details. Her descriptions were so vivid. For example, the perfumed bleach. I could smell it."

"The thick pink liquid soap—I could feel it on my hand," a voice says.

"The spreading black bruises. I could see them," comes another voice.

"Her mother's hand clutching the support bar in the bathroom… I've had that experience when I was in a hospital," offers Regina.

Marilyn, who took care of her dying mother, addresses her comments to Carolyn. "What I liked most was your willingness to engage with visceral body functions. I resonated with the clarity of your detail, the things we normally shy away from talking about, the messiness. The body talk was powerful. As I read, I visualized my body and the gallbladder scars I have, how I'm aging…"

"Similar to how I saw my body as I looked at my mother's body," Carolyn relates. "My body in 36 years. And now here it is…." She waves her hand over her frame, and the students chuckle.

"Well you wrote that more than 20 years ago," Art says.

"And a lot has changed in that time." Carolyn and Art share a smile that indicates their shared history.

"Do the details of the body talk bother anyone?" Carolyn suddenly asks.

"Not me. It transported me to different times in my life; for example, when I had major surgery at age 35 and my partner had to bathe me," says Marilyn.

"Reading about the support bar took me back 30 years. At that time, they gave you enemas and left you alone in the washroom while you were in labor. The only thing that saved me was holding onto that bar. That's why I mentioned it before," says Regina.

"Regina, I like how you called on one detail that carried you back to earlier experience," Carolyn replies. "Your comment points out that writers not only have to decide what to tell and what to leave out, but also to carefully choose the most effective details. These details have to bypass our cognitive processes and evoke a strong sensory reaction, which can stimulate readers to remember a scene where that feature was crucial. Sometimes a story can be too detailed. Or emphasize irrelevant minutiae that get in the way of the storyline. You probably all have read stories that take three paragraphs to describe what the characters look like and are wearing, when those specific descriptions are not necessary." The students nod.

"Yes," Art says, pointing to Inkeri, who has raised her hand.

"You asked if these graphic details bother us. They don't bother me, but they make me think about what details to include in my own writing about spinal cord injuries and sexuality. I'm never sure when to be suggestive and when to be more graphic."

"I asked this question," Carolyn replies, making a mental note to return to Inkeri's comment, "because I am aware that people tend to respond politely and in a positive manner in these workshops. Yet I know the graphic descriptions bother some people. I've had a few students in classes say they are troubled by what I reveal about my mother's body and grossed out by what I describe.

"What were you thinking when you wondered which details to include in your stories?" Carolyn asks, turning toward Inkeri.

"Sometimes I write graphically about my body," Inkeri says, "because I think it's an important part of conveying something deep about the experience of being disabled. But it makes people uncomfortable when I do, so I'm not sure it's a good idea."

"As I said when you introduced yourself, you should be the person who decides what you are comfortable including," Carolyn says. "Other peoples' discomfort is their problem. Though I know what you mean. You don't want to turn away readers. You should read…ah… Art, who is the sociologist who wrote 'Tell Me, Tell Me'?" While Art is thinking, Carolyn says, "It's a wonderful story, one of my favorites, about two people who are disabled having sex together for the first time. The story includes graphic details showing how difficult it is. Yet they manage, and it is beautiful and humorous too. They…well wait, I don't want to tell you too much because I want you to read and experience it."

"Zola," Art says. "Irving Zola (1982)."

"Yes, that's the author," Carolyn says. "Good memory."

Art calls on Tom, who has raised his hand. "I couldn't decide how I reacted to the graphic details, which I guess is a mixed reaction. At first, it seemed a little off-putting and clinical when you named body parts and functions. At the same time, you're so present and your feelings are so strongly grounded in the concrete reality of what you're experiencing. Reading the story reminded me of my mom's visit last week. She was trying to feed my young son, who wanted to feed himself. The result was butternut squash all over his face, his high chair, and the floor. When that happened, my mom commented wistfully, 'You know, I did this for your stepfather.' My stepfather had Alzheimer's," Tom explains.

"Good storytelling. You drew a picture," says Art, making eye contact with Tom. Art waits, but Tom does not follow up.

Into the silence, Carolyn says, "That's what you want to do—give a visual and sensual representation. I felt I couldn't draw a picture of taking care of my mom without writing about her body and describing the smells that were so much a part of the caring experience we had shared together. You always have to think about how much to include, and sometimes it can be a suggestive image without going into specifics. For example, the perfumed bleach…I don't have to describe it; if you've been in an institutional setting with sick or old people you know that smell."

"Like poetry…," a voice says.

Carolyn nods and then turns toward Tom. "And you gave us that detail by showing us your mother trying to feed your son who has butternut squash all over his face."

"Yes, another story of multi-generational connections," Tom says.

"Yes, similar to my saying, 'I'm doing this for my mother and she did it for me,'" says Carolyn.

"But how did you know which details would work?" comes a voice from the corner.

"By putting myself back into the experience and paying attention to my senses," Carolyn responds. "What did I smell, see, hear, feel, think? What stood out then; what stands out in my memory now as I write? What do I think would stand out if I were in that scene again? How might I directly stimulate readers' senses?

"Take how I was feeling, for example. I wanted to describe my feelings succinctly in a way that would elicit a visceral reaction, an identification from readers. So how did I do that?"

"You said you were 'falling in love' with your mother," Jane responds.

"I'm wondering how you responded to that," Art asks. "Did that expression bother anyone?"

"At first it did," says Tom. "I thought, you don't fall in love with parents. But then I came to see that expression as coming closer than any other to describing the tender feeling that Carolyn was experiencing. So I thought, why not?"

"I loved it," says Toni. "We all probably know what that feeling is, or at least what we think it should be." She laughs. "How all-encompassing it is. You can't think of anything else when you're falling in love. And the expression is so unusual in the context of child-parent relationships that it startles you a bit, gets your attention, makes you identify with how Carolyn feels."

"Another important detail for me," Carolyn says, "was helping my mother move from the bathroom to the bed. She's looking into my eyes and trusting me to guide her to the bed. She is walking forward and I'm walking backward." Carolyn enacts the movement. "I wanted to grab onto that moment. The trust. We hadn't always been that trusting of each other in the past. This connection pinpointed for me what was happening now in our relationship. Then once I had the moment captured in my mind, I asked myself how to convey it to readers and hold them in it with me."

"And when we get to the issue of how to convey, we are being writers," chimes in Art. "We dip and angle in between fiction and nonfiction, not to pull them apart but to put them together. We use fictional writing strategies to convey what happened and evoke reactions."

"We connect creative nonfiction to ethnography—a way to describe what actually happened vividly and sensually," Carolyn says.

Composing a Title and Ending the Story

"How did you get to the ending, about the babies?" Toni asks, reflecting her personal and research interests in having children.

"I hadn't planned to include that scene. But as I put myself back in the hospital and wrote, the memory of going to the nursery came to mind. About the same time, the title 'Maternal Connections' came to me in a flash of imagination. Including this scene seemed an 'of course' moment."

Art says, "That's writing as inquiry. Laurel Richardson (1994a) talks about how when you're writing, these connections start appearing to you."

"They do," Carolyn says. "So then I had to figure out how to convey my feelings about having my own child in a way that enhanced the story about my mother without getting too far removed from the main plot or taking it over. The side story—what turned out to be the ending—had to link to the primary theme. What details did I need to tell? Enough to show the parallels between the connection from me as an imagined mother to my imagined child and the link from me as a daughter to my mother. I didn't think cognitively about this at first; I merely let myself be in the feeling space—the flow—of connection across generations."

"It's interesting that you don't resolve the ending," says Jane, who seems to appreciate stories that hold her in experience. "We don't know if you decided to have children or not. You just turn back to your mother, which is a nice move because you bring us back to your focus."

Carolyn smiles.

"I can't help but wonder—and maybe it's not appropriate to ask," says Toni, "but did you and Art ever have children?"

"Please ask anything. No we didn't, partly because we got together later in life. I also think our choice not to have children reflects a cultural story that helps to understand the personal story I tell here. Stories of unique experience point toward cultural and social issues that transcend the personal and are important to all of us. So to what issue does this story point?"

Story as Theory: Thinking about the Story

"I think you mean the tension that comes up at the end of the story between having children and having a career," says Toni.

"Good," Carolyn says. "So 'Maternal Connections' can be viewed as an historical story about a particular group of women who grew up in the cultural milieu of the 1960s and 70s. The story concerns decisions they faced not only in terms of having children but also in the kind of relationship they would have with both their parents and their partners. The canonical story of that time—the one I likely would have embraced had I stayed in my hometown—promoted the ideal above all else that women should get married and have children, live beside and take care of their parents who had helped with the grandchildren early on. Since I went to college, was surrounded by professional women, and was influenced by feminism, I was receptive to a resistant, counter narrative that emphasized how important and meaningful a career could be for women. We are all freed and constrained by the choices available to us at particular points in our lived history and social location."

"Are you happy with your choice?" Toni asks.

"Yes I am, though I'd like to have two lives to live so I could try both."

"Art?" Toni asks.

"Adam Phillips (2013) says we all have a hundred lives within us, but we get to live only a few. I'm loving how this one is turning out." Art and Carolyn share a smile.

"Did anyone see any other themes?" Carolyn asks.

"I was intrigued by what you say about your mother not wanting to be a burden," says Marilyn, indicating her interest in aging studies. "Your story is about caregiving elderly parents in a society where family members often do not live close by. Yet we do care for our parents somehow and that caregiving doesn't have to be a burden, which is how it usually is discussed in the literature (Pinquart and Sörensen, 2003). We see in your story that caregiving was a meaningful experience for you and led to a closer relationship with your mother."

"Good," says Carolyn. "I like that you noticed that."

"It's about the importance of the body in understanding illness and caregiving," says Inkeri. "Often the body gets left out."

"I read it as a case study of intergenerational relationships," says Tom.

"I think it speaks to all those issues," Carolyn says. "When we move from responding to a story with our stories to finding themes, we have turned from thinking *with* to thinking *about* stories." The nodding heads of the participants make Carolyn feel that they get the distinction now.

"Amazing how theoretical a story can be, isn't it?" she asks. "So even though there is no literature review and no focused discussion of themes, these are present in the story, aren't they? Citations or no citations, stories explain, analyze, and theorize."

Honoring the Relationship

"I'd like to change the topic to ethics," says Regina.

"We're going to talk in depth about that tomorrow," Carolyn says. "But go ahead and ask your question, as long as it is specific to 'Maternal Connections.' Some of you have mentioned privately that you have had problems getting approval for your studies. Let's hold that topic for later." She nods for Regina to continue.

"When you write, how do you decide what you have the right to say about someone else? Especially if they aren't in on the decision making? For example, how did you deal with writing about your mother's body in 'Maternal Connections'?"

"That's always a question in autoethnography," Carolyn replies. "You're never writing about yourself in a vacuum, but in relation to others. Other people are characters in your story. I wrote 'Maternal Connections' without seeking approval from my mother. Of course, this was in the early 1990s, before we'd had much time to think about how to handle ethical issues in evocative autoethnography. Still it bothered me that I had published this story without telling my mother and revealing what I had written about her. I was reluctant to show it to her because I was concerned that she would be upset about the way I talked about her body. She was a fairly private person in that regard.

"When I then wrote a second piece about caring for my mother, 'With Mother/With Child' (Ellis, 2001), I decided that I wouldn't publish it until I had shared both stories with her. On my next visit with my mother, I read this second piece to her. As I read, I found myself skipping passages, such as how her body had deteriorated and her hands were shaking. So the article I published then ended up including two intertwining stories—one account detailed caregiving for my mother and the other dealt with my experience of reading the story to her.

"I ended the article with a discussion about why I made the decisions I did about omitting some passages, and how my relationship with my mother and her feelings were more important to me than being able to claim to my readers that I had read every word to her. After I had finished with that story, I read 'Maternal Connections' to her....and, yes, I skipped some of that as well." The participants laugh. "But then I left both printed stories with her in case she wanted to read all the words."

"Did she?" a voice asks.

"I'm not sure, though she did give both of them to my siblings to read. I felt satisfied with my decision. I hadn't forced her to listen to me reading these passages, but I did make them available. When I asked later how she felt about my writing about her, she looked me in the eye and said, 'You can write anything you want, anything.'

"But here's the rub. I didn't know for sure what she meant by that statement. I concluded that our relationship had grown so close that she trusted me to write in a way that would be respectful. I loved her so deeply that I wanted to deserve that trust. But could I ever be certain that my interpretations and decisions weren't slanted toward my own interests?" Carolyn pauses and looks down, contemplating what she is saying and how it is being interpreted by the workshop participants.

"Why do you think the two of you became so close?" asks Debra, interrupting the silence. Carolyn is reminded that Debra said she wanted to work on her relationship with her mother.

Carolyn thinks for a moment and then says, "Partly from the experience of caregiving and partly from engaging in writing about it. Through the writing, I reflected more deeply on the complexities of our relationship. I paid attention to my mother in ways that I had not done before. I became more committed to making our relationship the best it could be and in being there for her. Imagining her experience of me, I recognized that she must have felt rejected at times when I went away to school, passed through my hippie 'anything goes' phase, and tried to hide my life from her. I came back home from college a different person and—as often happens when working class kids go to college—someone my family barely recognized (Rodriguez, 1983). After writing about my mother, I became more forgiving and more loving, more willing to reveal myself to her, and more thoughtful about the role I had played in any disagreements or misunderstandings between us."

"Is that what you mean when you write that autoethnography can be therapeutic?" Debra asks.

"Yes, through autoethnography our relationship improved, and I became extremely grateful for all my parents had done for me. I especially came to appreciate my mother's positive characteristics—her independence, organization, strength, appreciative spirit, sense of humor, practicality, and desire not to be a burden. She changed too and became much more giving and receptive to my love. Of course, growing older helped both of us see the other's position and realize how much we loved each other.

"It's 'about time,' as Art likes to say (Bochner, 1997). The rest of the time we had together—thankfully another eight years—was wonderfully close and loving.

"But the good feeling doesn't have to stop with the writing, or when the person dies. I highly recommend that you read the evocative dissertation Blake Paxton (2015)—who I mentioned earlier—wrote on continuing bonds (Klass, Silverman, and Nickman, 1996) with his mother after she died at a young age. I, too, have continued to be bonded to my mother through the pieces I have written about her. I revisit her every time I reread one of my stories or talk to someone who has. I feel close to her now, as I share this story with you and hear your stories in return. I can call up her smile, smell her baby powder smell, remember events, and feel my love for her that continues to grow and change. The story's vivid prose helps me to remember and re-experience the details and feelings I had as I took care of her. The story keeps my mother in my life now. I 're-member' her in the sense of continuing to keep her as a significant person in my life. Activating your memory is a powerful and therapeutic way to continue to be with someone (Ellis, 2009, pp. 190–193). Art will have much more to say about memory work on the last day of the workshop.

"Okay, we better end now," Carolyn announces. "Tomorrow, we will deal more thoroughly with the ethical issues aroused by 'Maternal Connections' and applicable to other evocative autoethnographies. We'll focus on treating others in our stories ethically.

"But before we conclude for the day, I want you to divide into groups of three or four people and talk informally for 30 minutes. Discuss the kinds of ethical dilemmas you've encountered in your work. That will get you ready for our session tomorrow."

The students move around the room and form groups. Carolyn and Art walk among them, enjoying and participating in the enthusiastic conversations When time is up, Carolyn watches as several of the people who shared their stories in response to 'Maternal Connections' seek out each other. She hears them making dinner plans together. She feels exhausted but happy about how the day went.

"How about getting a pizza delivered to our room tonight?" Art asks, as they gather their papers and exit the room. "A little rest before going to Murphy's would be great."

"You read my mind," Carolyn says, just before they are pulled away by other autoethnographers who stop them in the hallway.

Part Three

Ethical Dilemmas and Ethnographic Choices

Ethical Challenges

"Good morning, everyone," Carolyn says into a cacophony of voices emanating from all corners of the room. "I hope you had a good evening and slept well. We sure did." She nods toward Art, who smiles.

"I was glad to see so many of you at Murphy's last night. A lot of education takes place in informal settings like Murphy's. As an ethnographer, I could feel the excitement in the bar as I watched some of you meet and talk to authors we've mentioned here. Guess many of us are burning the candle at both ends," Carolyn continues. Several participants cover yawns.

"Today is my opportunity to lead, but Art will jump in occasionally." Art pretends to leap from his seat and the students laugh.

"This morning we're going to focus on ethical dilemmas that arise in writing personal narrative and doing research that includes people in your life who may be identifiable or with whom you have—or may develop—a personal relationship. In our discussion of 'Maternal Connections,' many of you raised questions about your right to publish stories about other people and your responsibilities to them when you do. You also asked questions dealing with the ethics review board at your university. These issues came up again in your small group discussions at the end of yesterday. Today, I'll address these concerns in more detail. This session will be more lecture than conversation, but feel free to ask questions or make comments."

The participants get out their notepads and tablets and prepare to take notes.

Introduction to Procedural, Process, and Relational Ethics[1]

"First, make no mistake, all approaches to studying human behavior present ethical dilemmas for investigators. Even surveys can tap into traumatic and personal concerns. For example, sociologist Rachel Einwohner (2011) found that working with secondary data sets of Holocaust survivor stories presented moral and emotional anxieties for her. When she identified survivors by numbers, she was reminded of how Nazis classified Jews.

"In order to protect the welfare of research participants and their own potential liability in case of harm, universities in the United States have set up formal institutional review boards (IRBs) to determine in advance whether researchers have put in place ethical procedures for conducting research (Farrimond, 2013). As most of you know, these review boards require investigators to institute measures prior to conducting research to protect human subjects from harm, obtain informed consent, maintain confidentiality, uphold honesty, and respect privacy. Though these boards must follow federal regulations, their procedures and review process can differ greatly (Farrimond, 2013).

Many other countries, such as Canada, Australia, the UK, and South Africa, also have equivalent boards, though their responsibilities and scope vary as well.[2]

"In most cases, research boards provide little guidance about 'process ethics' (also called 'situational ethics' or 'ethics in practice' [Guillemin and Gillam, 2004, p. 4])—those unanticipated situations and dilemmas that arise and demand immediate attention in the course of conducting research. Ethical decision-making is not a one-time occurrence; doing research ethically involves a process of continual monitoring and circumspection (Frank, 2004; see also Swim, St. George, and Wulff, 2001). A researcher figures out in each situation how to create the most ethical relationship and outcome for participants by recalling past experiences, learning from each event as it happens, imagining future sequences of events, and considering consequences of actions.

"Process ethics leads us into an area I call 'relational ethics,' which usually is neglected by review boards. Doing ethical research requires that we honor our relationships with participants and make wise decisions about fulfilling our responsibilities toward them, especially when we engage in research about intimate and/or traumatic events that might engender strong emotions (see Ellis, 2007). Relational ethics includes mindful self-reflection about the researcher's role, motives, and feelings during the research process. This mindfulness extends beyond ourselves as investigators to our participants and the communities in which they live, as we figure out ways to contribute positively to them (see González-López, 2011, pp. 448–450).

"Relational ethics can offer needed guidance to autoethnographers. I'll explore that idea in detail later. But before I do, I want to concentrate on procedural ethics, and some of the practical problems you may face in getting formal approval from your review board."

Ethical Quandaries in Interpretive Qualitative Research

"Though I appreciate the purpose of ethical review boards, I caution you not to be lulled into thinking that you're doing ethical research simply because you have secured approval for your project (see van den Hoonaard, 2002; Tolich, 2015). Most qualitative research raises ethical issues far more complicated than those covered by procedural rules. Take confidentiality, for example. The groups and communities we study may be recognizable to readers no matter how hard we try to camouflage the locations. The identity of some participants (for example, the town mayor) may be obvious to outsiders. Often participants in our stories may be known by community members and recognizable to themselves, which Tolich (2004) calls 'internal confidentiality.'

"No matter how much we plan ahead, many unanticipated questions and ethical dilemmas emerge only when we are deep into the research process, engaged in day-to-day interactions and in the process of forming relationships with participants. Most IRBs view research as short-term, bounded, and controlled physically and emotionally by the researcher, who is considered separate from the 'strangers' studied (see Ellis, 2004, 2007; High, 2014, p. 27). But often we develop friendships or longer-term relationships with our participants (see, for example, Huisman, 2008), invite participants to share authority or coauthor with us (see Sheftel and Zembrzycki, 2013; High, 2014; special issue of *The Oral History Review* on sharing authority), or include participants with whom we have extended connections (Ellis, Kiesinger, and Tillmann-Healy, 1997; Tillmann-Healy, 2003). Relationships with participants can be fraught with tensions as we try to maneuver through and among groups of people and negotiate changing positions and responsibilities.

"Also we must continually consider how to balance what we owe our readers and academic colleagues in terms of telling a 'true' story, and what we owe participants and the groups they represent in terms of loyalty, friendship, and confidentiality (Ellis, 2007; see also Josselson, 1996). Tasha Rennels (2015) confronted these issues in her dissertation about white working class people, which included interviews of others and reflections on herself as both a white working-class woman and an academic. She writes:

> Among the many challenges I encountered, figuring out how to ethically present participants was the hardest. I wanted, more than anything, to present them as contradictions to common stereotypes about white working-class people so I could confront the judgment that plagued my childhood. At the same time, I knew I needed to honor and remain true to what I observed and what participants shared with me, even if this information reinforced the stereotypes I was trying to debunk. I constantly struggled with what details to share, like Randy's mullet haircut and Ellen's kitschy décor. These details were important to the stories I composed but contradictory to my desire to invite readers to understand, not judge, white working-class people. (p. 141)

Ethical Quandaries in Autoethnographic Research

"As you can see, the ethical complications in autoethnography are not as different from those in ethnographic and qualitative interviews studies as many people think. But ethical issues in autoethnography can have greater consequences for our personal lives and for other individuals in our stories too. In autoethnography, we often write about friends and family members who can recognize themselves or be recognized by other people in our communities. Must you obtain consent from all the people who appear in your story? And in every situation that includes them? What if you feel apprehensive about safety; fear retaliation, exclusion, or shaming; or simply believe this is your story to tell (Mairs, 2008)? What if the person you write about does not want to be a part of the story, has a different and incompatible version from yours, or is unavailable because of death, illness, or lack of contact?"

Responding to Ethics Boards and Doing Ethical Research

"So what do you do? Going back to the questions you raised about 'Maternal Connections,' what do autoethnographers have a right to say and what do we owe those we write about, as Art insisted you keep in mind?" Carolyn asks, pointing to Regina, who has raised her hand.

"Here's an issue I brought up in our small group discussion yesterday, but one we didn't know how to think about." Carolyn nods for her to continue. "I submitted a proposal to our IRB to write about the divorce of my parents and how it affected the rest of our family. I never got to the point of thinking about process or relational ethics since the IRB immediately raised a barrier because I did not have consent from those in my story. I didn't know how to respond to the IRB, since some of the people involved had died and others were not on speaking terms with me. So I decided to postpone the study. What do you think I should have done?"

"Wow, nothing like diving into the fray," Carolyn says, and everyone laughs. "Since IRB responses are varied and individualized, I am more comfortable addressing your question by calling on my experience with our particular university board rather than talking about boards in general."

"That would be helpful," says Regina, and several students nod.

"Okay, stay with me. This is a long story. When our students first started doing autoethnography in the early 1990s, I told them to describe their work as 'reflexive ethnography' in order to avoid confusing members of the ethics board, who would not know what we meant by the term 'autoethnography.' When autoethnography became more familiar, board members began asking increasingly complicated ethics questions, such as whether family members had given consent and if they could exempt themselves from the project. Then our students began to question me about whether they were permitted to write about people and events in their past if they got permission now, or to use interviews they previously had done for classes but for which they had not yet requested approval. When

I inquired several years ago about the possibility of 'retrospective approval' for these situations, responses from IRB staff members ranged across the spectrum from 'you must obtain retrospective approval' to 'there is no such thing as retrospective approval.' Imagine the quandary that produced!

"More recently, our IRB has taken the position that autoethnographies are not under their oversight," Carolyn continues. "Here is an excerpt from an official letter sent to Blake Paxton in January 2014: 'The IRB has determined that the activities described in the application are not designed to be a systemic investigation that will contribute to generalizable knowledge under the criteria required by Health and Human Services. The activities therefore do not constitute research per USF IRB criteria. As a result, IRB approval is not required for this activity. The study is marked closed—never approved.'

"Was this after the student did all that work to submit a proposal?" asks Maria, who is working on her Ph.D.

Carolyn nods. "Yes. This is the dissertation study I mentioned earlier in which Blake was investigating grief surrounding the sudden death of his mother. Blake proposed interviewing family members and friends of his mother, as well as writing a story of his own grief (Paxton, 2015). I was shocked at the board's response since previously they had taken the position that any study published or presented in a public forum was deemed 'research' and needed approval. While our board continues to define research in terms of presenting our work in public—such as at conferences and in print, they now classify proposals for autoethnographic research as not falling under the purview of IRB since autoethnographers do not seek 'systematic' and 'generalizable' knowledge. Of course, autoethnographies should be as systematic as any other kind of research; and most small sample qualitative research is not generalizable either, yet is under the control of IRB. I suspect they just couldn't keep up with the workload they've created."

"Nothing like bloated bureaucracy," a voice shouts out. Carolyn chuckles and Art nods in agreement.

"I should point out that Blake's case wasn't all that clear-cut. When I followed up, a representative from the IRB told me that Blake's plan to interview friends of his mother was a 'gray' area that provoked a lot of disagreement. Some IRB members felt these interviews required approval, but others felt that would be the case only if the people interviewed were outside the family circle."

"That sounds pretty arbitrary," says Maria.

"Yes, you can see a lot of gray in how these boards respond."

"But that's good, right?" asks Maria. "I mean now your students don't have to go through this process."

"I admit to feeling somewhat relieved by the board's decision not to review autoethnography proposals. Though we had always gotten our studies approved, we had to answer questions formulated mainly for biomedicine and the physical sciences, not the human sciences, which is where I locate autoethnography. The process was lengthy and many of the questions asked by IRB seemed unconnected to what students were doing. Some students began to shy away from proposing the studies they wanted to do, and the IRB presented a stumbling block for others, often holding up their projects for months.

"But this change also troubles me. Preparing to submit a proposal to an IRB can provide a good exercise in thinking about the procedural ethics in your research and considering ethical issues upfront. Tullis (2014, p. 258) says we should 'use, rather than resist' the federal ethical guidelines, and I agree."

"Isn't it also problematic that our work is not considered research by these powers that be?" asks Erica.

"Good question, Erica," Art says, as he rises to answer. "I think what the 'powers that be' mean is that autoethnography is not strictly scientific research. Of course, exactly what they may mean by 'scientific' is arguable, but that's another story. We don't buy into their conception of what is or is not 'research.' So we feel no need to respond. But the change does mean that our own oversight of student projects must continue to be a top priority."

"Though it's not considered research, autoethnography is still seen as a valid method by ethics boards, right?" asks Inkeri.

"Ethics boards have nothing to do with deciding whether a method is valid," responds Barry. "Their role is to protect human subjects and to insure that the university is not vulnerable to a lawsuit. That came up in our small group session yesterday."

"That's true, Barry," Art says. "Blake's committee members—and I was one of them—agreed that he was doing original research and that autoethnography was a legitimate methodology for achieving his goals. That approval was what counts."

"So what is the best way to handle review boards when you're doing an autoethnographic dissertation?" Eric asks. "I'm confused now. We haven't traditionally consulted ethics boards in doing dissertations in our performance and theater program, though we do have research ethics boards (REBs) in Canada. But now that we've branched out to doing more empirical research—including autoethnography—that issue is relevant. I don't know what to advise my doctoral students to do." Karen, who is in a similar program in the arts, nods in agreement.

"Eric and Karen—all of you really—here is my advice," Carolyn says, again taking the floor. "When you or your students propose a research project that involves human subjects, I suggest calling your university's review office and asking questions about their position on autoethnography. Inquire as to what steps you need to take. In talking to colleagues in the United States, Canada, England, and Australia, I have been impressed by how reasonable the procedures are becoming. I'm not sure what the process is like in other countries."

"Don't all dissertations have to go through review boards?" asks Jake, who has been quiet until now.

"For a long time all dissertations involving human participants—at least in the social sciences—had to go through the IRB at my university. This was true in most universities in the United States. But now dissertations in oral history and autoethnography do not *necessarily* have to go through the IRB if the student is not proposing to generalize beyond the individual—whatever that means.[3] As you might imagine, this is another hazy area, and highly dependent upon the specific review agency and actual person doing the review. Keep in mind that review boards normally specify that they, not the applicant, must determine whether a formal review process is needed or not. So I'd recommend erring on the side of submitting your proposals, even if you think you won't need to go through the whole process. Your dissertation or thesis is too important to you to risk making an irretrievable error in judgment."

"Is that how you advise your autoethnography students?" asks Eric.

"Yes, I tell them to fill out the first page of the IRB application and answer no—as angst producing as that may be—to the question, "Is this research?" Then a short form will open; answers to those few questions will determine if a student needs to complete the long document. Filling out the short form should give you institutional protection if a problem comes up. And if a journal editor or book publisher raises issues of consent—and that can happen—you will be able to certify that you have done what is required by the IRB."

"Unlike your university, we need IRB approval for all theses and dissertations at my university," says Regina. "I started my project on my mother's mental illness in a class on autoethnography that didn't require approval. But then, as I told my group yesterday, I decided to use the interviews of my family for my thesis. What do I do now?"

"Again, I can only answer according to what I know to be the case at my university. Classroom work done for an educational purpose with no 'intention' of producing a systematic, generalizable project that constitutes research does not need to be submitted to USF's IRB. After Blake's proposal was returned, I asked for clarification about this matter as well. I was told that if a student decides to pursue a classroom project in a systematic, generalizable way, then IRB approval is necessary. At that point, the student should request 'retrospective approval of data collected,' as well as 'prospective approval' for data yet to be gathered. If the student is not able to obtain consent for any of these data, then he or she must ask for a 'consent waver.'

"At some universities, ethics boards still examine autoethnographies closely and ask questions more appropriate to bio-medical projects; at the same time, some of you haven't had to deal with ethics boards much at all. So our experiences might be very different.

"Whatever the case, we need to make sure our research is as ethical as we can make it. That's the point I want to emphasize. Even if my students don't have to go through the IRB, I still require them to take our IRB's ethics training and to get consent forms signed from participants in their studies, if feasible. I also ask students to revisit the consent process frequently with their participants to make sure nothing has changed, and to discuss any problems with me. I revisit consent with my participants as well. You have to think about the ethics of your research and writing *at every point in the process* because relationships and the goals of the project can and do change."

"These decisions are so complex; they're never black and white," says Sophie, who is a teacher educator. "How do you ensure you're making them ethically?"

"The complexity is what makes them ethical decisions in the first place," Carolyn answers. "I don't have a definitive black and white answer for you either. I advise you to figure out what to do the same way you figure out what it means to live an ethical life in your everyday world. As a researcher, you should be tough on yourself and work to make certain you're not just drawing conclusions in your favor to give yourself permission to write what you want to write. It's your story, and you get to decide how to tell it and what to tell, but along with that privilege comes additional responsibilities."

Ethical Responsibilities to Family Members, Intimate Others, and Ourselves

"What you say is helpful," says Betty. "But I'm still confused about our responsibilities to people who are characters in our personal stories. They are in our lives, but they haven't consented to being participants. So how do we think about including or implicating family members in our autoetnographies? Should we consider them the same way we consider participants (Tullis, 2014)?"

"These are tough questions you're asking. You're getting to the heart of ethical dilemmas in autoethnography. I don't have magical, set-in-stone solutions. You have to think deeply about all the people in your research, even—or especially—those you think have behaved badly toward you. If you decide not to let them read what you're writing or not to ask them for permission to include them as characters, then you need to have good reasons. These reasons should not only make other people feel comfortable about what you do, they also should make you feel satisfied with how you've resolved the issue. You have to be able to live with yourself and your own ethical choices."

"Are you saying we have to take our work back to those in our stories? If they don't approve, do we have to omit the information or change it?" Jennifer asks, no doubt thinking about the project she wants to do with her therapist.

"No, and no. I'm saying that you need to look at each dilemma you encounter on a case-by-case basis. Susan Chase (1996) makes the point that while our participants should have some say in the details that are included in their stories, researchers should have 'interpretive authority' to reframe and analyze participants' experiences. You may decide to include counter interpretations from your respondents or omit claims your respondents might not appreciate, but as a researcher you are accountable for what you do or do not include and how you interpret your results. Phillip Lopate (2013, p. 85) says he does not want to give another person the power to decide what gets included in his story. He feels these decisions are his moral dilemma, his ethical burden, and he should not make them someone else's.

"Even if you get consent from those in your stories, that is not a ticket to write what you want or what you think your characters will approve. Consider, for example, Robin Boylorn's (2013) study, *Sweetwater*, about her hometown community, in which she focused on the women in her extended family. Concerned about how her book might impact participants, Robin asked her mother how she felt about the stories that would be in it. Her mother said, 'That was how it was...but it makes me look so bad.' Paralyzed by her mother's response, Robin wrestled with what to tell and how to tell it. So she approached her mother again. Her mother instructed Robin to write truthfully whatever she needed to write. The trouble with that mandate though was that Robin's mother desperately wanted to help Robin get her Ph.D., so perhaps her mother had little choice but to encourage her."

"Similar to your mother," Kalisha says, "when she told you to write anything you wanted."

"Good connection," Carolyn responds. "Certainly my mom loved me and wanted to be helpful. In these situations, acting ethically requires us to think about the larger situation, not just whether we have the person's consent at that moment or whether those in our stories have read what we've written. For example, Robin also had to consider how her words might affect the larger community of southern black women. In my case, I felt I had to acknowledge how harmful it could be to my relationship with my mom, and to her self-image, to force her to listen to me reading the entire story to her. Better to hand the finished manuscript to her, as I did, and let her make the decision about whether to read it from beginning to end."

"How do we know when we've considered these matters sufficiently?" asks Marilyn.

"Anybody want to answer Marilyn?" Carolyn asks.

Tom nods. "You really don't. All you can do is try to be aware of the ramifications on all levels. Keep asking questions and questioning your premises. And ask others to think through them with you as well. Then make the best decision you can at each step."

"Nice response, Tom," Carolyn says. "This should be our process no matter who our research participants are—whether strangers, strangers who become friends, or those who are family members or friends from the beginning. I believe it is important to act from a 'relational ethics of care,' a series of ongoing, uncertain processes where relationships and relational ethics guide you. Often what is ethical to do in any situation may not be clear, but, as Tom indicated, something must be done and/or decided. You can't evade ethical issues!

"As is true with the rest of life, sometimes we do it right and sometimes we make mistakes or in hindsight see a better way of doing things. I discussed this in my book *Revision* (Ellis, 2009), where I looked back at ethical choices I had made about doing research with the fisher folk and also with my mother. One is never finished making ethical decisions as long as one is interacting with or writing about others. We must be fully present to what we are doing and, as Tom said, continually ask questions—endless questions—about 'what is going on here,' 'what to do now,' and 'what is needed to make this interaction go well, to honor the other person, and to take care of myself' (Bergum and Dossetor 2005, pp. 9, 24; see also Adams, 2008).

"When you're writing about family members or intimate others, you have to go to great lengths to take the role of the other, to interrogate your own role and motives, to imagine how other people will respond and how you and they may feel later. You may want to ask yourself how they would tell the story and incorporate that into your version or use their story to enhance your own. Will you create a world/relationship you later have trouble living in, or act in a way that you wish you had done differently? Are there other solutions or ways to say what you want/ need to say to take care of yourself without hurting someone else? Can you write to understand how others in your life put their worlds together? Can you write yourself out of the trauma or figure out a way to be a survivor of the situation you've been handed that doesn't involve demonizing others (Ellis, 2007)? These predictions can be perilous and paralyzing. At some point, after you've weighed alternatives, you must decide and move on. You will likely have plenty of opportunities to qualify or explain your decisions in print."

"I solved this problem for myself by waiting until my parents had died. Or at least I thought I had," Marilyn says, hesitantly. "Now after listening to you, I guess I'm not so sure."

Carolyn nods to Jane, who wants to speak. "Marilyn, I don't think waiting for someone to die solves the problem. Dead people can't give you permission. Thus there is always tension surrounding what you can say and how you can say it. The dead can't talk back, but others in the community, who were in relationship with you and those who have died, will have feelings about, and reactions to, what you write. You'll still have to deal with them. And they might lash out and hurt you as well."

"Besides, there's always a chance you may die before them," Art quips.

"Good points," says Carolyn, grinning at Art's intervention. "Writing autoethnography inevitably makes the author vulnerable, as Art noted yesterday. Re-experiencing a traumatic situation might mean you relive the trauma, as April Chatham-Carpenter (2010) did when she was pulled back into an eating disorder as she wrote about it. Or if you clean up the story too much in the telling, it might set up a situation where you (and readers) come to believe you should be on top of a trauma even when you are not (Tamas, 2009). What you write also might cause you personal or professional difficulties (Medford, 2006). For example, Barbara Jago (2002) risked writing about depression and the effect it might have on her career. Carol Rambo has written about dangerous topics, such as being abused as a child (1995), having a mother with mental retardation (1996), and attempting unsuccessfully to become chair of her department (2015). She also wrote a performance ethnography of resistance after being told by her IRB office that she could not ethically publish a story about her relationship with a student who had a history of sexual abuse, though the article already had been accepted by a journal (2005).

"The crux here is that we can't always know the effect our words will have on another—or ourselves—or what will harm our lives or cause offense to others," Carolyn suggests. "Sometimes folks will even get upset about not being included in your stories or about not being given a central role (Lopate, 2013, p. 83).

"We write about our emotions, often those associated with pain. Thus, there's always the chance that our stories will cause discomfort. We can never completely get rid of that feeling, nor would we want to (see Andrew, 2015, p. 178). But we should do everything in our power to minimize hurt. We can be fair-minded and make sure to move beyond revenge narratives and settling scores (see Spry, 2011, pp. 36–37; Adams, Holman Jones, and Ellis,

2015, p. 96). Sometimes this means leaving out things, investigating more closely the part we played, and doing what we can to protect the identities of those in our studies."

"Assuming we need to protect identities, how do we do it?" Jennifer asks.

"Whatever you do, your goal should be to reproduce what happened in ways that preserve the reality you are seeking to depict for the reader. Some autoethnographers create composite characters, collapsing several characters into one. I've also experimented with putting characteristics of one person into different people (Ellis, 1995a).

"Other autoethnographers write in ways that take the focus off the specific identity of *who* they are writing about. For example, Norman Denzin (2003, 2008, 2015) highlights places and historical events with unnamed narrators, numbered voices, and contemporary historical characters who speak his words. Tony Adams and Stacy Holman Jones (2011) camouflage which experience belongs to each of them. Chris Poulos (2008) leaves characters nameless and identifies them solely by their roles—a father, a son—so that the identity of the actor is unclear. The reader can't tell whether Chris is talking about his father, his father's father, or himself as father. A few authors use *nom de plumes* to camouflage the characters in their stories and what happened (Carter, 2002).

"Some autoethnographers invent fictional stories, using what Yalom (1991, p. 169; see also Speedy, 2008) calls 'symbolic equivalents,' by which he means fragments of real occurrences presented in a fictionalized way that preserves the meaning, complications, and feelings of the raw events (see, for example, Pelias, forthcoming). Others cleverly blend fiction and nonfiction. You'll see that later, when Art discusses his story about an imagined conversation with his father in which he recalls actual events through what he calls 'memory work' (Bochner, 2007).

"All of these approaches help, but they are not magic bullets. Sometimes we just have to put our story out there and accept the consequences. We have to figure out how important it is to tell it, think about the potential rewards and risks, and determine if the work has something important to offer others by putting meanings into motion. Nobody can make these judgments for you. What to do is contingent on a context; our ethical decisions involve struggle and uncertainty. That's what makes them dilemmas.

"There are no perfect answers. Sometimes you just have to put your struggle and uncertainty on the pages and invite readers to enter your consciousness as you grapple with writing ethically. Revealing that struggle too is a contribution."

From his chair, Art says, "I advise that you don't get too bogged down in unresolvable ethical dilemmas. While important, they should not be your sole consideration. Take heart! Ideally, what you write can be considered a 'gift of the truth of your feelings' (Lopate, 2013, p. 84)."

"Guess I do tend to get heavy sometimes," says Carolyn, chuckling. "But imagine this: Art Bochner is showing the bright side." Art pantomimes a meditating Buddha, a mindful expression on his face, one hand resting gently atop the other.

Carolyn raises her eyebrows, her dimples deepening. "It's true," she says, "that many autoethnographers report improved relationships stemming from their autoethnographic investigations and stories. That's what happened with my mother and me. And with my connection to Jerry, a Holocaust survivor I'll be telling you about after our next break.

"Look at the bibliographies in the autoethnography textbooks Art and I brought with us today. You'll find that many people before you have confronted these ethical dilemmas, and many have written effective, evocative, and sensitive stories about the trials in their lives and the people who were part of them (see, for example, Bochner and Ellis, 1992; Adams, 2006). You can too.

"Okay, good place to stop. When you return from your bathroom break, enjoy the sodas, water, and cookies in the back of the room."

A Relational Ethics of Care[4]

When participants are settled, Carolyn says, "I'd like to concentrate now on working from a 'relational ethics of care.' I offer this approach as a way to think ethically about doing research from an autoethnographic perspective that focuses on the lives of others, while also including you—the author—as a character or storyteller. I'll end with an example from my current research.

"By relational ethics of care, I refer to how people connect to each another in their various roles and relationships from moment to moment (Bergum and Dossetor, 2005, pp. 3–4). Following a relational ethics of care does not mean that you reject an ethics based on justice; we need both reason and heart, and we exist in an 'ongoing tension' between justice and care as we aspire to both (Gilligan, 1988, pp. 35, 47). Virginia Held (1995, p. 3) suggests that justice sets 'moral minimums' and 'absolute constraints' while '[c] are deals with questions of the good life or of human value over and above the obligatory minimums of justice.' Nel Noddings (2002, p. 3) made a case for the close relationship between the two principles in her description of justice as 'caring about' the welfare of others at a distance from us, which generates the motive and content of justice, while 'caring for' involves relating face-to-face.

"Relational ethics of care focuses on the particular, local, concrete circumstances at hand, not the universal, abstract and theoretical (Bochner, 1994). Rather than relying on objective standards, acting ethically depends on engagement; it relies on building trust rather than drawing conclusions. Though some ethical issues can be anticipated, it is impossible to know ahead of time all the moral conundrums that might arise in any research project. As in any relationship, a researcher and participant must try to negotiate and resolve misunderstandings and disagreements that might occur in moment-to-moment interactions, repeatedly asking ethical questions, and working from specific cases to guiding principles and back again (Ellis, 2009, p. 317). As Vangie Bergum and John Dossetor (2005, p. 128) said about health workers and patients, 'Dialogic conversation involved give and take, back and forth, being strong and being vulnerable, listening to stories of pain and staying in pain, and confronting death and staying with the dying.'"

"This is all interesting," says Jake, "but it sounds like the same principles and practices that apply to doing any good ethnographic research. What makes this an autoethnographic perspective?"

"Good question. Anyone want to speculate?"

"You have to interrogate and try to understand the self to understand the other," says Barry, whose work focuses on ethics.

"The researcher is part of the conversation being examined, as Art's first precept indicated," says Regina, who also has voiced an interest in ethics. "So I'd think the researcher would have to do a continuous self-examination to ensure he or she is doing ethical research (Jacobs, 2004, p. 236). Also, part of the mandate is to care for ourselves as we care for them. That should be part of the self-examination too (see Fahie, 2014)."

"And you have to examine the space and dialogue between researcher and respondent," adds Barry (see Ellis, 2007; also see Jacobs, 2004; Bergum and Dossetor, 2005, p. 11; Etherington, 2007).

"Great," says Carolyn. "You guys don't need me anymore. Okay, now one more question: Are there any precautions you might suggest for someone doing this kind of research?"

"It demands a certain level of researcher vulnerability," says Regina, "and a willingness to share your stories, reflect on your own issues, and reveal yourself as participants reveal themselves. That can be hard."

"If it's so hard, why would you want to do it?" Carolyn asks.

"Because that is how relationships develop. That's what mutual respect means," says Inkeri.

Carolyn smiles. "Any other warnings?"

"We must be self-aware but not self-absorbed, all the while keeping the focus on them and their stories," says Barry (Bergum and Dossetor, 2005, pp. 81–82). "That can be difficult to balance."

"What is the payoff?"

"In the process we—researcher and participant—can together seek out new questions and understandings about ourselves, each other, and our relationship, as well as about the issues and topics to which our research collaboration is directed," says Inkeri.

"Bravo," says Carolyn. "You just did my lecture for me." The students clap.

Compassionate Research and Collaborative Witnessing with a Holocaust Survivor[5]

"I'd like to move now to what I call compassionate research, an approach done within a relational ethics of care. Here researchers and participants work collaboratively, sharing authority and responsibility. They listen deeply to, speak responsibly with, feel passionately for, share vulnerably with, and connect relationally and ethically to each other with care. Researchers—sometimes in collaboration with participants—write and tell stories empathically and respectfully, accompanied by a desire to relieve or prevent suffering (Patti, 2013, 2015; Ellis and Patti, 2014).

"In this process, we are a witness to those who tell their stories. We are intimately present to the other, open up to that person, hear and try to understand the world through the other's being, and feel close to what this person feels. Though we know we can never fully imagine another person's experience, still we try with all our might anyway, and do so without losing a sense of ourselves (Bergum and Dossetor, 2005, p. 55). As we 'give priority to the other' (Freeman, 2014), we extend as much compassion *for* the other as we might have for ourselves. The other, in turn, develops compassion for us, as his or her life and goals intersect with ours. We become a witness to the other and to ourselves (Laub, 1992, p. 58).

"Now I want to share a collaborative research project I am doing with Jerry Rawicki, an 88-year-old survivor of the Warsaw Ghetto. I first met Jerry in 2009 when I videotaped a traditional oral history interview about his experiences his experiences before, during, and after the Holocaust. We continued working together in videotaped sessions, follow-up conversational interviews, and informal meetings. Our project assumes that stories shared conversationally in long-term, close relationships present openings to tell untold stories, and to revise, develop, and analyze the stories revealed along the way.

"As I said on the first day, I work from the premise that research should be helpful (and heartful); if not, I don't want to do it. Because of my close relationship with Jerry, and the sensitive nature of our project, I have been determined to make certain our collaborative work doesn't bring any harm to him, but instead provides a positive experience. I focus on Jerry's wellbeing and the possibility of renewal and purpose in his life (and mine). I can do the research I do, which involves emotional sharing, because Jerry and I are close friends (see Tillmann-Healy, 2003). Our friendship formed around a mutual interest in the Holocaust, trauma, and loss, but now includes much more—caring for each other's families, other survivors, and day-to-day concerns and problems in living."

Carolyn pauses. Into the pause, Jake says, "I can't help wondering, given your close relationship with Jerry, what happens when you end this project?"

"When we end this project, if we do, we will remain friends," Carolyn replies. "I have no intentions of leaving the field, because I am committed to this work; besides there is no field to leave since Jerry is part of my life and will continue to be as long as the two of us are alive and living near each other.

"Our relationship is our project. I am now a character in Jerry's life story, as he is in mine. We exist in each other's stories, which are self-other stories, and we try to understand ourselves in the presence of the other. I am a person Jerry speaks with and tells his stories to in this present moment; I am a recipient and co-creator who allows herself to feel Jerry's stories; I am a person who speaks and listens empathically from a place of my own losses, and shares those losses when it seems appropriate; I am a person who tries to understand my own pain as I listen to Jerry's and to understand Jerry's pain through my own. In turn, Jerry tries to understand himself and his experience through the questions I ask, the stories he tells, the emotions he feels, the experiences I relate, and our conversational back and forth.

"Witnessing stories about traumatic experiences requires 'being with' the teller, which means to allow oneself to be in communion with the other as an ethical idea. Ultimately, this perspective asks autoethnographers not only to live 'with' but also 'in' the stories we tell and hear from others. I am committed to be with and bear witness to Jerry's story in whatever ways I can."

Becoming Compassionate Readers[6]

"In June 2013, I accompanied Jerry on his return to Poland for the first time since he left at the age of 21. While in Warsaw, we produced a video, *Behind the Wall*, featuring Jerry in situ exploring his memory of his past and his feelings about forgiveness toward his homeland. I also accompanied Jerry to Treblinka, where his sister and mother were killed. Now I want you to read the story I wrote about our Treblinka experience, which I hope conveys how a relational ethics of care might take place in practice.

"I don't want to say too much about the story before you read it, just two invitations and a warning. First, the invitations. I invite you to imagine the moment-to-moment concrete and emotional experience Jerry had while walking through Treblinka. Feel with and for Jerry as a survivor. Think about what happened and how you have felt in situations where you grieved a loss. Hopefully, reading this story will provide an opportunity to remember, empathize, compare, and understand what happened to you and to Jerry more fully. If you have not had an experience of loss, then this story offers you a chance to try to understand something unfamiliar. In either case, I invite you as a reader to become a compassionate participant observer, opening up to and trying to understand life as lived.

"Second, try to put yourself in my place, as a researcher negotiating the intersection of my roles as friend and researcher ethically. I invite you to enter my feelings and thoughts, as I experience Jerry's grief and the grief produced from the source of my own remembering. Take in my moment-to-moment decisions, as I try to participate fully in this important event with Jerry and give him my support, yet also preserve our experience for the telling. Become a witness to how Jerry, his family, and I try to create meaning in our trek toward and away from Treblinka. In the process, call on the ways you make meaning in your lives and on the ways in which you can understand this story in the spirit of a relational ethics of care.

"Now the warning. This is a difficult piece to read with ghastly images of murder and emotional images of grieving. Some researchers critique using these images in our stories and say we should respect the 'void' of the unspeakable and unthinkable nature of the Holocaust (see Lang, 2005). My philosophy is more akin to that of Charlotte Delbo (1995, p. 86), a member of the French resistance who survived Auschwitz. She advises us to 'try to look. Just try and see.' As an ethnographer, that is what I try to do—look, see, relate to, and feel, exploring what goes on in my surroundings and in my heart and mind, and what I see and imagine goes on for Jerry as he and I move through Treblinka.

"You'll find 'Groaning from the Soul' in Appendix B of your packet. Please read it now."

$\sim$

A few attendees retrieve sodas and several talk quietly, while most begin reading the story. Art and Carolyn remain in the front of the room, observing, and occasionally talking quietly with each other. Soon there is silence. Occasionally, Carolyn hears a sniffle and sees students wipe their eyes.

"Are you finished?" Carolyn asks when all appear to have stopped reading. She thinks of asking for responses, and then decides instead to respect the silence for those who need it. "Maybe you'd like a long lunch break today, a chance to breathe. It might be good to take a walk before lunch and think about what you just read, either alone or with another workshop participant. It's a gorgeous day outside. Go and bask in the warmth of the sunshine. I'm here if anyone wants to talk to me about this story. If you do, perhaps we might take a walk together."

A few students remain behind to talk with Art and Carolyn. Barbara asks Art about the writing in this piece and how she might learn to write that way. Then Eric asks Art to take a walk with him so that they might talk about how to bring a collaborative approach to his work in music. Several mention to Carolyn how much this story touched them and a few offer hugs.

"Excuse me," says Jake, as Carolyn starts to exit the room. "I have a question."

"Go ahead."

"What about Jerry? Aren't you hurting him by including these passages? How did he feel reading it?"

"I wondered that as well, and I offered in an email to take out the explicit description of murder before I sent the story to him for approval. I told him I didn't want him to feel what I had felt when I looked up information on the internet about my brother's plane crash. Hearing the conversation of the pilots and the cockpit sounds when the crash happened was really disturbing to me, and as I'll talk about later, I think that sometimes we don't need to revisit these details. I have the note Jerry wrote back right here."

While Jake continues to stand near her, Carolyn picks up the note from the table and reads. "'Carolyn, do not delete a single syllable in your paper. Though the pain will never cease, by now I'm inured to all the tragedies of the Holocaust. Nothing will ever assuage the memory of the night in Starahowice after trekking there from Bodzentyn, when I realized I would never see my mother and sister ever again. So please make your writing as vivid as you possibly can, even as you have to draw on your personal tragedy the way you described it in *Final Negotiations* (Ellis, 1995a), or as I remember the airplane plunging into the Potomac River from your story about your brother's death' (Ellis, 1993)."

"So Jerry was fine with your recording this experience?" asks Marilyn, one of several participants listening in.

"More than fine. I gave him some photos from the visit and told him about the footage. He said he was glad we had images of Treblinka and asked me to send them to his son, who could not be with us that day. Now, you might want to again question how much of his response was because he wanted to support me. I do ask myself that, but at some point we have to trust that what people say is what they mean."

Carolyn sees Silvia waiting quietly near the door and approaches her. Silvia asks Carolyn if she could take her up on the offer of a walk. "I'd like to talk about the trauma I experienced during the shootings at Virginia Tech that took place in 2007," she says, wiping her eyes (Tilley-Lubbs, 2011; Tilley-Lubbs and Bènard Calva, forthcoming). "It continues to affect me, especially with the latest gun violence at schools and colleges. The debate about openly carrying guns on campuses keeps me awake at night."

"Sure," Carolyn replies. "Let's walk around the quad."

After her walk, Carolyn texts Art:

"Meet in the room in ten minutes? I need a break. I'm emotionally drained."

"Me too, and mostly all I did was observe. There is yogurt in the room for lunch."

"Perfect. I want to make sure I'm prepared emotionally for this afternoon. I have a lot of information to share in our session on ethnography."

"Yes, that's going to require quite a cognitive and emotional shift from how you ended this morning."

Ethnographic Alternatives

"I hope you had a peaceful walk and good lunch," says Carolyn, amid the chatter of the participants. "Art and I enjoyed the quiet meal we had in our room and our talks with some of you during the break. I appreciate comments I received about my Treblinka story, especially how you identified with me as a researcher and sympathized with Jerry as a survivor. Thanks for the hugs too. Sometimes hugs mean more than words.

"Let me give you the website for the film that Jerry and I did together in Poland, since some of you asked about it." Art goes to the whiteboard and writes: www.youtube.com/watch?v=w9es0TQkj8s. "The film provides another example of compassionate research."

www.youtube.com/
watch?v=w9esOTQkj8s

Autoethnography as Interpretive Ethnography

"Yesterday Art focused on the 'auto' and 'graphy' aspects of autoethnography as he discussed precepts, definitions, and fundamentals of story writing. This afternoon I will concentrate on the 'ethno,' how autoethnographers incorporate ethnographic practices and principles into their research. Our decision to separate these is a pedagogical convenience, since autoethnography as a research practice integrates the auto, the graphy, and the ethno. We observe and write others as we observe and write ourselves, and we observe and write ourselves as we observe and write others. We ethnographically examine and analyze context, culture, and self-other interactions in reflexive and introspective stories as we describe our thoughts, feelings, bodies, motives, and experiences.

"The ethnography part of our workshop is enormously challenging. There is so much we could cover and time is limited. Art and I talked about this earlier today, and we want to adjust as much as possible to your concerns, providing as many examples as possible to illustrate the use of ethnographic methods in autoethnography.

"Here's our plan. We will divide you into six groups. Keeping in mind that our topic is the 'ethno' in autoethnography, each group will have 30 minutes to address one of these areas: 1. Producing Stories; 2. Analyzing Stories; and 3. Telling Stories. One person in each group should volunteer to take notes, recording issues, topics, and the group's consensus on questions to bring to the larger conversation. These questions will determine the direction of this session when we come back together, though I invite you to add other questions as our discussion advances."

The students count off and rearrange their chairs to form their assigned groups. Groups 1 and 2 are responsible for 'producing,' Groups 3 and 4 for 'analyzing,' and Groups 5 and 6 for 'telling.' After some discussion about what these 'categories' mean, Carolyn and Art move among the groups and participate in the spirited conversations.

Intersecting Ethnography and Autoethnography

"As I walked around the room, I heard some of you discussing the relationship between ethnography and autoethnography in general," Carolyn begins. "So let's start there."

"Should we move back to our original seats?" asks Tom.

"No, stay where you are," says Carolyn. "You might need to confer with each other."

"I was the note taker for Group 1 on 'producing,'" says Erica. "We spent a lot of time trying to figure out what fits into the definition of ethnography. For example, we wondered whether a story like 'Maternal Connections' can be considered ethnography."

"I approach all my writing as ethnographic," Carolyn replies. "Even when I write episodic short stories, such as 'Maternal Connections,' I observe myself and the world around me as though it is an ethnographic project of immersion into a relationship, an institution, or a culture. I recommend the same to my students.

"But as you can see from reading my work, I am partial to an interpretive, creative, and artistic ethnographic mode. Rather than taking a realist perspective that tries to represent what happened accurately from a distanced, nonbiased view and seeks to analyze experience, I desire to write from the closeness of my experience. I want to tell an evocative story that connects with readers, incorporating a transgressive and critical perspective when appropriate (Denzin, 1997, 2014; see also Van Maanen, 1988).

"Most evocative autoethnographers view themselves primarily as interpretive ethnographers who work between art and science. We blend these perspectives—some more, some less—depending on the goals of the project at hand (see Ellingson, 2009). Thus, we rely on our skills as ethnographers as well as our abilities as writers and storytellers."

"May I ask a related question that came up in our group?" asks Kalisha.

"Certainly," says Carolyn.

"I'm wondering if realist ethnography and autoethnography have had an effect on each other. Are the two positions compatible?"

"I think it safe to say that realist ethnography and autoethnography have had a significant effect on each other (see Ellingson, 2009). Autoethnographers commit to being observers of not only their internal states but also of interactions, social groups, and the culture they are part of. In their research, some autoethnographers focus on the study of others, though they might include themselves as characters, as I did in the story with Jerry. Moreover, many autoethnographers incorporate traditional analysis in their stories.

"At the same time, many ethnographers have begun more and more to embrace good writing, position themselves in their work, and reflexively write themselves as participants who speak, ask questions, make comments, and occasionally even have feelings and tell stories" (see, for example, Duneier, 1999; Tracy, 2004; Goffman, 2014). Carolyn smiles. "Of course, that's truer for interpretive ethnographers than it is for those with a realist orientation, most of whom have been socialized to believe that what they do is not storytelling."

Art adds a comment. "Some of the influence on ethnographers to be more reflexive comes in the shift from focusing on 'participant observation' to focusing on the 'observation of participation' that

Tedlock (1991, 2000) wrote about—where researchers observe the interaction they have with participants. This shift was inspired by the epistemological doubt associated with the crisis of representation and the changing composition of those who become ethnographers, with more women, working class, ethnic and racial groups, gay, lesbian, transgender, and third-world scholars now represented."

"What Art says brings up another issue for me," says Jake. "You talk about autoethnographers being ethnographers, but what about the opposite: Are ethnographers who focus on their participation with others considered autoethnographers?"

"I think most effective ethnographers also are autoethnographers in that they are open to learning from their feelings and interaction in whatever group they are observing. But not all realist ethnographers would agree. I tend to be inclusive," Carolyn responds, "and welcome anyone who claims the identity of autoethnographer. Researchers who position themselves in the text or take on the role of an active participant in their research can consider themselves autoethnographers. That would hold especially if the author wrote narratively, including the detail, dialogue, and plot that Art talked about yesterday. And showed vulnerability, caring, and concern for all involved, which fits within an autoethnographic worldview. I'd even include analytic autoethnographers in this group," Carolyn says, turning and smiling at Art.

Producing Stories

Systematic Sociological Introspection and Emotional Recall

"Okay, I think we're ready to focus on the topic of 'producing stories.' Group 1, you had an interesting discussion about how we gather information to write autoethnographic stories. Erica, give us your group's first question."

"Sure. We were interested in how to recall details of experience in situations that we want to write about. What is the process?"

"I call this process *systematic sociological introspection*, which means actively recalling thoughts and feelings from a social standpoint. Introspection emerges in and represents social interaction and occurs in response to bodily sensations, mental processes, and external stimuli, while it affects these same processes. As you introspect, you are not just listening to one voice arising alone in your head; usually, you access multiple interacting voices, which themselves are products of social forces and roles (Ellis, 2009, p. 101)."

"How do you do systematic sociological introspection?" asks Erica. "That was our main concern."

"I use a process of 'emotional recall' similar to 'method acting' in which actors relive in detail a situation in which they have felt this emotion before. They use their senses, emotions, and imaginations to reexperience events from the past as though they were happening now. When I use emotional recall, I imagine being back in the scene emotionally and physically. Revisiting the scene in that way leads to recalling other details, which produces deeper emotional remembering.

"Initially, I concentrate on the lone, loud voice screaming inside my head or the raw fear gnarling within my gut. Then, embracing the multiplicity of selves that all human beings harbor, I try to bring to my consciousness the contradictory and ambiguous thoughts and feelings that I also experience. I write down what the many competing voices in my head are saying (Ellis, 2009, p. 108; see also Ellis, 1991a)."

Feeling she is talking too abstractly without providing illustrative material, Carolyn stops, picks up an article from the desk, flips through it, and says, "Let me give you an example from a piece I wrote about events that occurred at our summer home in the mountains (Ellis, 2013). In this scene, my dog Buddha has badly injured a rabbit. I call on my partner Art to do something:

"Art, come kill the rabbit," I yell, trying one more time. "It's suffering."

"I'm not going to kill the rabbit," Art's voice sounds out.

"I can't stand seeing this," I say.

"Then come away from it," the voice replies.

"I can't leave the rabbit like this."

"Well, then, don't look at it."

"I can't stop looking," I say.

"Then let Buddha kill it. It's a dog's natural instinctual process."

"Then I introspect about the exchange," Carolyn explains to the workshop participants and continues to read:

> I experience an ambivalent mixture of hoping Art might intuitively understand and respond to my stress, thinking I should be able to handle this on my own, not wanting to make a big deal out of something that isn't one in the larger scheme of things, desiring comfort and companionship anyway, being somewhat irritated, and finally accepting that this is my problem to solve.
>
> I look again at the rabbit and at Buddha, who is making movements toward the gate and then looking at me quizzically. As I once again visualize hitting the rabbit with the shovel, I decide instead to open the gate. Letting Buddha finish him off feels less horrible than doing it myself. I hope that Buddha won't kill the rabbit and then I hope she will. She runs toward the rabbit, gives a sniff as the rabbit frantically turns flips with its injured body in a final desperate attempt to get away. Suddenly Buddha pounces, takes one bite out of the middle of the rabbit, and shakes the body with her mouth. (p. 37)

Carolyn looks up from the article, and raises her eyebrows quizzically, seeking a response. "Did you write this right after it happened?" asks Tom. "Is that how you recalled all the things going on in your head and in your feelings?"

"In this case, I did," Carolyn responds. "And that's helpful because it doesn't take much effort then to access details or lived emotions—they're often there whether you want them to be or not. The disadvantage is that being so involved in the scene emotionally means that it may be difficult to get outside it to analyze from a more emotionally distanced cultural perspective. Yet both of these processes, moving in and moving out, are necessary to produce an autoethnography that reveals multiple and often contradictory thoughts and feelings that affect one's actions. That's why, if you have the opportunity, you should write about an event while your feelings still are intense, and then go back to it once you're more emotionally distant, when, as Art likes to say, you have 'lived through' the experience (Ellis, 2004, p. 118; see also Bochner, 2015).

"For example, listen to how I analyze Buddha's behavior after I've had more time to think about what happened:

> Rat terriers—able to run low to the ground, quickly change directions, and move rapidly—were bred to kill rats and other small vermin, probably in just this instinctual way. Does instinct relieve her from responsibility? From now being a killer? Perhaps thinking that Buddha is "bad" for killing the rabbit is akin to thinking my Australian Shepherd is "bad" for herding! (Ellis, 2013, p. 37)

"I didn't think about this during the event Carolyn describes," Art interjects, addressing the workshop participants. "But it occurs to me now that we are much more likely to forgive animals for their animalistic instincts than humans. Because of our capacity to reflect and introspect, we expect humans to control and manage their instinctive reactions. And fit into whatever is deemed appropriate or civil in the society in which they live."

"Of course, you and I think of our dogs as near-humans," Carolyn responds, "so that makes us cringe when we are reminded that they are indeed animals with uncontrolled instincts."

Art nods, and adds, "But, of course, humans have a survival instinct too—a powerful one, and sometimes the arousal of that instinct reveals how animal-like we can be."

"Reminds me of Jerry's fascination with the wildebeest," says Carolyn, "and how these animals use their cunning, or survival instincts, to sometimes outsmart the faster cheetahs who pursue them. Jerry compared being a Jew in the Holocaust to being a wildebeest in that his survival instinct kicked into high gear (Ellis and Rawicki, 2015)."

Writing and Using Field Notes

"Let's follow up on this discussion later," Carolyn says to Art. "Group 2, what do you have for me?"

"How do you do the ethnographic part of autoethnography? Do you recommend working from field notes? If so, how should we go about doing that?" Toni asks.

"Good topic," Carolyn says. "When I am involved in writing about an ongoing experience, I write extensive field notes. My first goal is to write down what happened, in as much detail and with as much remembered feeling as I can. In the first draft, I am not as concerned about the plot of the story as I am about the specific descriptions and emotions of the events and where and how they took place.

"In *Final Negotiations*, I had recorded field notes during the last year of Gene's life. I also generated chronological details for the previous eight years of our relationship, since I wanted to express how we came together as well as show what we went through at the end of his life as we approached his death. I wrote the first draft of my narrative from these hundreds of pages of field notes and constructed chronological details, including material from interviews, physicians' records, diaries, calendars, and tape recordings. The first draft of the manuscript turned out to be 700-plus typed pages that read more like edited field notes than an emplotted and evocative narrative.

"Sorry about that, Art," Carolyn chuckles, turning toward Art.

"But many drafts later—and with the help of Art's editing—the text became a more focused and storied 300-page version.

"In the final drafts, my goal was to turn these chronological notes—this happened, and then this—into an evocative tale that had the elements of a good story that Art talked about yesterday. I wanted the story to stay true to the experience as I had recalled and recorded it in my notes. But that didn't mean that I tried to describe events exactly as they happened or even precisely as I recalled them taking place. I had a more important goal, which was to write the most evocative story I could, one that had dramatic tension and an interesting plotline, yet stayed true to the meaning of my experience."

"May I interrupt?" asks Toni.

"Certainly."

"Someone in our group said that autoethnographers don't care about accuracy. Is that true?"

"That was me," says Jake. "Sometimes it seems that way, given all the attention paid to a dramatic plot."

"Our group discussed this topic as well," says Toni, the note taker from Group 2, "and one person said that the difference between ethnography and evocative autoethnography is the emphasis on accuracy of the stories we tell. Could you comment on that?"

"I'm glad you brought that up, Jake," Carolyn replies. "As you can see, others were thinking that as well. Art will discuss the nuances of this in some detail when he talks about memory and truth." Carolyn looks at Art, who nods. "So I'll be brief.

"Nothing Art or I have said should imply that evocative auto-ethnographers eschew facts. Most autoethnographers work back and forth between, on the one hand, generating meaning and narrative truth—which requires depicting experiences as believable, lifelike, and possible—and, on the other hand, staying close to the facts as we recall them. For me, this alternation produces the most effective story with the greatest possibility of deep understanding. It's what Art and I try to teach our students to do (for examples, see Tillmann-Healy, 2001; Foster, 2007; Herrmann, 2007; Adams, 2011; Patti, 2013; Paxton, 2015; see also Lopate, 2013)."

Art interjects, "Please remember that facts don't tell you what they mean or how they feel."

"Though I never lost sight in *Final Negotiations* of trying to write as honestly as I could from the data I had," Carolyn continues, "still I collapsed events, changed the time line, left out events to protect myself and others, and invented dialogue that represented who we were and how we related. I reordered the events into scenes that had a particular focus, were not repetitious, described a particular activity, and made a point. These are all writing strategies used by realist ethnographers, I might add."

Collaborative Autoethnographic Research

"Okay, we have time for one or two more questions about producing stories ethnographically," Carolyn says.

"Several in my group want to do collaborative work using an autoethnographic approach," Sadira says. "For example, I'm planning to do compassionate interviews with people in India about what home means to them. Collaborative autoethnography and ethnography are mentioned in the literature, but we're confused about how they're similar or different. Would you elaborate on collaborative approaches for us?"

"We could spend a whole session on this question," Carolyn says. "I understand your confusion. It stems from the many different labels attributed to recently developed collaborative methods. They all describe ways for qualitative researchers to collaborate with other researchers or participants and to share authority as they write and interpret (Frisch, 1990; Rubin and Greenspan, 2006). When researchers work together, they jointly tell about their lives; when researchers collaborate with participants, they generally focus on evocatively communicating the lives of the participants in shared storytelling and conversation. In the latter case, the sharing of researchers' lives is secondary, and the goal is to add to rather than get in the way of the coconstructed story told about others.

"Collaborative autoethnographic research is about and for others as well as about and for the researcher (Ellis, 2004; Chang, 2008; Ellis, Adams, and Bochner, 2011); it is a relational practice that asks us to enter the experience of the other as much as we think about the experience of the self (Ellis and Adams, 2014); and it requires us to take others' roles as fully as we can, and to reflexively consider why, given their histories and locations, they act on the world and respond the way they do (Ellis and Rawicki, 2013; see also Freeman, 2014).

"Let me mention briefly some of the recent collaborative approaches. Handout #10 will summarize these types, and you can follow up on any techniques that interest you."

HANDOUT # 10

Collaborative Approaches to Autoethnography

1. <u>Duoethnography:</u> In duoethnography (Norris, Sawyer, & Lund, 2012), several researchers work together to juxtapose their own autoethnographic accounts about a research question and integrate their separate findings to provide multiple perspectives on a social phenomenon. For example, Richard Sawyer and Joe Norris (2004), one who is gay, the other straight, compare their perceptions, experiences, and how their socialization influenced their attitudes and behavior toward sexual orientation.

2. <u>Collaborative autoethnography:</u> In collaborative autoethnography (Chang, Ngunjiri, and Hernandez, 2012), several researchers write individual autoethnographies and simultaneously contribute their individual findings for collective analysis in a series of standardized steps. Patricia Geist-Martin and collaborators (Geist-Martin et al., 2010), for example, write about their individual experiences with the complexities of mothering. They perform their stories publicly, look for commonalities, explore the literature, and then do a feminist critique of the scripts they have reproduced in their collective story.

3. <u>Collaborative writing:</u> In collaborative writing (Gale, Pelias, and Russell, 2012; Gale and Wyatt, 2009) multiple writers, who may not be in the same place or writing at the same time, co-produce an autoethnographic story about their relationships that also points toward issues of social justice. Marcelo Diversi and Claudio Moreira (2009), for example, write a

coconstructed autoethnographic narrative to explore the spaces between their lives as two Brazilians, one born privileged, the other not. In their examination of their experiences of race, class, identity, sexuality, and pedagogy, they seek to decolonize knowledge production, pedagogy and praxis, and in the process promote inclusive social justice. Ken Gale and Jonathan Wyatt (2009) also write 'between the two' in their joint dissertation. They send emails back and forth and comment on their own and each other's words in their reflexive and sensitive writing about the practice and theory of collaborative writing (see also Speedy and Wyatt, 2014, for different kinds of collaborative writing).

4. Community autoethnography: This approach is closely connected to collaborative writing. It is a form of working together where mutual exploration of the personal experiences of researchers-in-collaboration serves to illuminate a particular social/cultural issue, such as whiteness, and provides opportunities for social intervention (e.g., Toyosaki et al., 2009). Much like Gale and Wyatt, Pensoneau-Conway et al. (2014) use collaborative autoethnographic writing to try to understand the politics and ethics of their multiple relationships with each other and the dynamics and polyvocal constructions of their collaborative writing group.

5. Participatory action research: This approach is similar to other collaborative methods in terms of work-ing together and focusing on social justice. But here researchers work with laypeople—rather than other

2.

researchers—and orient their projects toward practical outcomes, with their primary goal being to identify and solve problems and unjust social conditions of the group with whom they are working. This is an engaged research practice where researchers desire to get things done, and in the process to come to some understanding. Action then is joined with research, collective practices, and self-investigation (Rahman, 2008).

6. Coconstructed narrative: This is a process in which two people record and then share their stories about a joint experience, attempting to write a story that brings together their separate versions into a single version satisfactory to each of them (Bochner and Ellis, 1992; Ellis and Bochner, 1992).

7. Interactive interviewing: Sharing dual roles of researcher and research participant, small groups of researchers well acquainted with each other investigate an emotional topic by recording multiple conversations. They focus on the stories that are created in the process as participants become closer and converse, write, and analyze their experiences (Ellis, Kiesinger, and Tillmann-Healy, 1997).

8. Compassionate Research: This approach includes compassionate witnessing, interviewing, and story-telling. Researchers share authority with participants as they connect in a caring and ethical relationship, coconstructing stories empathically and respectfully, accompanied by a desire to relieve or prevent suffering (Ellis and Rawicki , 2013; Ellis and Patti, 2014; Ellis and Rawicki, 2015).

3.

duoethnography
collaborative
    autoethnography
collaborative writing
community
    autoethnography

"Duoethnography, collaborative autoethnography, collaborative writing, and community autoethnography," Carolyn says slowly, writing each topic on the board. "All these are approaches where researchers work and write autoethnographically *with other researchers*. Similar in orientation, goals, method, and flexibility of procedures and guidelines, they overlap, intersect, and extend one another. Researchers who do collaborative forms of autoethnography have a common desire to achieve understanding of a topic from multiple perspectives through dialogue. Collaborative approaches value positive social change that can arise from this understanding. They diverge only in minor respects, such as when, how, and with whom collaboration takes place; when, how, and by whom data are collected, represented, and analyzed; and the degree of emphasis placed on individual and collective stories and on the analytic process (Chang, Ngunjiri, and Hernandez, 2012)."

"Thanks for the overview," says Sadira. "That's helpful. But our group was primarily interested in the two perspectives you developed with colleagues—coconstructed narratives and interactive interviewing."

"That was more than 20 years ago, but they have held up pretty well and they may have played a role in some of the more recently developed collaborative autoethnography. They also fit with the principles of evocative autoethnography, as Art and I have developed it. So I am happy to go into detail about them." Carolyn flips through her notes until she finds what she wants.

Coconstructed Narratives

"In the early 1990s, Art and I were interested in listening to, understanding, and feeling compassion for our own and others' stories, especially narratives of pain and sorrow. Our focus was on working out collaborative ways to understand deep emotional and relational experiences. Our first foray into a collaborative approach began in 1990, when we designed *coconstructed narrative* research, a process of inquiry that we thought could help us understand the decision we had made to forego having a child at that time, our emotional reactions, and what the choice we made meant for our relationship (Ellis and Bochner, 1992; Bochner and Ellis, 1992). We wanted to open up a conversation about what had happened and figure out how to work through our decision for the good of our relationship.

"A coconstructed narrative process emerged spontaneously. First, we wrote independently about our experiences. Then we exchanged our stories, read each other's, and had many conversations about our responses, interpretations, and increased understanding of this joint experience. Finally, we set about writing a coconstructed story about what had happened, one that we both could live with, that would describe our complex thoughts and feelings alone and together. We chose to write our coconstructed story as a script."

Carolyn pauses. The students are quiet; you can hear a pin drop. Finally Toni asks, "Was this therapeutic for the two of you?"

"Amazingly so. I think it is always helpful to take time to understand your partner's perspective and to convey your own in a loving way, especially when you confront a problematic issue. If the two of you are committed to your relationship, this examination can strengthen it and give you resources to understand the interpersonal dynamics in a deeper way. Preserving the relationship and improving it becomes your joint goal.

"Of course, Art and I also are two relationship communication junkies." The students laugh, glad for some levity. "So we appreciated what we learned about interpersonal dynamics through this process, as well as what we learned about ourselves and each other. For us, it felt more ethical to explore out own emotional trauma within our relationship than to risk doing emotional harm by asking other vulnerable people to talk about this topic.

"We developed this approach so that other couples might examine their relationships and communication in similar ways, if they desired. And we also encouraged other researchers to serve as intermediaries in this process, assisting laypeople to conduct this kind of research. With a mediator, participants might talk their stories into tape recorders rather than write them, and the researcher would transcribe the accounts and assist in assembling them into a collective story. A researcher might include herself in the narrative in the character of researcher observing the interaction, or as a person who has had similar experiences to the participants. The approach should be flexible, and a coconstructed story could take various forms. Our main concern was that the project be designed to meet the needs of the particular study, the researcher, and the participants, hopefully resulting in increased understanding of what had happened for all involved."

"Isn't that contradictory though?" asks Jake. "I mean, as you said, it could be damaging to vulnerable people? And researchers aren't therapists."

"Good points," Carolyn says. "In the wrong hands, done insensitively, this process could cause problems in a relationship rather than help it. And of course when you put your story out there so vulnerably, others may respond to you in hurtful ways, as some did to ours. I think we've said it before, autoethnography is risky, and anyone engaging in it has to be aware and sensitive at every point in the process. The riskiness and vulnerability though are what make autoethnography so potentially valuable. For now, let's hold off on the question of research as therapeutic. Art will address that when he takes up memory and truth.

"Let me try to summarize coconstructed narrative before I move on to interactive interviewing. In general, Art and I wanted to study relationships in ways that would more closely reflect how we live them in everyday life. We wanted to show couples engaged in the details of daily living, coping and trying to make sense of the ambiguities and contradictions of being partnered. Our procedures were based on several premises about how relationships are practiced. We assumed, for example, that relationships between people are jointly authored, incomplete, and historically situated. Connections hinge on contingencies of conversation and negotiation that often produce unexpected outcomes. One of the actions we take in relationships is to assign significance and meaning to vague experiences and events in an attempt to bring order to, and make sense of, events, ourselves, and our relationship. We do this by telling stories about what we've experienced. These stories are coconstructed by partners continuously over time and are, in that sense, unfinished. Each person's views and actions affect the other person's, and the joint activity and mutual identification that result (or fail to develop) become part of the relationship. Successful relationships, we believe, are a result of each person taking into account the other's perspective and integrating it with their own as they keep the conversation going (Bochner and Ellis, 1995; see also Ellis, 2004, pp. 71–82; Ellis, 2009, p. 196)."

Interactive Interviewing

"Now let's turn to *interactive interviewing* (Ellis, Kiesinger, and Tillmann-Healy, 1997), a research process that also came from an attempt to understand emotional experiences of people to whom I felt close. In this project, I worked with two graduate student women struggling with body image. We decided that all three of us would act as both researchers and research participants. We met and taped our conversations about eating and appearance. From these group interviews with each other and reflections on each other's writings, we then explored the meanings and embodiment of bulimia. We examined the accounts each of us brought to the interaction, but more importantly we focused on the stories that evolved as we interacted, developed close relationships, and came to trust each other deeply.

"One of the scenes in the article we wrote describes us eating together. In the middle of having dinner in a restaurant one evening, we suddenly realized what a rich ethnographic encounter we were experiencing. Thus, we decided to independently write our impressions of eating together and then share them with each other. From that we coconstructed a story where readers are inside our consciousness as we observe each other and ourselves.

"As we convey our thoughts and feelings, it becomes apparent how what we eat, and how much we eat, depends on our perception of others and their actions. We note how self-conscious we are about being watched and judged. Thus, readers witness us enacting an activity that we had been talking and writing about for months. In the performance of eating, then writing and sharing our thoughts and feelings, our understanding of women and eating was deepened as a personal consideration and broadened as a social concern."

"Did you continue this work?" asks Maria.

"I continued exploring the method," Carolyn says. "Lisa made several documentary films on food, eating, and body consciousness, and both she and Christine have written other pieces and given talks to young girls about women and body image (Kiesinger, 1998a, 1998b, 2002; Tillmann-Healy, 2009; Tillmann, 2014, 2015). The three of us have recorded some follow-up interviews with each other, but we haven't yet published anything from them. That still may happen."

"Could you give us another example?" asks Silvia.

"Sure." Carolyn picks up a manila folder, and scans her notes. "Bryant Alexander, Claudio Moreira, and hari kumar (2012) are three men from different racial and cultural backgrounds who decided to write about their relationships with their fathers. They wrote individually and then together, commenting on and following up on each other's stories. Writing performatively between feeling and critical thought, they included reflections on their unique stories to try to understand masculinity, resist repeating similar relationships with their children, understand themselves and each other, and become 'better men' and parents.

"What impressed me about their work was how within their resistance to being like their fathers they still could see their fathers' reflections in how they themselves acted. For example, Bryant's father often gave little gifts to his children, but when he lost patience he would escape into a television movie or into his room listening to music alone. Following his example, Bryant usually had treats in his pocket for his nieces and nephews, but also ran away when his tolerance was tested. On one occasion, Claudio caught himself acting like his father, impatient and exploding with his children. He begged forgiveness, walked out of the house and back in to begin again. And hari found himself paying more attention to the food on the dinner table than to his family, as had his father. All vow to do better, expressing hints of forgiveness as they consider their privileged positions relative to their fathers.

"Their collaborative writing incorporates elements of both interactive interviewing and coconstructed narrative. Note how the authors extend our work, and in the process expand the range and reach of evocative autoethnography."

Compassionate Research

"I'm curious now," says Kalisha. "How do you think your compassionate research with Jerry is related to interactive interviewing and coconstructed narrative?"

"The term 'compassionate research' signifies an orientation toward doing research more than a particular strategy. Emphasizing a relational ethics of care, this approach builds on these earlier interviewing and storytelling practices."

"How is this approach different from other collaborative autoethnographic approaches?" Kalisha asks.

"Let me admit first that I've added to the confusion about kinds of collaborative autoethnographic methods by using different terms at various times for the work I do with Jerry. I've referred to this research as 'compassionate research' (Ellis, forthcoming), 'compassionate interviewing and storytelling' (Ellis and Patti, 2014; Ellis, forthcoming), 'intimate interviewing' (Ellis, 2014b), 'relational autoethnography' (Ellis and Rawicki, 2013), 'heart-ful autoethnography' (Ellis, 1999), and 'collaborative witnessing' (Ellis and Rawicki, 2013, 2015).

"Let me simplify these terms for you. The most appropriate *umbrella term* for this genre of work is 'compassionate research.' 'Collaborative witnessing' describes *the kind of relationship* that is desired between researcher and participants; 'collaborative inter-viewing' refers to *the methodological process* by which stories are elicited, and 'collaborative storytelling' depicts *the product* result-ing from these practices.

"There are more similarities than differences in all the col-laborative autoethnographic research approaches. But note that compassionate research involves working with lay people rather than researchers and addresses multiple audiences—in this case, participants, their families, and similarly positioned collaborators, in addition to academics. While the researcher is present, his or her story is secondary to the story of participants..

"Though compassionate researchers also are committed to social justice, our focus is on making change one story, one life, at a time rather than on more macropolitical change (Ellis, 2002). While our goals include understanding, knowledge, and social jus-tice, we emphasize compassion for, and protecting the well-being of, our participants."

"Sounds like you've come full circle back to ethnography," says Tom.

"You could say that," says Carolyn, "but I think of it as extend-ing the stance of autoethnography to ethnography, and thus bring-ing to ethnography a caring autoethnographic sensibility about how to live and do research.

"I see refreshments have arrived. Perhaps we should take a short break before beginning the questions about analyzing stories."

Analyzing Stories[1]

"The students slowly make their way back to their seats after the break. Since the breaks take longer and longer and the conversations grow louder and more spirited, Carolyn and Art assume that the students are getting to know one another better and debating issues that come up in the workshop. The group discussions seem to have brought the participants closer together.

"Okay, we're ready for the next question," Carolyn says. "Groups 3 and 4 had enthusiastic discussions about how to do analysis in autoethnography, an issue that routinely comes up in these workshops. Anyone want to start us off with a specific question?"

Narrative Analysis and Narrative-Under-Analysis

The students begin talking to each other. Amid the conversations, a voice rings out. "Group 3 has a question." Carolyn recognizes the voice of Sophie, and turns in her direction. "Writing autoethnography with vivid and introspective descriptions of thoughts and feelings is starting to make more sense to me. But I'm still confused about the analysis part, and I was one of the people that raised this issue in my group. I've heard you and Art say that a good story is theoretical. What do you mean by that?"

"We mean that storytellers use analytic techniques to interpret their worlds and that stories themselves are analytic. Storytellers, as well as theorists, address the questions: 'what is going on here and what does it mean?'

"I think it might be good here to give you some background. Art, since you published a handbook chapter on the different kinds of narrative analysis, perhaps you'd like to answer this question (Bochner and Riggs, 2014)."

"Sure," says Art, standing and facing the class, while Carolyn takes the opportunity to sit for a moment. "Donald Polkinghorne (1995) differentiated two kinds of narrative inquiry: narrative analysis and analysis of narrative—or as I like to call it, 'narrative-under-analysis.' In narrative analysis, the research product is a story—a case, a biography, life history, autobiography, or autoethnography—that the researcher composes to represent the events, character, and issues that have been studied. Here we are concerned with what the story does, how it works, what relationships it shapes or animates, or how it pulls people together or breaks them apart. We take the standpoint of the storyteller who wants a listener to 'get into' the story, as I was saying yesterday (Bochner and Riggs, 2014, p. 204). We are concerned with communication: Do our stories evoke readers' responses? Do they open up the possibility of dialogue, collaboration, and relationship? Do they help us get along with each other? Change institutions? Promote social justice? Help us think through values and moral dilemmas? (Bochner, 2002; see also Rorty, 1991; Ellis, 2004, p. 195).

"In narratives-under-analysis (Bochner and Riggs, 2014), we treat stories as 'data,' and we analyze them to arrive at themes, types, or storylines that hold across stories. That's what grounded theory does, for example (Charmaz, 2000). Stories are analyzed from the perspective of the analyst and presented in the form of abstractions, as a traditional social science report does. Analysts are interested in what they can 'get out of,' or take away from, a story (Bochner and Riggs, 2014, p. 205; see also Greenspan, 2010; Kim, 2015).

"When we privilege the standpoint of the storyteller, we attend to different goals than when we privilege the standpoint of the analyst. In the former case, how a story makes sense is an ethical and relational question; storytelling is a means of being with others in order to understand and care for them. In the latter case, how a story makes sense is a 'scientific' question; analyzing a story or a collection of stories is a way to advance theory (Bochner and Riggs, 2014, p. 205). In narrative analysis, we see ourselves as storytellers connecting and communicating with readers; in narrative-under-analysis, we see ourselves as scientists representing reality in order to develop theory and reach generalizations."

Carolyn stands and enters the conversation. "Arthur Frank's distinction between thinking *with* a story and thinking *about* a story bears repeating here. This distinction might help illuminate the difference between narrative analysis—which assumes, as Art and I do, that a good story itself is theoretical—and narrative-under-analysis—which treats stories as information to be categorized. In *thinking with a story (narrative analysis)*, Frank says, you take the story as already complete instead of trying to go beyond it. Thinking with a story means to experience it as affecting your life and to find in that experience a truth about your life. In *thinking about a story (narrative-under-analysis)*, we reduce the story to content and then analyze it, hoping to find larger categories, themes, or patterns (Frank 1995, p. 23; Ellis, 2004, pp. 194–197; Bochner and Riggs, 2014).

"Does that answer your question, Sophie?" asks Carolyn. "I know it was a long-winded reply." Sophie nods.

"Oh and one more thing," Art adds. "Not everyone uses these terms the same way. Try not to let that confuse you (see Riessman, 1993)."

Blending Narrative Analysis and Narrative-Under-Analysis

"Group 3, what else came up in your discussion?" Carolyn asks.

Maria raises her hand. "We were curious about whether and how we can connect traditional analysis to an autoethnographic story. For example, what if I want to tell my story about living in a community populated by immigrants and ask readers to think 'with' the story; but I also want to say something about relationships that go beyond the specifics in my story and think 'about' the story? My dissertation committee is willing to let me tell the story of my mother who lives in this community if I analyze it traditionally. I'm not sure how to do that. Could you talk a bit more about that?"

"Sure, you can put the two forms together. I think we did that earlier with my example of our terrier killing the rabbit. We thought *with* the story, and then Art and I analyzed Buddha's behavior in terms of instinct, what it might mean to be 'bad' in the animal world, and how and why our reactions to and expectations of animals compare to our reactions to and expectations of humans.

"So yes you can analyze evocative autoethnographic pieces, but the story itself should always occupy a prominent position. In deciding the best way to do analysis in autoethnography, one consideration is whether you are interviewing other people in your study. In many autoethnographies, the author is the main character and there are no other designated participants. Here I do mean 'participant,' and not character. As we've discussed, other characters are always part of our personal stories since we live relationally, not in isolation. By participant, though, I mean people who have consented to be part of our study, whom we formally or informally interview and/or observe (Tullis, 2014; Andrew, 2015).

"If you wanted to include traditional narrative-under-analysis within your autoethnography, you would treat your stories as information to be interpreted. You might decide to analyze these stories as you would any qualitative 'data.' You would, as Art says, put your narrative 'under analysis' (Bochner and Riggs, 2014, p. 210). You would tease out the concepts and patterns within the text; work back and forth with available literature to compare similar insights or patterns in other stories or studies; bring in concepts from other studies that might be relevant; determine the main argument of your piece; frame your work accordingly in terms of this idea or problem; then show how your story and its analysis make a contribution to theory. For example, your work might show a relationship researchers haven't explored before, raise questions about the literature, fill a gap in what we know or have studied previously, extend our understanding of some process, or challenge what we have assumed to be true" (see Ellis, 2004; Bochner and Riggs, 2014)."

"How would you analyze the stories if you have interviewed or observed other participants?" asks Inkeri, clearly thinking of her own project interviewing people with spinal cord injuries.

"The process is not that different," says Carolyn, "except that you have more information from more sources with which to work. One possibility would be to interview others and ask yourself similar questions, treating yourself as one of the contributors (Crawley, 2012). You might weave your story, as a researcher with related experience, in and out of others' tales. Or you might observe others ethnographically and consider yourself as one of the main participants. You would observe your interaction with them, as well as your thoughts and feelings, as part of what you are investigating.

"Otherwise, your analysis might follow the conventions of social science in terms of looking at processes, patterns, and types. For example, Alice Goffman (2014) includes herself as a feeling, thinking, and acting participant in her study of a poor black neighborhood in Philadelphia, though the larger framing story focuses primarily on young black men's accounts of engaging in crime, going to prison, policing, and surveillance. This is what Tedlock (1991) was getting at with her idea of 'observation of participation.' Observing yourself observing is a reflexive move that can provide new insights about how you came to learn what you did."

Creative Analytic Practices

"Group 4, let's hear more from you," Carolyn says. "Silvia, you were the note taker. How about starting us off?"

"Okay, our group's members were curious as to how the idea of creative analytic practices (Richardson, 1999) fits with autoethnography. How do you go about designing analytic processes that are creative?"

"It is possible to honor the goals of traditional analysis, but to design the analysis in a more creative way that integrates social science and humanistic perspectives, invites conversation, and is useful for helping us know how to live. Laurel Richardson (1999) coined the term 'creative analytic practices' or CAP for ethnographies that seek to do that," Carolyn continues. "Many of our students use some form of CAP to analyze their stories. We want them to have the skills of analysis in their toolbox, but in many cases a traditional analysis of narrative does not fit their projects.

"How might CAP take place?" Carolyn asks rhetorically. "For one, you could gather all interviewees to participate in a conversation about what each other's stories mean. After all, who decreed that only the researcher should have interpretive authority? Let the participants generate important ideas, concepts, processes, and patterns too. If you followed this scheme, you would write the analysis as conversation, drama, or in any form you wanted, and yet this section would still meet the goals of traditional analysis in the ways we have discussed.

"For example, in her ethnography of a children's mental health care treatment team, Christine Davis (2013) checked in with her study participants throughout the course of her fieldwork. They had dyadic and group conversations in which she and the participants jointly constructed their interpretations of the findings of the study. Cris wrote her dissertation as a novel and included these conversations as natural dialogue and turning points in the plot."

"You make it sound so easy," says Shing-Ling. "Could you give us more examples?"

Carolyn chuckles. "It's anything but easy. I'd say that analysis is the part that autoethnography students struggle with the most. That's not surprising. You find autoethnography because of your interest in storytelling and lived experience. Then we ask you to abstract and theorize. I want to remind you, though, that a theoretical frame should be thought of as just another story, though usually a less concrete one. To theorize, think about how your experience might relate to others' experiences. What are the interesting properties they might have in common? Work inductively, keeping the analysis close to the experience."

"Examples?" Silvia reminds.

"Oh yes. Let's see. I have several in mind," Carolyn says, opening her computer and scrolling through files.

1. Bereaved Parents: CAP with Autoethnography, Interviews, and Narrative

"This first one shows research in which the respondents are invited to participate in the follow-up and analysis. For his dissertation, Greg Roberts (2015) interviewed eight people who had lost a child, and he included his own story. He was interested in the creative activities in which parents took part in order to cope with their grief. First, he gave respondents an opportunity to write an introduction about the things they had done after their child died. Then he interviewed each person. He listened to the recorded stories several times and then transcribed them, giving the transcripts to the interviewees to read and check. He turned each person's words into a lyrical story, which participants read and commented on.

After several years passed, he gave them an opportunity to provide comments and reflections from their current perspective about the significance of the activities they had talked about at the beginning of the study. These reflections served as the conclusion or analysis for each story. Roberts then wrote a creative synthesis in the form of a found poem about each person's experience in an attempt to find the essence of the experience.

"Here is an excerpt from one reflective story, written by a participant whose daughter had drowned in the bathtub:

> The story/scrap book I created about Ariel's life was certainly something to immerse myself in during the months follow- ing her death. The way I understand it now as I approach eight years since she died and five years since the interview is that I wanted to be immersed in her. I didn't want to forget the little things about her...Ariel died in such tragic circumstanc- es which I felt so ashamed about and speaking of it brought unbearable humiliation as I hadn't at that point begun to dif- ferentiate between Ariel and who she was/the tragic way she died/the part I played in her death...It was easier to just pass the book around and receive some little bit of healing from the tears of others paging through it....
>
> [About the poems I wrote] I was in such a state of disbelief that it was hard to believe that it was actually my life that I was reading about. Now that I've spent the last couple of years actu- ally processing the trauma, I actually find them very edgy to read....It makes complete sense to me now, how some family and friends criticized me for sending it around to them as it would be pretty horrible to read through! (Roberts, 2015, pp. 135–137)

"Wow, that project has so many levels and such depth," says Betty. "I'm getting fresh ideas for how to use poetry and incorporate respondents' comments in analysis."

"Good, Betty. I'm glad the description was helpful," says Carolyn.

2. White Working-Class Experience: CAP with Autoethnography, Interviews, and Critical Analysis

"Here's another example that also has many levels; this one is auto-ethnographic but also critical analysis," says Carolyn. "The writer, Tasha Rennels (2015), did her dissertation on the relationship between mediated representations and lived experiences of white working-class people. After introducing her early life of living in a trailer park, Tasha told the stories of three white working-class families she interviewed. During the telling of these stories, she reflected on her experience of growing up as a white working-class person who was bothered by the mediated portrayals of this group. She also examined her ambivalent and contradictory roles of identifying with the white working class while at the same time acting as an academic researcher. At the end of the dissertation, she returned to her own experience, reflecting on how the insights she gained from participants had enabled her to think differently about her working-class background and relationship to media.

"Tasha included her own personal stories. She also used a critical cultural lens to analyze interviewees' responses to media depictions of white working-class life, incorporating theories, such as Stuart Hall's (1973) analysis of the positions from which audience members decode media messages. Finally, she interpreted her data through a social science lens, examining patterns in working-class families, such as lack of socioeconomic mobility.

"Let me read you a couple of segments that illustrate how Tasha put all these elements together in a very creative dissertation."

Carolyn scrolls through her files and then says, "Oh good, here it is." She clicks through a few pages.

"This first example shows Tasha reflecting on her experiences growing up to help her decide how to depict the people she interviewed:

> I see a young white man with a pierced ear, dark clothing, and a brown mullet haircut standing on the side of the road smoking a cigarette. I do a double take. He is a carbon copy of my ex-stepdad to whom my mother was married for ten years, the

'epitome of white trash' my peers used to say. My chest tightens as I recall their ridicule…I contemplate whether or not to share details about his appearance for fear of perpetuating the 'white trash' stereotype. (Rennels, 2015, p. 72)

"This second example shows Tasha reflecting on her life, and working-class life in general, after analyzing her interviewees' stories:

Witnessing happiness in Ben's and Ellen's life was a pleasant surprise. I didn't expect them to be so positive about their situation because of how dire it seemed compared to mine growing up. My family may have struggled to make ends meet but we rarely relied on governmental assistance, and access to proper and affordable healthcare was never a concern…. I was more advantaged in many ways, yet I still complain. However, reflecting on the happiness expressed by Ben, Ellen, and many of my other participants encourages me to reflect, rethink, and reframe my working-class past; maybe it wasn't so bad after all…(p. 76)

"In the third example, Tasha raises methodological questions as she ponders the difficulties of conducting research as an insider/ outsider:

As a member of both the academy and working-class, I often find myself moving between two different worlds, which was difficult throughout my fieldwork. Instead of being able to comfortably immerse myself into the working-class communities and families I studied, I felt pressured to make choices about how I looked, acted, and spoke. I dressed 'down' in jeans and a t-shirt, behaved modestly, and refrained from sounding verbose. I wanted to blend in, but I also didn't want to seem fake. I worried that my participants would see right through me and think I was disingenuous. My insider-outsider position made me hypersensitive to their voices, experiences, and opinions. Perhaps I brought this pressure upon myself, but I wanted them to know that I cared. I wanted to be included, to have them see me as a member of their working class. (p. 93)

"Thanks for the examples," says Silvia. "I hope we aren't expected to include all those modes in our work."

"That's unlikely," says Carolyn, smiling. "The important thing is to recognize all the choices open to you."

"Could you give us an example of analysis in an autoethnographic piece that focuses on the author's life without other interviews? That's what I'm most interested in. How would you handle that?" Betty asks.

3. Long-Term Grief: CAP Focused on the Researcher's Life

"Let's see," Carolyn responds. "Here's a chapter I wrote on long-term grief in which I focused on how I felt 30 years after losing my brother in an airplane crash (Ellis, 2014a). In it, I told stories about re-membering my brother through photos. I included stories I had written in the past, told in the classroom, and shared with family. These stories explored long-term grief, which is rarely discussed in the literature other than to warn that grieving too long can be pathological (Stroebe et al., 2000). I also wanted to put a face on the concept of 'continuous bonds,' 're-membering' those you have lost and maintaining them as part of your community, instead of trying to forget and move on (see Hedtke and Winslade, 2004).

"Wanting to re-member my brother in as many ways as I could, I looked online for information on his plane crash, which I had not done before. I found videos and first-hand, detailed, emotional, and vivid descriptions of the accident. I listened to audios of the pilots' last words, synchronized with an illustration of the crash and stories of pilot error." Carolyn pauses, struggling to hold back tears. Art rises from his chair, moves toward her, and lightly touches her arm. "Suddenly I was reading about and watching the survivors of his plane being rescued. I thought I could hear their screams."

Carolyn wipes away a tear. "I'm okay," she says to Art. Then, "And I knew at that moment that this kind of re-membering was not positive, that there were things about this loss that I shouldn't bring to mind (see also Gannon, 2013, p. 242). You'll recall that this experience was what stimulated my offer to Jerry to omit the details of murder in the Treblinka story.

"Writing this story taught me something about my own grief. Also, I wanted readers to think in a deeper and more nuanced way about positive and negative ways to maintain connections to family members who have died and about how the experience of grief changes over survivors' lives (see also Paxton, 2015)."

The room quiets. Carolyn shakes her head and breathes deeply. "Sorry to end this part of our session with such a sad story," she says. "Really, writing that piece about long-term grief was good for me. It was a way of doing something, of continuing to create something to symbolically memorialize my brother that would be solid, concrete, and sustainable. As Roberts (2015) suggests, engaging in a project like this is healing."

When the students don't say anything, Carolyn asks, "How about a bathroom break?" She understands how difficult it can be to respond to grief in a public setting. The students nod and quietly leave the room.

Art asks Carolyn to take a quick walk with him outside. She agrees, thinking the fresh air will be good for her. "It's amazing how emotional that story always makes you feel," he says, grabbing her hand.

"Yes, even 35 years later," Carolyn responds. "Some losses you never get over, nor should you. They become a meaningful part of you that you don't ever want to lose."

Telling Stories

After participants return, Carolyn says, "Okay, let's all stretch and stimulate our brains a few minutes. Everybody stand and reach for the ceiling. Breathe deeply. That feels better, doesn't it?

"We're ready now for the next set of questions on telling stories. What I'm looking for here are questions or comments about the forms our stories can take. 'Telling stories' has a double meaning: our stories should have force and produce a strong effect, and we as authors should be aware of how we are telling them and how form affects content.

"Group 5, your turn."

"We talked about the different forms autoethnographic stories can take," Jennifer says. "We got stuck on literary stories, such as 'Maternal Connections,' and several of us wondered about the process you went through to write that story. But we also are interested in other arts-based forms, such as poetry and performance. In what sense do you consider them ethnographic?"

Episodic Short Stories

"'Maternal Connections' is one of several short stories I have written that purposely evade the trappings of conventional social science," Carolyn begins. "As you saw, I do not cite other works in these stories; nor do I include literature reviews, methods sections, or theoretical frames. Instead, I compose a concrete, episodic narrative that is uninterrupted by academic jargon and abstractions. I use some of the literary devices that Art talked about to write evocatively and to draw readers emotionally into my experience. But I still want the story to generate conceptual ideas about caregiving, and I think our discussion of 'Maternal Connections' revealed that. Many of you responded by sharing stories from our own life about caregiving and maternal connections, and ideas and concerns about your child-parent caregiving, gender and caregiving, and parenting in general. This was how I hoped you, as readers, would respond.

"On the one hand, autoethnographic stories must be artful; while on the other, they must be pointed toward the workings of history, social structure, and culture. Though I don't explicitly mention larger cultural forces in 'Maternal Connections,' the language, dialogue, character development, and action in the story work to open up conversations about social structure and culture. By reflexively discussing episodic stories in classes, workshops, and other public venues, readers and writers of episodic narratives can gain a greater awareness of the complexities, contradictions, and choices people face in such situations, enhancing the possibility of coping better with them. The goal of the story is to resonate with the lived experiences of readers, inviting them to use the depiction of one person's experience to explore and understand their own."

Barbara joins the conversation. "I love this kind of writing, and I feel moved to try it. But my group wondered about writing without citations or a literature review. Is this an acceptable way to write autoethnography? Will we get published?"

"Stories that stand alone, such as 'Maternal Connections,' are not nearly as common as autoethnographies that are more integrated with ethnographic accounts or analysis," Carolyn responds. "Writing this way can limit your options for publication since this form breaks from many of the standard conventions of writing in social science journals. Without the signifiers of scholarship and 'science'—citations, methods, jargon, and theory—journal reviewers may not consider these stories sufficiently academic or scholarly; they may view them as creative nonfiction or memoir. For similar reasons, poetry, performance texts, scripts, photographic essays, music, video, and fiction are not universally appreciated or considered legitimately 'academic.' But certainly opportunities to publish work in blended and alternative forms are expanding (Singer and Walker, 2013). Art and I illustrated some of these possibilities in *Composing Ethnography* (Ellis and Bochner, 1996a) and in monographs published in our two book series, *Ethnographic Alternatives* and *Writing Lives*. These and other arts-based practices are increasingly accepted as genres of ethnography (see Leavy, 2015)."

From Group 5, Barry waves his hand. "How do you decide when and what to write about your life? I'm afraid people won't be interested in what happened to me."

"Good question. I am moved to write autoethnographic stories when I experience an epiphany, an event in which I am so powerfully absorbed that I'm left without an interpretive framework to make sense of my experience (Denzin, 2014). For example, I wrote about the death of my brother (Ellis, 1993) and the illness and aging of my mother (Ellis, 1996a). Sometimes the event I am moved to write about is less dramatic than an epiphany. For example, I published a story about receiving the news from a physician that I had arthritis in my hip, and how it affected my sense of self and my relationships (Ellis, 2014b). I felt a strong need to make sense of what was happening, and I thought people in similar situations would identify with what I had gone through.

"Often the topics I focus on are about an event occurring now, such as my arthritic hip, or about ongoing emotional issues I might experience, such as living with a lisp (Ellis, 1998b). Other times, the phenomenon of interest is an incident from my past that is unresolved or that I now look back at with new eyes, such as race relations in the small town where I was raised (Ellis, 1995c). In each case, I felt convinced that what was happening extended beyond me and could yield insights about culture, social structure, relationality, and communication.

"In all these cases, I used a more traditional social science form. I made the story central, but I also included a literature review and analysis."

Poetry

"Do you consider poetry a form of autoethnography?" asks Barry.

"I do," Carolyn replies. "Let's look at two examples. In the first, Deborah Austin wrote a narrative poem entitled 'Kaleidoscope,' describing an interview she had over dinner with a woman from Africa (1996, pp. 206–230). Her poem captured the sensuality of sharing food and talk. As they investigated their cultural experiences together and sought to understand one another as two women of color, one African and the other southern African-American, the bodily nature of qualitative exploration became apparent. Feeling that her own experience and history, her eyes and body, were integral to their interaction, Deborah expressed the 'tension, lyricism, and circularity' of their interaction through lyrical poetry (p. 207).

"Listen as I read an excerpt from Deborah's poem (Austin, 1996, pp. 207–209):

> *Africans are the same*
> *wherever we are, she says to me*
> *   matter-of-factly*
> *I look at her and smile*
> *And ask*

like a good researcher should
How so?
I can't explain, she says
    With that voice that sounds
    Like the rush of many rivers
It is the way we all are
    The way we move
    The way we think
I look at her again
    And see her smile
    With full lips closed over pearly white teeth
We do look alike
    High cheekbones under taut brown skin
    Cheekbones that my family
        claimed
        were a sign that we had Indian blood
        in the days when nobody
            wanted to be African
But I am the daughter of slaves
    as some Africans
        So quickly remind us
Still, she says
    as she looks at the pictures
    of me
        pasted all over my kitchen refrigerator
    while I cook barbecued chicken, collard, greens
        macaroni and cheese
    butternut squash, homemade biscuits, and ice tea
    the kind of dinner
    my grandmother would make
        I hope she does not consider me vain
        And I tell her that
        the pictures
            story part of my life…
You look like
A true African woman

I wish I looked like that, she exclaims
I am surprised and honored
　How can an African woman
　Say that I look more African
　than she?

Carolyn pauses. "So what do you think? Is this ethnographic research? That really is the question you're asking, right? Can a poem be ethnography?"

"I could visualize both women from the words," says Kalisha. "I could smell what's cooking. That's the kind of food we had when I was growing up in the South. I felt I was in the kitchen making dinner and eating with them."

"I also identified with the African woman who wanted to look more African, more like Deborah, since sometimes I wish I looked more distinctly African too," says Jennifer. "Often people I meet think I'm from the U.S.—that is, until they hear me speak. I thought Deborah and her friend seemed more similar than different."

"That may be because I didn't read the section that points to cultural differences," Carolyn says. "Later, the African woman talks about polygamy in her culture, the patrilineal authority in the family, and she asserts several times that Africans have the ability to 'just know' things. Although she begins with the statement that 'Africans are the same wherever we are,' the poem shows that she and Deborah are similar *and* different. Thus, we grasp ethnography as both about the universal and the particular.

"Watch the screen now, as Deborah performs her poem," Carolyn says and nods to Art. Art inserts the DVD and pushes 'play.'

Afterwards, Jennifer says, "Deborah appears just like I imagined her, and she does look African. Her voice also sounds as I anticipated. The writing is so vivid, but I have to say that seeing her and actually hearing her say the words made the poem even more evocative."

"Yes," Carolyn agrees, staring at Deborah on what is now a frozen screen. "Many social scientists, such as Laurel Richardson (1994b) and Sandra Faulkner (2014), write lyric poetry. Laurel's 'Nine Poems' (1994b) about marriage and family is a classic, and the way she groups the poems provides a metanarrative about relational life. I want to read a short one, so you can see how her poem provides plot and the pauses invite readers' interpretive responses (see also Faulkner, 2014; Janesick, 2015; White, forthcoming). This is called 'Being Single' (Richardson, 1994b, p. 5).

> **Being Single**
>
> *drying a wishbone*
> *by the kitchen window*
> *'til the bone is chipped*
>
> *to bits by trinkets*
> *placed beside it,*
> *or it rots, because*
>
> *there is no one*
> *to take one end*
> *you the other*
>
> *pulling, wishing*
> *each against each*
> *until the bone*
>
> *breaks.*

Carolyn summarizes. "In 'Being Single,' the sound and rhythms, along with a concrete image—a wishbone rotting—evoke the emotions and turning points associated with not having a life partner (Richardson, 1994b; see also Denzin, 1997, p. 211). No doubt we could talk for hours about what this poem signifies for each of us, personally and sociologically."

Performance

"These examples connect to my group's interest in performance," says Eric. "Especially for Karen and me, since we're both performers and artists. I know we're running out of time, but could you speak to performance as autoethnography and ethnography?"

"Sure. But I'll only be able to deal briefly with it in this session. For those of you interested in performance, I recommend reading Alexander's (2005) chapter and Denzin's (2003) book on performance ethnography. They both are on the table. Also keep in mind that we're leaving out art, photography, dance, film, video, and music, among others (see Spry, 2001, 2011; Scott-Hoy and Ellis, 2008; Bartleet and Ellis, 2009; Carless and Douglas, 2009; Bartleet, 2013; Stévance and Lacasse, 2013; Leavy, 2015; McRae, 2015; Harris, in press).

"This example is from Ron Pelias (2004, 2011, forthcoming), a communication scholar who has published autoethnographic poems and performance texts. He also has written texts on writing performatively (Pelias, 1999). Here is an excerpt from a script portraying his relationship with his son, who has fallen out of the middle class. Without casting blame, Ron composes scenes that show their failure to communicate; not hearing each other, they talk past one another. His opening passage metaphorically sets the stage for the problems in communication he describes in the scenes that follow:

> The curtain opens. Two phones sit on a table. A man looks at the phones. A phone rings. He picks up the receiver of the one not ringing. 'Hello. Hello?' he calls out. He hangs up and cries out, 'There must be more phones.' He leaves the stage only to return with another phone. The pattern repeats itself until the stage is filled with phones. He never selects the phone that rings. His final words are, 'Hello.' 'I said, 'hello.' Can't you hear me? Is anyone there? Hello? Hello? Curtain. (Pelias, 2002, p. 36)

"I don't have a film of this piece, but I think that hearing this setup helps you visualize what he describes. Ron uses phones as a metaphor to move readers deeply into the conflict between father and son. This story always generates a lively class discussion about father-son relationships and the responsibilities and rights these relationships entail. At first students want to figure out which one is the 'good guy' and 'bad guy' in the interaction. But as the conversation progresses and the students are privy to each other's multiple interpretations and reactions, they begin to realize that the father-son relationship is more complicated than they initially thought.

Ron's story provides a good exercise in 'taking the role of the other' as students move from considering what it would be like to be the son to this father to what it would be like to be the father to this son, and back again. The discussion inspires a deep examination of relationships, encouraging a complex and sympathetic reading of autoethnography as students recognize the vulnerability it took for Ron to open himself up to critique. They begin to question their impulse to judge him for his confessions about not being the perfect father and they become sympathetic to the life situation of the son."

"That's really cool," says Barbara. "I want to write like Ron and Deborah."

"You should give it a try," Carolyn says. "I do have some concerns though since you said you were in a traditional psychology program. Mainstream psychologists might not be receptive to these forms, though the social psychologists Mary Gergen and Ken Gergen (2012) have been at the forefront in advocating the enrichment and broadening of social science through performance and performance texts. But until you have some success in publishing, or at least don't have to answer to a traditional dissertation committee, you might consider trying something closer to realist ethnography than a literary short story, a poem, or performance. Actually, I'd give that advice to all of you working in traditional social science departments."

When several of the students frown, Carolyn says, "Don't worry. You can have fun with more conventional forms as well. You'll see."

Closed, Open, and Breadless Sandwiches

"Our group focused on autoethnographies with traditional analysis," says Regina from Group 5. "We all had different ideas about how to insert analysis so that it adds to, rather than detracts from, the story. Do you frame the story with theory and analysis? Or does the analysis go at the end, as in most grounded theory qualitative pieces that focus on generating concepts and theory from data? Can analysis appear throughout the middle of the text?"

"That's a mouthful," Carolyn jokes. "First, consider how you want to engage the audience. Do you want to set up an analytic puzzle or pull readers immediately into the emotions of the story? I usually try to immediately engage readers upfront, but whether I do or not partly depends on the audience I'm trying to attract. Editors and readers of traditional qualitative work will expect framing of the main issue at the beginning and an analysis at the end; those involved with more creative outlets will want to be engaged quickly by a story and may not care about traditional analysis. Decide what best fits your project. You have to figure out the voice and form that best suits the information you're trying to convey or the feeling you're trying to evoke.

"I tend to think about making a sandwich when I think about where to place analysis," Carolyn continues. Appreciating the comic relief, the students chuckle with her.

"What do you mean? Full of bologna?" someone shouts.

Carolyn laughs some more. "Hopefully not. Let me show you what I mean by giving you some examples.

"First, you might want to construct a *closed sandwich*, with the traditional framing at the beginning and the theoretical conclusions at the end, encapsulating the narrative meat—or tofu, if you're a vegetarian—in the middle. That's the form I used in *Final Negotiations*. Instead of analyzing the content of the story, I used a methodological and epistemological frame at the start that described the narrative and autoethnographic approach in the book, and then I returned to this theme in the concluding chapters. I made a case for opening up conversation about the story rather than proclaiming what the story meant.

"A second alternative is to prepare the *open faced sandwich*, which would include both a traditional analysis and a creative narrative, one framing and the other concluding the main story. In 'Speaking of Dying' (Ellis, 1995d), I wrote a story about a difficult encounter with an old friend who was dying of AIDS. Though the narrative contained no citations or literature review, it ended with a theoretical paragraph that described our inability to enter each other's consciousness as a result of intersubjective failure. This failure came from the difficulties of communicating across the boundaries of the living and dying, between those residing in the temporarily well and the terminally ill communities." Carolyn picks up her notes and reads: "'When you're inside IT [meaning dying], it's hard to imagine there's a world outside IT. When you're outside IT, you can't fathom life on the inside, even when you've been there before and know you'll be there again' (p. 81).

"Third, and highly recommended for dieters, is a *breadless sandwich*, with narrative at the beginning and ending and analysis in the middle," Carolyn says. "I used that layout in the article I wrote about my experiences during the terrorist attacks of September 11 (Ellis, 2002). The stories focus on what happened, but in the middle of them I included a discussion of framing and sense-making. I explored the frames I called on to understand my experience of danger and loss during these events: my location on a plane during the attacks, my personal experience of loss, both current (my mother's and mother-in-law's deteriorating health) and past (my brother's death in a commercial airplane crash). The ending described a return visit to Ground Zero, after which I traveled by plane again to visit my dying mother. These last two scenes provided a space for me to examine through story what it means to 'remember absence.' I gave story the privileged beginning and ending slots. Who says that analysis should always get the last word?"

"You're assuming the bread is more important than the meat and veggies inside," someone shouts.

"You have a point," Carolyn jokes back. She pauses, waiting for the next topic.

Seamless Writing

"Our group had read some of Art's stories," says Eric, "and we were impressed by how he wove theory and story together."

"I call that *seamless writing*. It represents more of a stew or potpie than a sandwich. This form mushes all the parts—the bread, meat, and veggies—together," Carolyn jokes. "I don't write much in this style, but you're right—Art is a master of weaving theory and story together in the same paragraph and moving the reader effortlessly thorough a story that is both theoretical and evocative (for other examples, see Gingrich-Philbrook, 2005; Spry, 2011; Tamas, 2013;

Durham, 2014). One of my favorite examples is Art's story about the death of his father where he inserts a theoretical discussion of how university professors split the academic from the personal self. These disconnections then lead to isolation and institutional depression and inhibit risk taking and change within universities and academic disciplines (Bochner, 1997). Another favorite is the seamless prose in Art's book about coming to narrative (Bochner, 2014). There he interweaves theories and stories of his professional and personal life with the social and historical contexts of the times, and presents the information in engaging and multiple forms.

"Art, would you read us the example from your book that we selected last night?"

"Be happy to." Art stands and opens his book to the page he has marked.

Carolyn sets the scene, "Art is returning home early from an academic conference to attend his father's funeral. Note how Art places you on the plane with him as he reflects on the gulf between his academic and personal life. He takes you into his consciousness, seamlessly weaving his thoughts and feelings with Ernest Becker's (1973) observations about the denial of death."

Art reads:

As I looked out the window of the plane and saw how small the roads, farms, cars, and houses looked from above, I was reminded of Ernest Becker's (1973) remarks about the puniness of life in the face of the overwhelming majesty of our universe. I felt confusion swelling within me as competing parts of my self struggled for supremacy. A voice inside me questioned the motivation for my drive and dedication as a social scientist. 'Admit it, Art, your work sucks energy away so you don't have to face the reality of the human condition.' I had no ready response, but I was inspired to scribble some notes on the pad on my lap:

Academic life is impersonal, not intimate. It provides a web of distractions. The web protects us against the invasion of helplessness, anxiety, and isolation we would feel if we faced the human condition honestly. Stability, order, control—these are the words that social science speaks. Ambiguity, chance, accidents—these are the terms that life echoes. Suppose we achieved the stability, order, and control we seek— what then? No variance—no differences—no chance—no fun—no adventure—no vulnerability—no deniability—no flirtation—no love.

The notes didn't help. They only exaggerated the divisions tugging within me. I felt an obligation to answer back to the first voice, but the only thing I could think of was to reaffirm my commitment to the Deweyan premise that no matter how honest we are about the tragedy of the human condition, we still have to point ourselves toward some hopeful, creative activity. What was it Ernest Becker (1973) said in the final lines of *The Denial of Death*? 'Fashion something—an object or ourselves—and drop it into the confusion' (p. 285). But these words begged the question of how to narrow this large gulf between my academic life and my personal life. In the aftermath of my father's death, it now seemed obvious to me that life had a different shape and texture than the ways it was sculpted in the classroom and in scholarly journals. (Bochner, 2014, p. 280)

"Thanks, Art," Carolyn says, and then to participants, "We'll get to experience more of Art's writing tomorrow when we discuss 'Bird on the Wire.'"

Layered Accounts

"Okay, we've left out the *double decker sandwich*," Carolyn continues. "Anyone know what I mean by that?"

"I assume it means to have many different layers," says Barry. "We talked about the *layered account* in our group."

"Exactly," Carolyn responds. "Many young scholars are attracted to this form, which is essentially a multi-layered sandwich with lots of meat and vegetables and more than two slices of bread. This is one of the more popular ways to blend traditional and creative forms, with analysis and story coexisting side by side.

"Carol Rambo coined the term 'layered accounts,' by which she means combining different ways of knowing, such as statistics, theory, ethnography, personal stories—not necessarily in chronological order, and reflections on the vignettes she tells ([Rambo] Ronai, 1995). In a story about her mentally retarded mother, Carol juxtaposed literature and statistics of mental retardation, with episodes of interaction with her mother at various times in her life. She included emotions and attitudes toward her mother and doing this research. Here is a passage demonstrating how she layered these ways of knowing in 'Multiple Reflections of Child Sex Abuse' ([Rambo] Ronai, 1996, pp. 118–119):

> According to researchers, I don't have a good reason to bring my own genetic status into question: '90% of the known causes of retardation have nothing to do with heredity...' (Kantrowitz, King, and Witherspoon, 1986, p. 62)...[but] it was the parents of other children who brought my status into question....When [my friend] Lisa's mother finally met my mother, I was not allowed to play at Lisa's house again. Debbi's mother, on the other hand, let me play with Debbi, but only when Debbi's father was away. On the one occasion he came home early, I was asked to sneak out the back door.

"Would you describe how you make the pieces fit together in a layered account?" asks Barbara. "That's what my group was not so sure about. I tried to write like that once, but my prose ended up being a jumbled mess of different kinds of things on the same page."

Minor Bodily Stigma: An Example of a Layered Account

"Let me think," Carolyn responds. "In my article on minor bodily stigma, I combined stories from different periods, literature on stigma, and observations of others. Similar to Rambo, I moved back and forth between story and these other modes, and I separated each change with asterisks.

"In that story, I met a clerk in a store who had a lisp, which made me think about my own lisp—how I experience it, and how I perceive others hearing it. At the same time, I noticed a woman ography*

who had a scar on her face, and this made me think about the minor 'blemishes' we all have, how we think about them, and how others react to them.

"My observations led me to develop the category of 'minor bodily stigma,' which include imperfections we can see, such as buck teeth and scars, or missing or damaged body parts, such as chipped teeth, and impeded bodily movement, such as limping; those we can hear, such as lisping; those we can smell, such as body odor; or those we can identify by the presence of an aid, such as a hearing aid. Though rarely do these features stand in the way of performing everyday life, they are involuntary and perceived by self and/ or others as undesirable. They are difficult to hide, leading many people to develop concealing tactics. They also generate ambiguity about whether and how this blemish is perceived by others and how a blemish is experienced and coped with by the holder. Interactants are in a double bind about how to respond: Should it be mentioned by the holder or other interactants? If so or if not, what does that mean? You end up in a double bind about how to think about your stigmas. You feel shame for having the stigma and metashame for feeling ashamed about your shame for a seemingly trivial blemish."

Regina's hand goes up. "So even though you are writing a personal story about having a lisp, you also are an ethnographer looking around to see how stigmas might occur for others."

"And you also are an analyst looking for patterns and common properties that reach beyond the particular story," says Jennifer.

"Good observations. In this article, I argued that categories and personal stories work together." Carolyn reads: "'The categorical story offered a name to my experiences where before there was only dread; the personal story connected real people with feelings to the labels, where before there were only tactics of concealment and denial' (Ellis, 1998b, p. 535)."

"Could you speak to the differences between your piece and the layered accounts of Carol Rambo?" asks Karen.

"There are more similarities than differences," Carolyn replies. "For both of us, the more traditional theorizing segments are related to, though distinct from, the story segments. Carol and I both

208

shift between more conventional forms of social science reporting and narratives that communicate emotionality. But I stay in each mode for a lengthy time, desiring to hold the reader in my emotional experience or in my theoretical story. For both of us, though, the separated sections in our texts end up merging in surprising ways, and stories continue to be prioritized over traditional analysis, which is true in most layered autoethnographic accounts."

"I really appreciate that we don't have to follow chronology in layered accounts," says Karen. "These texts show the messiness, ambiguity, and contradictions of lived experiences."

"That's true," Carolyn agrees. "Nonetheless, I sometimes caution students that writing layered accounts does not mean that they can write anything in any order. I find that as a reader I often long for a logic, progression, and integration in storytelling, even in layered accounts. I feel that way though I understand that life as lived is more fragmented than can be depicted in this arrangement."

Montage and Bricolage

"Of course, not all autoethnographers think as I do or make their stories unfold in the ways Art and I write," begins Carolyn. "For example, Stacy Holman Jones is a bricoleur who begins with story fragments, conversation clips, or lines of stories that come up over and over for her. She purposefully delays her plot and conclusion, preferring to generate multiple storylines connected to ideas from what she is reading, objects that recur from different sources, transposed texts, and a montage of images that arise (Adams, Holman Jones, and Ellis, 2015, pp. 71–76; see also Holman Jones, 2011). The result is a layered account of stories that take the form of aesthetic, poetic, and fragmented texts contextualized and integrated with complex theoretical and citational interpretation.

"Another writer, Jane Speedy (2015), has written a beautiful text filled with poems, visual images, and fragments of experience that serve to bring readers into the chaos, confusion, and repetition of her stroke and its afterlife. Her book is an aesthetic performance and montage of her fragmented and disjointed experience as she stares at the park near her home. Through this amplified experience, she realizes that 'the linear narrative [she] had been living' and the sense of the 'perfection of able bodies' were just conceits (p. 13). Her text resists narrative coherence as she tries to bring her experience to life as she lived it (p. 14). And bring that experience to life she does! Sometimes artistic fragmented texts are needed to convey disconnected and messy experience."

"A Dagwood sandwich," someone says quietly.

"What?" Carolyn asks, then, "Oh, never mind! I think we need a bathroom break. We're getting punchy, and your bladders and your minds must be ready to explode from all the information I've been pouring into them. Mine too."

Analytic Autoethnography

When the students return, Carolyn stands with her hands folded. She doesn't say anything, waiting to see what the attendees will bring up next. After a few moments, Tom breaks the silence. "Aren't there any more topics to cover about forms for telling stories?"

"You've mentioned all I had planned to cover," says Carolyn. "What else is on your minds?"

After a pause, Shing-Ling says, "I'm curious how these forms connect to grounded theory and Anderson's (2006) version of analytic autoethnography, which was brought up in an earlier session."

"Glad to give you my take on that topic," Carolyn responds. "I'd categorize Anderson as a realist ethnographer who employs traditional analysis to arrive at themes that illuminate the content and hold within or across stories. Though he also is an autoethnographer who includes his own stories among others, he primarily seeks a storyline that contributes to a theoretical understanding of broader social phenomena (Anderson, 2006). Art and I agree that analytic autoethnography neglects how stories can function as theory. In an analytic approach, stories are used either to illustrate a proposition or to reach a theoretical explanation akin to the 'discussion' section of traditional research reports. Analytic autoethnographers tend to treat stories as data useful for abstracting and generalizing.

"Analytic autoethnography is different from Art's seamless autoethnography, Stacy's aesthetic approach, and Carol's layered account. These three perspectives value and include theoretical understanding, but these authors view theory as a kind of story and story as a mode of theorizing and analyzing. Theory and story are interwoven, put into conversation, and work together, side by side. These writers seek to evoke with theory as well as story. They do not claim to be abstracting or generalizing, though they do seek resonance, which Art will discuss tomorrow. Offering impressionistic sketches of layers of experience, they make room for readers to enter the text. Stories, for them, provide a means of opening conversation about how to live, as 'equipment for living' (Burke, 1974; Myerhoff, 2007), and a way of putting theory into action (Adams, Holman Jones, and Ellis, 2015, p. 90).

"To be fair, though, Anderson's recent work blurs the boundaries between evocative and analytic autoethnography. He claims to be blending emotional autoethnography with the theoretical goals of analytic ethnography, though he remains 'committed to an analytic model of autoethnographic writing' (Anderson and Glass-Coffin, 2013, p. 64). When I look at his analytic autoethnography on skydiving (Anderson, 2011), I see a form akin to a layered account.

"Anderson now makes the case for similarity in goals among autoethnographers, in terms of visibility of self, strong reflexivity, engagement, vulnerability, and open-endedness. The primary difference is where each autoethnography is located on the evocative/analytic spectrum. Though he is still wed to thinking about the value of story in terms of its role in the development of sociological analysis of larger trends (2011, p. 136), Anderson now says that he is seeking self-clarification—to understand things about himself better by integrating personal stories with analysis.

"I applaud his openness, but I doubt analytic autoethnographers will ever acknowledge the ways that a story alone can do the work of theory—that there is always a moral to a story. Nonetheless, I am delighted to see ethnographers incorporating aspects of personal experience, emotionality, and vulnerability in their writing."

"Silly, when you think of it," Art interjects. "Nobody ever asked Charles Dickens to say what his stories mean." Participants giggle. Carolyn calls on Inkeri, whose hand is waving.

"As long as I name what I do 'analytic autoethnography,' my committee members have no trouble with my including a story of my life, though they cringe sometimes at what I am willing to tell," Inkeri says.

"Go for it then," Carolyn advises. "If calling your study 'analytic autoethnography' and using your lived experiences to formulate abstractions and generalizations allows you to sneak the precepts of evocative autoethnography into your more traditional work, well so much the better. You have to start somewhere."

Evaluating Autoethnography

"There's one more issue that came up in our group," says Erica. "How do you go about evaluating autoethnography, especially since there are so many ways to do it?"

"That came up in our group too."

"And in ours," voices echo.

"Yes, this issue is raised in every workshop," Carolyn says. "First, depending on the kind of autoethnography you are doing, the criteria by which it should be evaluated will be different. Manning and Adams (2015) divide kinds of autoethnography into social scientific, interpretive/humanist, critical, and creative/artistic. If you are planning to do something akin to analytic autoethnography, the criteria should be more social scientific, such as considerations of validity, data collection, categorization processes, and generalizability across cases. Given that evocative autoethnography generally falls into the areas of interpretive/humanist and creative/artistic, both with critical elements, most of you doing this work will not be so concerned with these issues.

"Art, you've been quiet. Would you like to jump in here about the criteria you use in evaluating evocative autoethnographies?"

"Sure," Art responds. "I covered some of this implicitly in the session yesterday, and I will elaborate on evocative autoethnography's conception of 'truth' tomorrow. But I am happy to summarize in this context. First, I look for abundant, concrete details. I want to feel the flesh and blood emotions of people coping with life's contingencies. I am attracted to structurally complex narratives that are told in a temporal framework representing the curve of time. I also reflect on the author's emotional credibility, vulnerability, and honesty. I expect evocative autoethnographers to examine their actions and dig underneath them, displaying the self on the page, taking a measure of life's limitations, of the cultural scripts that resist transformation, of contradictory feelings, ambivalence, and layers of subjectivity, squeezing comedy out of life's tragedies. I also prefer narratives that express a tale of two selves, one that shows a believable journey from who I was to who I am, and how a life course can be reimagined or transformed by crisis. I hold the author to a demanding standard of ethical self-consciousness, as Carolyn highlighted earlier. I want the writer to show concern for how other people in the teller's story are portrayed, for the kind of person one becomes in telling one's story, and to provide a space for the listener's becoming. And finally, I want a story that moves me, my heart and belly as well as my head; I want a story that doesn't just refer to subjective life, but instead acts it out in ways that show me what life feels like now and what it can mean."[2]

"Thanks, Art."

"I'm looking forward to all of you thinking with 'Bird on the Wire' tomorrow," Art says.

"Me too. Don't forget to read Art's story tonight. It is in Appendix C in your reading packet," Carolyn reminds participants.

"If you have time, you also might want to look at the criteria that others have mentioned for evaluating autoethnography," Art tells participants. "We have copies of articles here from the special issue of *Qualitative Inquiry* on assessing alternative modes of qualitative research (2000, volume 6, issue 2; for example, see Bochner, 2000; Ellis, 2000a; Richardson, 2000) and a more recent one by Manning and Adams (2015). Feel free to take copies."

"They won't have time to read all of that. We've scheduled drinks at Murphy's tonight," Carolyn says, and checks her watch. "Then they can read the articles at Murphy's," Art jokes, as participants move toward the table to retrieve their copies.

Part Four

Narrative Truth: Meanings in Motion

Thinking with "Bird on the Wire"

"Are you rested and ready to give us everything you've got today?" Art asks, cupping his hand behind his right ear and tilting it forward. A loud 'yes' echoes through the room as participants respond to Art's now familiar gesture.

"That's great," Art replies. "I'm going to need you at the top of your game.

"Let me begin with a concise summary of what we've covered so far in this workshop. We began by sketching the history of auto-ethnography. We outlined the social, cultural, and philosophical shifts of the mid-to-late twentieth century that gave rise to a 'narrative turn' and created an atmosphere of openness to experimenting with forms of expressing lived experiences new to the human sciences. After defining autoethnography and identifying several genres of autoethnographic research, we focused on evocative autoethnography, highlighting its goal of activating subjectivity and inducing readers to respond viscerally. We depicted evocative autoethnography as a genre of writing designed to put meanings in motion so that readers of social science texts could not only receive but also *feel* the truths of first-person accounts of lived-through experiences.

"In the second phase of the workshop, we concentrated on methods and ethics. We focused on the craft of storytelling, taking up the 'auto,' the 'graphy,' and the 'ethno' facets of an autoethnographic project. Our discussion of Carolyn's story, 'Maternal Connections,' drew attention to the personal and emotional connections that can be evoked by a vulnerable observer shaping an embodied text into a sensual story. By conveying intimate details that resonate with readers, Carolyn linked a specific event in her life to a widely shared predicament faced by many women. Her story raised a host of ethical dilemmas associated with writing, performing, and/or publishing autoethnographic research, which Carolyn addressed in her reflections on institutional review boards, relational ethics, and ethnographic forms.

"Today I want us to turn our attention to the question of how readers should listen to and connect with autoethnographic stories. I also want us to meditate on the kind of 'truths' these stories seek. Autoethnography makes different demands on readers than other forms of inquiry in the human sciences. My goal is to produce a greater understanding and appreciation of these differences.

"The more informed we become as readers of autoethnography, the more able we are to identify the most useful and evocative autoethnographic stories. Earlier in the workshop, I made the point that authors of evocative autoethnography do not abide by the same conventions of writing as authors of objectivist and realist social science. I want to make a similar claim about reading autoethnography. I don't read autoethnography the same way I read traditional social science research. The human sciences are large and diverse enough to accommodate both kinds of work. But writers and readers need to approach, engage, and assess them differently.

"Students often ask me, 'What should I get out of this autoethnographic story?'

"'That's the wrong question,' I tell them. You should be asking, 'How can I get into the story, not what can I get out of it' (see Greenspan, 2010). You aren't likely to get anything out of the story until or unless you can get into it.' Carolyn made the same point yesterday during her discussion of narrative analysis."

"What do you mean by getting into a story?" Eric interrupts. "How do I get into a story?"

"You start by giving priority to the stance of the storyteller. You're ready and willing to put yourself in the place of the storyteller. Recall our discussion of 'Maternal Connections' on the first day of the workshop. As readers you were dwelling in the story, living in it, and using it to reflect on your own lives by thinking *with* the story rather than *about* it (Frank, 1995). That's a distinction we've been highlighting throughout the workshop. Thinking about a story removes you from the story, and you analyze from a distance, like a spectator at a sporting event or a social scientist doing content analysis or grounded theory.

"Conversely, the autoethnographic storyteller wants you to interact *with* the story, to plunge in, using all the senses available to you, feeling the story's tensions, experiencing its dilemmas or contradictions, and living in its reality. When you engage with a story in this way, you allow yourself to consider the ways in which this story relates to your life and to find in that connection some truth about yourself—especially the good that you are seeking.

"We encourage readers of evocative autoethnography to resist the temptation to turn the story immediately into 'data' in order to test, analyze, or generalize theoretical propositions and thereby produce knowledge that can be received by others. Instead, we want them to link theory to story by resonating with the story's moral dilemmas, identifying with its ambiguities, and letting the story analyze them (Frank, 2004). Readers *think with* a story from within the framework of their own lives. They take the story to heart, concentrating on how they can use the story, what ethical direction it points them toward, and what moral commitments it calls out in them (see Coles, 1989)."

Revisiting 'Maternal Connections'

"Last night Carolyn and I had a fascinating conversation about the discussion of 'Maternal Connections' that took place earlier in the workshop." Art turns toward Carolyn and motions for her to join in the conversation. "Help me here, Carolyn. Share some of what you were saying last night."

Carolyn starts talking as she approaches Art to stand beside him. "I was so impressed with how many of you put yourself in my place, imagining what it would be like to take care of your mother as I was taking care of mine. I was thrilled to see how my story guided you to think about what kind of relationship you imagined having with your mother, what sort of relationship you desired, and what values you associated with these desires. Then Art said to me, 'We have to bring this up tomorrow because the workshop participants' discussion of 'Maternal Connections' was such a good example of what we mean when we talk about *letting the story analyze you.*'

"Thinking with the story enabled you to realize what was drawing you to it as well as what you may have resisted about it. Some of you were attracted to the warmth of a daughter/mother love exemplified by the affectionate care I was giving my mother. But others found the thought of connecting so intimately with your mother's body unseemly or indecent. In some of your responses, I heard you struggling to figure out who you could possibly be, and questioning what you could possibly do, in a situation like mine. You were actively considering what kind of story you would want to be able to tell other people in your life after you'd faced these circumstances?"

Carolyn pauses and Art interjects, "Mark Freeman (1997) calls this kind of contemplation 'narrative integrity.' By reflecting *now* about how to act *going forward,* you consider what story you want to be able to tell others *later on* about how you acted in the past. Notice how this kind of narrative activity merges several dimensions of the past, present, and future.

"When you think with a story in these ways, you are exercising your 'moral imagination' (Coles, 1989). You are called by the auto-ethnographic story to enact intense self-scrutiny. Carolyn's story does not tell you what to do when your time comes to face a similar circumstance. The way you take in her story may lead you in a particular direction, but the circumstances that you face will not be identical to hers. Thus, you are left to grope with the possibilities and difficulties of becoming the person you want to be at that time and in that place. You are asking what kind of life you want to live, which becomes a yardstick for measuring how meaningfully you live up to the standard you set for yourself."

"I guess what we're both saying," Carolyn adds, "is that evocative autoethnographic stories ideally provide the tools and inspiration to achieve this kind of narrative understanding. And that brings us to the goals of today's opening session." Carolyn pauses, gesturing for Art to continue.

"Thanks, Carolyn. I'm glad we had this opportunity to share some of what we talked about last night. That's a good segue into the exercise that we have planned for today, which is designed to give you additional experience in thinking with a story. I'm assuming that everyone has read the story we assigned for today, 'Bird on the Wire.'" The participants nod and reach for their copy.

The Back Story of 'Bird on the Wire'

"Before we start the exercise, let me tell you a little about why I wrote this story and the process by which I composed it. 'Bird on the Wire' fuses nonfiction, fiction, and essay, raising questions about the validity and usefulness of canonical boundaries that treat these as separate and distinct categories or genres of writing. I wanted to compose an autoethnographic story that would move along the fringes of nonfiction and fiction and show that writing nonfiction involves imagination and writing fiction often relies on autobiographical events. One of my goals was to write *through* these various forms while tacitly writing *about* them. Using conventions of narrative realism, I intended to produce a story that felt 'true' and 'real.'

"Early on, I tell readers that I had dreamed up this story, but then bend and blend the 'actual' and the 'real.' My goal is to create a palpable illusion of the real that would diminish the significance of any such distinction in the reader's mind. The story attempts to fashion something akin to what Margot Singer (2013 p. 242) calls 'an artful illusion of the real.'

"If I could make my story connect viscerally to readers, they would be inclined to move seamlessly back and forth between my experiences with my father and their experiences with theirs, diverting their attention away from the form. The conversation between my father and me would feel so 'real' that readers would forget that it never actually happened. Caught up in a story of events that seem real, they would move with me into these events, suspending or bracketing distinctions between the 'actual' and the 'real.' They would feel the 'truth' of the story deep in the bowels of their own lived experiences with one parent or the other.

"In 'Bird on the Wire,' I show how autoethnography can merge literary art and social science to enact memory through narrative. This co-mingling of fiction and ethnography calls attention to questions about the kinds of truth autoethnography seeks. It also prompts readers to consider what roles imagination and memory play in the pursuit of these truths. Some of you may want to speak to these issues during our discussion. After you converse for a while, I may want to weigh in on the differences I see between autoethnography's story-truths and the happening truths of traditional social science (Bochner, 2014).

"After we take a brief coffee break, we'll reconvene and begin a 'thinking with a story' exercise. During the break, Carolyn and I will rearrange the chairs into two circles, one inside the other. The inner circle will be populated by eight volunteers who we'll ask to share their responses to 'Bird on the Wire.' Their objective will be to show how they 'think with' my story. The rest of you, those populating the outer circle, will serve as the reflective team, listening carefully and preparing to comment and raise questions when the discussion period ends. Some of you in the reflective group may want to take notes during the discussion. When you return, you should take a seat in the inner circle if you want to participate in the 'thinking with' group. Those seats may fill quickly—I hope they will—so don't stay out too long. We should have the room set up in just a few minutes."

Thinking with 'Bird on the Wire'

"The circle of volunteers is complete," Art declares. "Bravo! I'm going to sit here with the observers just outside the inner circle.

"There is nothing complicated about this exercise. We simply want you to talk with each other about how you responded to 'Bird on the Wire.' What emotions and memories did the story evoke? What did it bring up for you? Let's begin."

The volunteers look at each other but nobody speaks. They sit in silence, the atmosphere heavy with apprehension. Then several volunteers look directly at Art, giving the impression they want him to take charge, but he shows no sign of intervening. A few volunteers exchange sideways glances at one another, while the rest squirm in their seats and stare at the floor.

"Somebody has to get this started," Vicki interjects into the palpable stillness. "It might as well be me. Art's story brought a lot of feelings to the surface that I'd buried. His dad reminded me a lot of mine. My father is an immigrant and he's a very angry person. Like Art's dad, he's obsessed with work. Art respected his father's work ethic, but that wasn't enough. I had to take a deep breath when he referred to his dad's fathering as phony and insincere. That's how I feel about my dad."

"My father was a big fake too," Jake interrupts. "I could relate to what Art wrote about learning to hate his father. Dad never beat me, but I grew to hate him for his disinterest. The scene that really got to me was the one in which Art's dad asked him to come to visit him more often. I thought about how my dad sends random texts to me out of the blue, especially when he's had too much to drink. That's when he's able to express the love I've wanted from him for as long as I can remember. He tells me he loves me and to come around and check on him more. I know just what Art means when he talks about how his fantasies of revenge dissolved. It's crazy how we live our lives seeking revenge on those who wrong us and then all of a sudden they express weakness and our desire for revenge melts."

"That was a heartbreaking moment in Art's text. It brought tears to my eyes," Monica replies. "I'd never thought about mourning together with a person who hurt me. But it made sense that it's mostly people you love who hurt you. You spend so much of your time defending yourself that you forget what you really want from each other. When you drop your guard and express your regrets together you may be able to set a new tone and direction. How sad that now it was too late for Art and his dad. That was one of several instances in which I was moved by Art's vulnerability. He showed a fearless disregard for how readers would judge him. His vulnerability touched me on a personal level, which evocative autoethnography is supposed to do. At least, that's how I'm grasping it."

"But the vulnerability wasn't completely one-sided," Vicki adds. "I got a sense of his dad's helplessness and hurt too. His dad had been poor and Jewish and he'd carried all that despair and those feelings of being discriminated against into his adult life. Art's only a little kid at the time. He's too young to truly understand a parent's wounds that run that deep. It got me thinking about how little I really know about what my parents' lives were like before I came on the scene."

"I want to say something about that too," Anna says, entering the conversation. "I have to admit that I find it nearly impossible not to demonize someone who has treated me badly. My relationship with my father is nothing short of what I desire. But I have other people in my past who have hurt me, and I carry around a lot of pain from those experiences. Art's story made me question my own ethics. Why do I hold on to so much anger and sorrow? I kept thinking about some of the lines Art quoted from that Leonard Cohen song. As long as I carry that resentment and am unforgiving, I won't ever be free of these past hurts. That's what those lines meant to me."

"I'm glad Anna brought up how Art uses 'bird on the wire' as a metaphor for his predicament," Vicki replies. "Does anyone else want to share an interpretation of his use of the song lyrics?"

"I love that song," Alex begins emphatically. "The band I'm in has played it many times. 'I have tried to be free *in my way*'—that's the line I resonate with. It's as if we're all trying to be free in our own way, but we don't necessarily make it. Some of us really mess up. In Art's case, he's still trying. He refuses to give up. The trouble is that the person he wants to break free from is stuck in his consciousness. He can't have an actual meeting of the minds with his father. They can't mourn the past together. Art's story appears to be a conversation, but I read it as a meditation. He's working through a meditation in order to let go of the past and move on. I'm excited to think about using autoethnography as a form of meditative consciousness. That could be a way of merging personal essay with ethnography."

"Monica looks like she's trying to get back into our conversation," Vicki says, inviting her to talk.

"Thanks for calling on me, Vicki. I consider 'bird on the wire' a metaphor for feeling abandoned and stranded. Like Alex suggested, the sudden death of Art's father left him high and dry. At home, we've occasionally had birds fly into our house and they flutter around desperately trying to free themselves from captivity. In the song, the bird is stuck on a wire, reaching for something to free it. When you're stuck—and I've had this happen to me—you reach out to other people, seeking their advice, but then what often happens is you get different views, sometimes totally opposite, about what to do, like the beggar and the pretty woman in the song. But real freedom can't be gained by attaching yourself to somebody else's version of who you should be and what you should do. Ultimately, you have to decide for yourself. That's what makes freedom such a burden."

"I don't mean to interrupt the flow, but we seem to be drifting away from the 'thinking with' idea," Erica intervenes.

"Go ahead," Vicki replies. "We're supposed to stay with the story."

"Art's story focuses on his father, but my mind kept drifting toward my mother," Erica begins. "I kept thinking about all the anguish my mom had put me through. I never felt like I could talk to her about anything because she voiced such strong opinions. She brought a lot of hurt into our family and that's something I will never forget. As I was growing up, my mom continually expressed her disgust for gay people and she warned me against ever dating a woman. I didn't want to disappoint her, so for years I kept my attraction to women a secret. When I finally decided to tell her I was a lesbian, she made cutting comments about my girlfriend and our relationship. I felt disrespected and humiliated. Shortly after my first semester in college my mom left home, and I found out she had been emotionally involved with people other than my father. I'm still angry about that. I don't know if I'll ever be free of resentment toward her, though I'd like to have that weight lifted from my shoulders."

"That's so sad, Erica," Monica responds. "I can only imagine how I would feel to be so rejected by my mother. I've never had to face anything like that. Several of us seem to be struggling with this 'letting go' issue. We don't want to be held in the grip of the past, but we don't know how to break free. We're kind of tied in knots. It sounds to me as if you've made up your mind not to give any more effort to improving the relationship between you and your mother, and I can understand why you would feel that way given what you've been through. But you also realize how that keeps you fastened to the past."

"I wonder if you could fabricate a conversation like Art did," Vicki asks.

"I suppose I could try that," Erica replies. "My mother isn't dead, though she might as well be, since I can't forgive her and I don't have any interest in seeing or talking with her. Though I'm studying forgiveness, I don't believe in forgive and forget. Maybe that's why I'm studying it."

"Then how about trying to forgive and remember?" Vicki asks, looking directly across at Erica. "That would mean taking a different ethical stance. You would uncouple the person from the act they committed. It was wrong of your mother to disrespect you and bring so much pain into your family. But you don't have to forget what she did in order to move past it. If you close down the possibility of redeeming your relationship with your mother, then you relinquish any chance of building a different and better relationship with her in the future. I'm not a psychologist, but I don't think you can heal unless you allow the feelings you have about your mother's actions to lead in a different direction, one that doesn't make her your mortal enemy. I know that's easier said than done, but that seems to be the direction in which Art's story moves."

"I agree," Monica replies. "The story brings together Carolyn's idea of relational ethics and Frank's narrative ethics of thinking with a story. Art's trying to show how fluid relationships can be—at least that's how I interpreted his story. Family bonds are continuous. They don't end even when the person dies. They still live on in your mind. Holding a grudge against a family member can eat at you and tear you apart. Resentment infects your mind and can build a dark cloud around you. One of my psychology professors likened resentment to taking poison and waiting for the other person to die. Art didn't get an opportunity to let go while his father was alive, so he's using his memories and imagination to achieve a kind of moral renewal that can free him from those feelings of bitterness and animosity. He's searching for a new narrative, one that will disentangle him from the feelings associated with the old one."

"This is a good place for me to jump in," Eric announces. "I've been listening closely and I appreciate how the rest of you are digging deeply into the meanings you can draw from Art's story. Reading about how Art worked through his fears helps me see how I might work past mine. I related in so many ways. My father was emotionally absent too. I got to the point where I pushed him and anything that made me think of him away. But that didn't help. He wasn't around, but I still felt his influence on my life, and it enraged me. Art put my frustration and all I was feeling into one sentence, which I wrote down on my notepad."

Eric grabs the pad from beneath his chair and turns to a page he has marked: "'Acting against is just another form of submission and dependence.' That sentence sums up what several of you have said. I'm sitting here thinking now about how I've been limiting myself, not reaching as high as I could because of my anger toward my dad. I've been guided by a self-defeating logic. I was afraid that if I became really successful, my dad would stand up and take credit, and I was damned if I was going to allow that to happen. I suppose that sounds crazy but it's true."

"That's one of the powerful things about autoethnography," Alex says, taking a deep breath and exhaling. "It can make you aware of your own consciousness, things you've not realized or you've forgotten. You become more aware of how you reason about things and react emotionally to them. I don't have a problematic relationship with my dad. But Art's story evoked a lot of emotion, a lot of sadness. I was in this situation a few years ago where a friend of about eleven years died, and I never got a chance to tell him how I felt about him. To this day, I still think about our relationship. I can't help wondering whether telling him how I felt might have changed things in our friendship before he died."

"I'm glad you brought that up," Toni says, joining in for the first time. "I've been holding back, because Art's story evoked a lot of fear in me, and I don't have as much courage as some of you to talk about it. I'm conflict-aversive, which may be why I'm doing my dissertation research on quarreling in close relationships. When I get in a fight with one of my parents, or even with a close friend or sibling, I worry about destroying the relationship and forever regretting that we had argued over something that wasn't all that significant in the total scheme of things. I need assurance that things won't escalate to the point of no return."

"So do I, but I'm sure you realize that's not always possible," Monica replies. "I was holding back too, but now I feel safer in this group. Like Art, I lost my father. I was only four years old when he passed, but a few of the issues Art wrote about in his story are things that I've thought of in the past, especially the concept of 'unfinished business.' I've always felt as if a lot of unfinished business existed between my father and me, probably because I was so young when he passed."

Monica stops for a moment. Tears form in her eyes and one runs down her cheek. She looks toward Art, clears her throat, and then continues. "Art, I really appreciated how you talked directly to your father in the story as though he were sitting in front of you. When you said that the relationship between the two of you lived on in your mind, but conversation had ended, I thought, 'well yes, that applies to me and my father.' I had never put it into words, but you did and I'm grateful."

Art nods, signaling his appreciation. The group falls silent for a moment, and then Vicki says, "Well, you probably know by now that I'm one of these people who can't stand silence. I was struck by what Monica said about Art's speaking directly to his dad in this story. I loved his use of the second-person voice. It was beautiful and powerful because it allowed me to mourn, regret, and forgive alongside Art. That's how I want to be able to write. The vulnerability was visceral. Does anyone else have specific reactions to Art's writing?"

"Some of the lines gave me goosebumps, like the one about death ending a life but not a relationship," Monica replies, still looking directly at Art. "The way you mixed your reminiscing thoughts with synthetic dialogue intrigued me and made the story fun to read."

"I liked the way it was written too," Anna says, turning attention back to the group. "Sometimes he was ranting about past grievances and sometimes he was interrogating what it all meant."

Alex nods his agreement. "Art's writing shows the complexity of his mind and of life itself. As a reader, I felt as if I were witnessing the movement of his mind. I was watching him come to terms with different layers of his relationship to his dad over the course of their lives. Like most people, his dad was a complicated person. Art forces himself to face up to how riddled with contradictions and ironies relationships can be. Like when he wanted to settle things while his dad was still alive, but he had to accept that his father was too fragile and not the same violent person he had been as a younger man. That was a poignant moment that rang true, and something I'd never thought about before."

"But there's an important difference between ringing true and being true," Jake interrupts. "That difference shouldn't be taken lightly. I've had this sinking feeling that you folks are going to let

Art off the hook. But I can't. As I said earlier, my father is a phony so I'm really sensitive to people who fabricate stuff."

"What are you talking about, Jake! Art isn't hiding anything," Erica insists. "He makes it clear upfront that he's imagining this conversation."

"But most of you seem to be treating the story as if it were real," Jake complains. "It isn't a true story. The conversation never actually happened. That's a fact. I'm a social scientist, and that means I'm compelled to respect facts."

"Good for you," Toni replies, a hint of sarcasm in her voice. "But I'm sorry, I don't see it your way at all. I think you're missing the point."

"That a girl, Toni. Now you don't sound like you're a conflict-avoider at all," Vicki chuckles, breaking some of the tension growing in the room.

"Seriously, the story may not be true in the sense of actually happening, but it's very real," Toni continues. "If it weren't real, I mean if it didn't relate to our lives, we wouldn't be sharing so much personal stuff. Haven't you been touched by the feelings some of us have expressed?" Toni looks directly at Jake.

"Yes, I was moved by some of the emotions," Jake admits. "But that doesn't make his story true. People have emotional reactions to lots of stuff. I'm just asking us not to get carried away by Art's imagination."

Vicki shakes her head in disagreement. "I beg to differ. That's exactly what you do when you think with a story; you let it carry you somewhere into the recesses of your mind and your own life experiences. You dig into it. You use the story to explore yourself."

"Not if it isn't true," Jake counters. "Don't get me wrong, I understand how imagining that you could have this kind of conversation can bring up hypotheticals for debate and discussion. That can be useful. But the result of that kind of exercise is philosophy not social science." Jake has a look of frustration on his face. He turns toward Art and says, "Even you concede near the end of the story that your dad really wasn't there, Art. I don't mean to sound insensitive. I'm just saying that your father wasn't around to say otherwise."

Art resists the temptation to be pulled into the conversation. A relaxed smile covers his face; he appears content, even delighted, to have the group work through these issues on their own.

Vicki responds. "What you're doing Jake is thinking *about* Art's story not *with* it. Art made it clear that he was purposely writing along the margins of nonfiction and fiction, and you could add social science, philosophy, or humanities as well. He's bending the genres. But, Jake, you seem to want to unbend them. Can't you see a middle ground between fiction and nonfiction?"

"Sorry, but I don't see any nonfiction in Art's story. He made up the story. There's nothing true in it," Jake negates.

Vicki interjects, "You talk as if you're completely certain what 'truth' means. I don't believe there's any such thing as naked truth. I consider truth rather elusive. It calls to us. We seek it. But it eludes and escapes our attempts to capture it."

"This conversation is starting to get on my nerves," says Alex in a tone of exasperation. "At the beginning of the workshop Art emphasized the importance of defining our terms. And both Art and Carolyn construed evocative autoethnography as a hybrid form of expression and inquiry that sits between social science and humanities, between facts and values. The primary focus is on meanings, subjectivities, and feelings."

"That's a great point. Even when facts enter, they still must be interpreted," Vicki says.

"Facts don't tell you what they mean or how they feel," Alex asserts. "Art's interrogating the meanings of his relationship with his father over the course of his life. He's not so much presenting what happened as trying to find out what did happen and what it meant. He calls what he's doing 'memory work.' He's trying to understand the past so he can move on in the future. It rings true because it's believable. I was persuaded."

"There you go again with 'rings true,' Jake says, frustration showing in his voice. "How can something that never actually happened ring true? Don't you have to admit that this story is not factual, so it can't be true?"

"No I don't and I won't," Erica holds her ground. "You talk as if there's such a thing as facts pure and simple. But there isn't. To me, the truth of Art's story is as real as any other kind of truth. When I teach narrative to undergraduates, I call this 'story truth.'"

"Some psychologists call it narrative truth," Monica says, "which means that the story is truthful to life as it is lived. Art's trying to restore some order to his life. I found it exciting to watch someone going through the process of creating a story in order to cope with the trauma he had experienced. At the beginning of this session, he told us that his plan was to write a story that would merge the aesthetic dimensions of storytelling with the investigative spirit of an ethnographer interrogating personal experience. He's an ethnographer seeking a story that will provide some continuity to his life, which has been interrupted and traumatized by his father's death. He brings together the 'auto,' the 'ethno,' and the 'graphy.' Maybe that's why he and Carolyn are ending the workshop with this exercise."

"The turn in this conversation fascinates me," Vicky says. "I've been jotting some notes as you all were talking. It looks like we have a number of kinds of truth of interest: factual truth, emotional truth, aesthetic truth, happening truth, story truth, and lifelike truth. Damn, I feel overwhelmed by all this truth. Maybe Art can help us sort through these." The participants fall silent, but Art doesn't move. Instead, he nods toward Eric who has been trying to get into the conversation for a while.

"I think even in this story, there is a happening truth," Eric begins. "What's happening in Art's story occurs right in front of our eyes. As someone who teaches and studies performance, I would say that Art is performing his desire to heal a long broken relationship. I had to laugh when I heard Jake refer to the conversation between Art and his dad as 'untrue' or 'unreal.' I venture to guess that at one time or another every person in this room has participated in an imaginary conversation with someone. We concoct scenes and play them out in our minds all the time. We use our imagination to produce these dialogues, allowing them to unfurl in our mind. You want a fact, Jake? Well, that's a fact. It's true, we do

this all the time. To a certain extent, we learn about our own consciousness—how we reason and think, how we feel and react—by
doing this. If we pay attention to these 'imagined' conversations,
we can gain a heck of a lot of self-knowledge. Think about the ironic
nature of this kind of performance. We imagine these conversations, but the activity of imagining itself is real, true to life, and
useful. As far as I'm concerned, the truth of Art's story is just as real
as any other kind of truth."

"I've had imaginary conversations with my father for as long as
I can remember," Monica says. "This may sound strange, but those
conversations help me to conjure an image of my father as a character and to cope with the loss. And I'm not alone. A lot of people
do this in the aftermath of loss."

"Eric, your comments make me think that Art's story goes a lot
deeper than I thought," Vicki declares. "Sometimes people worry
about whether the memories people enact and reflect on in autoethnographies can be trusted. But the primary event of Art's story
is not a memory, it's an event he creates and invites us, as readers, to witness and engage. The event itself, however, is layered with
memories, the accuracy of which can't be verified."

"Do they need to be?" Erica asks, looking around the circle of
participants. But nobody responds and the group grows silent.

"This might be a good time for me to reenter," Art says, standing and moving to the front of the room. He senses that some
fatigue may be setting in and wants to keep things moving forward
a bit longer. "But first let's take a short break."

Reflecting on Truth and Memory Work

As soon as the break begins, the silence is broken. Participants gather in small groups by the coffee and snack table, and carry on animated conversations about fact and fiction, the actual and the real, reading and writing, and narrative and historical truth. Carolyn and Art observe and listen in on the spirited banter from a distance. "I'd love to get closer and be a part of some of those conversations," Art whispers.

"Me too, but it's better this way," Carolyn replies. "Our presence would change how they're relating. They're going to remember these dialogues long after the workshop is over."

"Jake's dissent really stirred things up. I like that. Let's try to keep things lively through this final session."

"Given the excitement in the room, that shouldn't be difficult," Carolyn replies. "I'm amazed you were able to restrain yourself during the group discussion."

"I'm glad I did," Art replies. "But my tongue has some deep bite marks on it."

"I suppose we ought to get started. Don't forget to leave time for the closing we planned."

"How do you want to handle that?" Art asks.

"We'll give them a final break. Csaba and Erica should be here by then. I'll introduce them, and they'll do their performance."

The participants gradually settle into their seats and the room grows quiet again. "You think you know how readers are going to respond to your story, but you never do," Art begins. "That's one of the reasons I look forward to these workshops. I get to hear directly from readers. The opportunity to observe other people relating with your text is one of the great joys of being a writer. Today, I was delighted and occasionally surprised by your reactions to my story. Actually, I anticipated that more of you would side with Jake on the question of story truth and raise doubts about the accuracy of the memories I worked through in the story. I want to talk about these issues during this session, but first I want to give some of the participants in the observing group a chance to react to the discussion." Several hands go up immediately, and Art calls on Sadira.

Resonance

"I admired the way the group members were teaching each other about what it means to think with a story by actually doing it. It was fascinating to watch how their interaction with your story evolved organically into a discussion about truth."

"That's what good conversations do," Art interjects. "You can't predict where they may lead. They take on a life of their own."

"As it turned out," Sadira continues, "this one ended up focusing on truth, which brought me back to the question of how autoethnography should be evaluated. Carolyn mentioned some general criteria yesterday. Then in this exercise, we were given a specific story and we have listened to a number of readers reacting to it. So I'm wondering, how do we judge whether this story makes a significant contribution? Most members of the group expressed some personal resonance with your story. Vicki, Eric, and Monica each said—though in somewhat different ways—that you put what they were feeling into words. Doesn't that suggest that your story achieved generalizability? Can't resonance be regarded as evidence of validity?"

"You've hit the nail on the head, Sadira. Generalizability takes on a different meaning in autoethnography than in traditional social science research. The question we ask is: how does a particular story depicting a specific context—a story like mine—manage to acquire something akin to universal significance? The answer is through *resonance*. When a story resonates, it moves beyond itself by questioning, probing, and expressing feelings that connect to lives lived apart, often far away, from the time and place of the story. These stories do not tell people precisely what to do. Rather, they take readers into one universal struggle or another that exemplifies ways of dealing with the difficulties of living a good life.

"How is this resonance accomplished? As a writer, I reach for metaphors that can connect to readers. In my story, I'm not literally a bird on the wire. Nor are any of you. But most of us have experienced dilemmas in our lives that made us feel as if we were a bird on the wire. Recognizing the universal 'resonance' of this metaphor was a huge step in my process of creating a story that could provide an example of one person's struggle and resolve to figure out what he could do to move on from a serious and sudden loss.

"But I didn't know what I was going to write until I started writing. I didn't make an outline or a graph of the story's narrative arc. Though many years had passed since my father's death, whenever I thought of us—him and me—I would find myself immersed in grief and sorrow. I recognized that I desired something I would never have—a healing conversation that would end in an expression of love between the two of us. In a general sense, I set out to explore loss, pain, and sorrow. Indeed, most people read 'Bird on the Wire' as a story of grief and loss. I'm trying to figure out how to deal with the brute fact of my father's death, an event that millions of people face each year.

"As I wrote, I started to grasp a deeper motive for wanting to write this story. I was seeking an understanding of the relationship between my father and me that had eluded me while he was alive. Like many people, I had allowed my life to speed by unreflectively, not all that aware a day would arrive when I would need to achieve some kind of clarifying truth that greater understanding through hindsight could bring (Freeman, 2010). I came to this story feeling trapped and confined in and by the past. I'm a bird on the wire trying in my way to be free.

"But as I said, I'm not there by myself. Loss, remorse, and regret are universal experiences; they are not unique to me. When a story like mine—a particular story that takes place in a particular context—gains resonance, it achieves a universal significance, but it does not achieve truth with a capital-T. In the aftermath of my father's death, I face uncertainty about what to do with the lingering anger and conflict between us, and I struggle to figure out how I could understand him and our past in ways that would allow me to let go, with insight, and move on.

"The truth of my story is found in other people's struggles with uncertainty—those of my readers—and the protracted conflicts they bring to my story, as well as their own experiences of actual or anticipated loss. I've heard many readers say, as Eric and others did, 'I felt as if you were writing my life, putting my frustrations, fears, or feelings into words.' People who appreciate the gifts of autoethnography realize that when they dive deeply into the ocean of private thoughts and feelings, they can make contact with what is staunchly universal."

Usefulness

"Can you give us a firmer handle on the question of autoethnography's truth claims," Andrew interrupts. "I, too, was pulled into the group's conversation, but at the end of the discussion, I didn't feel resolved about how to explain to my committee, or to other reviewers of my autoethnographic work, the kind of knowledge my stories produce. How would you want the truth claims in 'Bird on the Wire' to be judged?"

"Oh yes, sooner or later we always get to the issue of 'truth claims,' don't we? It's hard to break free from the demand for criteria by which to judge academic work. Andrew and Sadira both pose questions about the benchmarks for judging autoethnographies. This obsession with criteria is left over from the old hypothetical-deductive model of science and the correspondence theory of knowledge, both of which were thoroughly debunked and deconstructed in the 1980s.

"Let's go back to something I emphasized the first day. Evocative autoethnography is a narrative practice aligned with a pragmatist orientation to inquiry that replaces the concept of 'truth' with the concept of 'usefulness' (Bochner, 1994). We need to burn this distinction into our brains." Art chuckles at the image. "The narrative truths of evocative autoethnography are pragmatic truths. The question is not whether autoethnographic stories convey precisely the way things actually happened, but rather what these stories do, what consequences they have, and to what uses they can be put.

"It is no secret that autoethnography has a wide appeal to people on the margins (working class, LGBTQ, and ethnic and racial minorities) because these populations often have been silenced, objectified, left out, or oppressed by value-free, disembodied social science. If we relapse into traditional ways of assessing the value or validity of research, we risk delegitimizing the very essence of what makes the evocative autoethnography paradigm powerful. I'm referring to autoethnography's capacity for self-reflexive and self-critical accounts of experience that can heal, change, validate, and engage others.

"Evocative autoethnography transgresses the old ways of judging the merits of a social 'scientific' argument. An autoethnographic text directs attention to meanings rather than facts, readings rather than observations, and interpretations rather than findings. Autoethnography gives up any illusion of producing an unmediated mirroring of reality. Instead, it acknowledges that all attempts to speak for, write about, or represent human lives are partial, situated, and mediated. Like all social research texts, evocative autoethnographies inevitably create value, inscribe meanings, and become a site of moral responsibility.

"But now I fear that I've strayed from your question, Andrew. That's a bad habit of mine that even Carolyn hasn't been able to correct," Art grins. "Let me give a more direct answer. My first impulse is to ask each of you to identify my truth claims. That would be devious, though, since I didn't make any specific truth claims in the story. Still, you could infer a proposition or two from my story. The poem from Ricoeur that opens 'Bird on the Wire' suggests one: 'A life story is always incomplete.' Another could be 'Re-describing the past can cast a new light on it, yielding relational and psychological insights.' You can probably come up with others. But clearly propositional knowledge was not my purpose."

Regions of Truth

"I don't mean to be a troublemaker," Andrew interrupts. "But it sure seems that you're evading the 'truth' question. Maybe I shouldn't have used the term *claims*. So let me rephrase. What kind of truth are you seeking? Isn't that a reasonable question to ask?"

"Of course it is. So let me rephrase the answer," Art kids. "I'm seeking a pragmatic kind of truth that rests at the meeting place of my story and the reader's life. Robert Coles (1989) exquisitely captured this pragmatic dimension of evocative truth when he said: 'The beauty of a good story is its openness, the way you or I or anyone reading can take it in and use it for ourselves...there are many interpretations of a good story, and it isn't a question of which one is right or wrong but of what you do with what you've read' (p. 47).

"But I want to be mindful of your needs too, Andrew. You won't have Carolyn Ellis or Art Bochner in the room when you're asked to defend the legitimacy of your autoethnographic projects. At that time, you'll likely feel an urgent need to have a concrete answer on hand if a challenging question is posed. So let's get back to the big 'truth' question.

"That question loomed large in the group's impressive discussion of my story, which came across as an epic struggle among participants to get to the truth about truth." Art chuckles as he points to the group and uses his right hand to span across the entire circle.

"But is there a truth about truth to reach?" Art inquires. "Is truth a *thing* we want to reach? Or is it a *place* in which we want to dwell. Freeman (2010), the psychologist I mentioned earlier, calls truth 'a kind of region, a psychic space that becomes inhabitable' (p. 181). 'Bird on the Wire' fits that description. I dwell in memories of my father's life, our connections and disconnections, his defects and virtues, and my desires and disappointments, applying narrative and moral imagination to reach a consciousness of the meaning and significance of this past *as I remember it*. I enter this region of truth to do 'memory work,' which takes place at the intersection of the past and the future. I am remembering *now*, using the present, which is the temporal domain of all memory work, to draw from the past with my eye on the future. I cannot reconstruct the past exactly as it was. I can only read the past through my experiential reality, and my readers will interpret my reading of the past through their lived histories.

"This memory work can yield the kinds of insight and understandings that are associated with pragmatic, emotional, and aesthetic forms of truth. The stories we tell ourselves and others in these moments rework, refigure, and remake our past in accordance with a future onto which we project our possibilities."

Ringing True: Verisimilitude

"Clearly, I do not consider my story to be exclusively a work of fiction. Even if it were, as an evocative autoethnographer I would still keep my focus on the reader's experience, which is the truth that I am trying to locate. Can readers comprehend and feel what I understand and feel? Is my story true of what my readers know of life? The term 'rings true' was tossed around during the group's discussion. The best way I have found to think about 'ringing true' is through the frame of narrative and sense-making. Does the autoethnographic narrative feel emotionally true and make sense?

"As I said in response to Sadira's question, when readers such as Eric say 'you put words to my feelings,' I take that resonance as evidence of truthfulness. His feelings become braided to my particular words or forms of expression, though I know that a gap remains between my experience and its expression in language. Life is not language, but language is one of the few means at our disposal to connect to and move us toward other lives. Convinced that my narration has tapped into his experience and the meanings he draws from it, Eric moves with me. People who move together remind each other of stuff. That's the point at which I know my words have landed."

"But does the end justify the means?" Jake blurts out. "I agree that you reached us. You made us feel stuff. We resonated. But you achieved that goal by making up a story. Your text is fiction not nonfiction, isn't it?"

"I'm glad you brought this up again, Jake. I appreciated the way you were questioning, doubting, and expressing personal misgivings about the truth of my story during the group discussion. This isn't the first time I've heard someone say these things. I interpreted your comments as an honest expression of concern grounded in your own experience as a student of social science. As I noted earlier, each person brings a somewhat different consciousness and way of thinking to the process of reading and reacting to autoethnographic stories. Sometimes in these sessions, participants hesitate to speak their minds. They feel pressure to go along with the majority. People who make waves risk bringing a barrage of attacks or disapproving comments on themselves. In groups that discourage dissent, tough questions and diverse opinions don't get expressed. But as a community of scholars we owe it to ourselves to remain open and responsive to people who want to understand evocative autoethnography, what it's trying to do, how it works, and how to judge when it succeeds and when it does not. As scholars, we can't afford to assume an uncritical stance in which anything goes.

"So let me try to address the concerns Jake expressed," Art says, redirecting his attention to the participants as a whole. "Let's start with fiction. As I said, I don't consider 'Bird on the Wire' to be a work of fiction. Even if it were, I would not want you to underestimate its potential as a means of expressing truth. The best fiction succeeds because it is true to life. As the anthropologist Michael Jackson (1989, p. 187) says in 'On Ethnographic Truth,' a brilliant essay, truth is not binding. 'It is in the interstices as much as it is in the structure, in fiction as much as in fact.'

"Besides, we don't need to inhabit the *actual* in order to satisfy our hunger for the *real*. Evocative autoethnography shares with fiction the desire to produce the effect of reality, *verisimilitude*, which seeks a likeness to life. I think of this kind of production as a performance of truth. Whether containing elements of fiction or not, an autoethnographic narrative must be true to life. Like all life writing, evocative autoethnography tells *a* story, not *the* story.

"Moreover, no matter how hard we try, we can never fill all the gaps between life experience and a representation of that experience in language. I don't find that discouraging, though. Our goal is to bring as much light as possible through the cracks.

"When we attempt to fit language to experience we become increasingly aware of the fissures between experience and words, between living through and narrating about, between the chaos and fragmentation of living a life and the smoothing orderliness we bring to it when we write, between what we remember *now* and what we can say with certainty took place *then*, between how we mourn and work through the past and what shape our grieving gives to our future. 'Language is all we have to connect us,' writes Shields (2013), 'but it doesn't. Not quite' (p. 207).

"As if the suffering we felt while living through the experiences were not enough, now we shed blood again as we try to put life and truth on the page. We bleed not so much because we have to relive the painful events of which we write, but because of the obligation we feel to produce a truthful account of the past.

"Where does this leave us?" Art asks, refocusing his attention on Jake. "You feel an allegiance to facts. I do too. My father died; that's a fact. Dad's death set in motion the meditative state that eventually brought me to this story. That's another fact. My meditative state stirred vivid memories of events that took place between my father and me in the past—yet another fact. These facts were significant in themselves and they provided my inspiration to write, but not my purpose for writing. My intentions were to pay attention to those memories, to interrogate and listen with an open mind to what they had to teach me, and to use what I learned to achieve a different relationship to the past. I wanted to revise what had been a harmful narrative inheritance (Goodall, 2005) and make it into an enabling narrative legacy. By concentrating on the *meanings* of our relationship, I was seeking to create something good out of the past—a lesson or moral that I could extend into the future."

Imagining Not Inventing

"So you're saying that 'Bird on the Wire' is based on facts, but written as fiction," Toni says. "Do I have that right?"

"More or less," Art equivocates.

"Then why not just call it fiction?" Jake grumbles.

"Because, it isn't fiction. As an autoethnographer, I worked under constraints that don't apply to novelists or short story writers. I did not have a license to make things up. I knew that certain things had happened—violent, harmful, unpleasant things—and I could not change that. I was constrained by the events themselves. They were fixed in my mind and there was no way to delete or erase them. Remaking the image of my father did not mean making him up or creating him anew. He was a real person, not a fictional character.

"Bonnie Rough (2007) provides a useful explanation of the differences between imagining in the autoethnographic ways I do and the fictionalizing of a novelist. 'Nonfiction writers imagine,' she says. 'Fiction writers invent. These are fundamentally different acts, performed to different ends' (pp. 65–66). I am asking my readers not only to imagine with me but also to believe me. I am not free to make up or tell any story or to be guided chiefly by a desire to tell a good story. I am bound instead by the particular events that I recall having occurred in my life.

"This is where hard and fast distinctions can get muddled. My claim is that an autoethnographic story like 'Bird on the Wire' is based on facts but not determined by them. Facts achieve significance and intelligibility by being situated in a temporal frame that links what came before—episodes between my father and me—to what comes next, a continuous bond after his death that will live on in my consciousness without shutting me in. The truth I seek is a deeper truth than the facts on which it is based. My interrogation of the past is an effort to realize the shape of the relationship between my father and me. It is not so much the events or experiences between us that concerned me. Rather, I was after what made the relationship operate the way it did. As the lyrics of 'Bird on the Wire' note, 'It was the shape of our love that twisted me' (Cohen, 1969). Memory work is the only means I knew that could reveal that shape. I was attempting to 'afford memory' to speak (Nabokov, 1989).

"Reframing the meaning of my father's past was an attempt to reclaim my past. I felt a powerful desire to own up to the experiences that had shaped me—for good or for bad—to reconstruct, reinterpret, and make sense out of my family history from the vantage point of my present situation. I knew there was no getting to the bottom, no final 'truth' to be rendered. Writing this story would not be the last time that I would ever consider these events.

"Remaking what my father meant to me and how I understood him was not a disinterested activity. On the contrary, I needed to create an image of my father that would release me from his grip and allow me to move into the future free of past inhibitions. This is one way to understand the work of the self-narration of auto-ethnography: to make a life that seems to be coming apart come together again by retelling and re-storying past events of one's life in order to provide meaning and direction to that life.

"My father's sudden death interrupted the well-planned life I had been living, disrupting my sense of continuity. Without warning, I had lost my bearings. My life felt incoherent and unruly. Moments like these occur in everyone's life. When you experience such moments, you face what I call 'a narrative challenge' in which you contemplate the possible meanings of a past relationship or a traumatic period of your life. In search of a narrative in which you can live more ably, you give voice to previously unspoken stories and feelings that help you inhabit a region of emotional truth about your life. Clearly, this is not a verifying-facts region of truth. These truths are not literal truths; they're emotional truths. Your concern is not with better science but with better living, and thus you are not so much aiming for some goal called 'Truth' as for an enlarged capacity to deal with the life challenges and contingencies you are facing."

Research and Therapy

"I love what you're saying, Art, but you make this sound a lot like therapy. Some critics of autoethnography make that argument, that autoethnography is therapy not research," Monica says.

"Then they've never been a therapy client or a student of therapy. Psychotherapy is a form of research on oneself. Autoethnography can be a healing practice too. But that's not all it is. Investigating my father's life in order to try to better understand his actions, his character, and his influence required me to examine, gather information, make interpretations, and reach conclusions about the shape of the relationship between us. That sounds a lot like research to me.

"My story reaches beyond me. It resonates with other people's lives. It deals with an issue of universal significance. Those are things we want research to do. People drawn to therapy want to live better lives and so do researchers attracted to autoethnography. Do we need to draw a line in the sand? No, we don't. Therapy and research can be quite different, but they also can overlap. Most of the active researchers I've known over the course of my life have been attracted to the topics of their research by events in their personal lives or family history. Often they were troubled by these events. They came to care about certain things or issues because of a personal connection to them. They want a better life, and/or social justice, for others and for themselves. Doing research that can help others also helps them. Their research is therapeutic."

Uncertainty

Art pauses for a moment and sees several raised hands. He nods to Vicki.

"You've made it clear that the writer must focus on how readers will respond to the text. But you also said you never really know what readers bring to their experience of the text. As a writer, how do you deal with this kind of uncertainty?"

"You can't eliminate uncertainty. But you can count on human curiosity. Most people are curious about how other people live their lives, especially what they do to get through trying circumstances. Moreover, our brains are hard-wired for narrative (Eakin, 2008). They compel us to want to make sense, understand, and remember our lives in a story-kind-of-way. We recall and retain stories much easier than we recall information, lists, or data.

"As a story-writer, rather than a data-analyst, you start with an advantage. People crave good stories. If you can create a narrative that responds to this yearning for story and deals with fundamental issues of existence, you have a superb chance to connect with most readers on a visceral level that encourages identification, attentiveness, concern, and questioning.

"When you begin writing, you face challenging artistic and aesthetic choices. Readers bring their quite different experiences and interpretive practices to what they read. So you want to provide sufficient room for their own meaning-making to breathe. The goal is to empower readers, not control them. After all, autoethnography is about connection. You have to accept and treat the reader as a co-constructor of the meaning of your text.

"Recognizing the diverse experiences and values readers bring to your text, how do you achieve connection and resonance with them? I think you do this by being present in the text, by coming across as honest and vulnerable, speaking from your heart, showing both sides—your narrative self and your reflective self—and acknowledging your own uncertainty about what things really mean. After all, Vicki," Art says, looking directly at her with a gleam in his eyes, "To be alive is to be uncertain.

"As I've said several times, autoethnography should be celebrated and appreciated as *the genre of doubt*. Unlike traditional social science, which usually comes across as an exclamation point (!), autoethnography emphasizes the question mark (?). Doubt and awe should remain in our stories."

"Are you certain about that?" Eric teases, evoking laughter throughout the room. As the chuckles diminish, he adds, "I'm intrigued by your emphasis on *writing lives.* That expression seems to have several layers of meaning."

"Indeed it does," Art replies. "As an autoethnographer, you are writing about events, experiences, and values that you care about deeply. The trick is to extend that same passion to your writing life. The term 'writing lives' has a triple meaning. First, you're writing about lives—your own life and the lives of other people. Second, you're living a writing life—a life as a writer. And third, your goal is to produce writing that lives, stories that breathe, move, and arouse. As an autoethnographer, you observe, document, interview, reflect, conceptualize, and theorize. As a writer, you shape, structure, organize, stylize, and/or dramatize. The 'ethno,' 'the auto,' and the 'graphy' are different activities, but they come together in your writing life, where you work to merge fictional and interpretive styles with scientific ones.

"As a writer, you always seem to have more work ahead of you. How are you going to stage the facts? How are you going to color and shade them? You become an artist fashioning an emotional experience for the reader. You keep in mind your allegiance to real events and experiences as you understand them, but your focus shifts to the work of making a story of them. You craft scenes, coin metaphors, and create dramatic expressions of what you recall taking place. Your vocation becomes storytelling, but not just any kind of storytelling. Evocative autoethnographies are bound by what actually happened. But the stories we write also are compositions that have texture and depth that differentiate this genre of the human sciences from the genres of factual transmission associated with traditional social science. Evocative autoethnography has to merge painstaking empirical work with taxing artistic labor. In autoethnography, the raw materials of ethnographic inquiry are transformed into a blended genre in which ethnography is fused with literary art. You use techniques of fiction writing to bring the emotional and subjective meanings of fact-based stories to life, encouraging readers to use their experiencing of your experience to reflect critically on their own.

"Are you sure you still want to do evocative autoethnography?" Art chuckles.

Memory Work

Carolyn clears her throat, drawing Art's attention. She glances down at her watch, tapping it several times with her index finger. "Oh, I must be running late," Art says. "We need to bring this part of the session to an end so we have time for the closing we've planned."

"I'll take one more comment or question. Let's see, "Art says, scanning the room for hands. "How about someone who hasn't spoken today? Leon, go ahead."

"Several times you've acknowledged how autoethnographies are steeped in memory. You even referred to 'Bird on the Wirc' as 'a work of memory' and you repeated that a moment ago. But I'm still a little fuzzy on how to do memory work. I'm constantly remembering things, but I don't think of that as work. I assume something more than everyday remembering is involved in memory work."

"You're right, Leon. Remembering is going on all the time, when we're awake as well as when we're asleep. Our existence and experience in the world are largely contingent on memory. My use of the term 'memory work' is intended to make autoethnographers more mindful about its importance. Also, keep in mind that memories are not only important in autoethnography; they're a crucial part of most forms of research in the human sciences. Whenever researchers ask participants to provide responses, accounts, or stories of events they've experienced in the past, they are relying on participants' memories. I use the word 'rely' intentionally because it calls attention to reliability. Are memories reliable? Can they be trusted?

"But let's keep our focus on autoethnography. When we write autoethnography we engage in the activity of remembering, which is so ubiquitous in our lives that we have little or no conscious awareness of the process of remembering itself. Most of us give little thought to what it is that we do when we remember (Casey, 1987). Is remembering akin to retrieving a file from our computer? Have we stored memories of events and experiences in our brains or our minds for use at a later time, the way we reprint an article on a copy machine and place it in a file? What do you think, Leon? Is that how memory works?"

"I'm not sure," Leon replies. "Sometimes I get flashes of memories that take me back to past events. I can visualize a scene that took place years earlier as if it's happening now, though I know it isn't. It just came to me out of the blue."

"Note how you describe this memory as a passive experience—something that happened *to* you. When we describe memory this way, we unwittingly treat remembering as something inert and inactive. This information processing model induces us to treat memory as akin to data processing by a computer. We register and store incoming impressions of events, experiences, feelings, people, and so on, a copy or replica of which can be accessed and downloaded at a later time. Was this true of your flash, Leon? Did it appear as if it were a copy of the event you were remembering?"

"I didn't question it. What I remembered seemed real and true. But I doubt whether it was an exact replica."

"Good. That's precisely the point. You didn't question why you were remembering this event *now*. Did your recollection have something to do with the place you were in, or the people with which you were engaged? The naïve empiricism associated with an information retrieval model of memory doesn't take into account what is inspiring you to remember this particular event. Treating memory as akin to a copying machine that replicates past experiences, this model ignores the time lapse between what took place in the past and what you remember having taken place *now,* and fails to include any examination of how memories are transformed when they are narrated. Nor can this model help you understand or explain important differences that may exist between remembering to, remembering how, and remembering that. Carolyn wants me to remember to do the shopping. I need to remember how to drive my car. I want Carolyn to remember that she needs to pick me up at the university at five o'clock.

"Remembering is an activity. It is dynamic, vigorous, and lively. The analogies to computer memory, photographic memory and the retrieval of files and disks won't hold up to close scrutiny. We cannot download copies of our past experiences. We do not memorize lived experiences like we do poems or equations that must be reproduced on an exam. Freud (1968) made no bones about the process of recollecting the past in psychoanalysis, which he referred to as an active process of 'working through.' When I use the term 'memory work,' I am alluding to an active process of working through the lived experiences depicted in autoethnographies.

"Subjectivity and temporality play a significant role in what and how I remember. Once the past was there; now it is gone. I want to be faithful to the past, but what I remember of experiences I lived through is anchored by what summons me *now* to remember; and my memory is, in part, a response to what presently inspires my recollections.

"Consider a brief example relevant to 'Bird on the Wire.' My father died suddenly of a heart attack and I was drawn back to memories of my childhood, my interactions with my father, my disappointments and our misunderstandings (Bochner, 1997). My memory was contextualized by current circumstances. Looking back on my childhood—remembering—was a response to my father's death and tied to the *respons*ibility I felt to better understand the relationship he and I had when I was a child. My memory was punctuated by present events, and what I remembered was addressed not only to my present desires but to the other writ large—to my father—whose shadow hovered over my recollections. Was I remembering for him, for me, or for us? What purpose did my memory work serve? How will I use these memories?

"By asking these questions, I place attention on how memory is used in the here and now, and the personal and relational functions it can serve. By doing so, I assume a phenomenology of memory that emphasizes remembering as *an activity that is always under the influence of the present* (Bochner, 2007). The present perspective or frame from which I look at the past *now* is something I must always contend with when I am engaged in the activity of remembering (Kerby, 1991).

"In autoethnography, we must worry not only about the connection between the present *in which* we remember and the past *of which* we remember, but also the relation between what we remember happening *in the past* and the stories we tell about what happened—how we retell or recount the past (see Larson, 2007). As I said earlier, our work as autoethnographers entails making stories, and this means we must find language that fits with the experiences we are recounting. Thus, autoethnography involves two kinds of interrelated work: (1) *memory work* and (2) *story-making work* (Bochner, 2007).

"As works of memory, stories about the past are made, not found. The work of memory begins with the activity of remembering, a working through and toward the past, making what has been absent come into presence. Kerby (1991) points out that the material of recollection, the content of what we remember, is like the product of an archaeological dig, a trace of the past in need of interpretation. Terms such as 'remembering' and 'recollecting' remind us that the result of memory work always involves transformation; it is not the past, only a form or representative of the past. Thus, we are engaged in an active re-making of the past, transforming *then* to *now*. Freud saw that the truth of the past could not be reached directly, but required a long and painstaking excavation of the traces, tokens, and images of the past (Brill, 1938) expressed through the activities of remembering and narrating.

"So to answer your question more directly, Leon, when I talk about memory as *work*, I signify that remembering is active and continual; it is personal, political, emotional, and relational. Memory is also a destination, a place we inhabit or revisit in order to question and reflect on the meaning of the past. That's what I mean when I say memory is inquiry. My research into the past requires me to dwell awhile in the space of memory, urging memory to speak.

"Even if we bracket the difficult challenge of grasping the truth in our memories, we still come up against the narrative challenge of finding language that is adequate to represent the past in order to achieve a narrative truth. Every autoethnographic story returns the storyteller to the past, and all such stories can be viewed as retroactive re-description and re-experiencing of human actions and behavior.

"My memory of events is my memory *now*; it is what I know and remember *now*, not what I knew *then* in the past; the most I can say is it is knowledge *from* the past and not necessarily knowledge *about* the past (Hacking, 1995). Freud went so far as to question whether we have any memories at all *from* our childhood. He believed that we possess only memories *relating* to our childhood (Harrison, 2008). The point is not to question whether the events actually took place but rather to question whether the events under the descriptions we apply to them took place. We should not underestimate the complexity of this question. As time passes, we rethink, re-describe, even re-feel the past as part of our ongoing sense-making endeavors.

"When we compose stories from memories of our lived history, we can't help but revise the past retroactively, using processes of languaging and describing that modify the past. What we see and claim as 'true' today may not have been 'true' at the time the actions we are describing were performed. Thus, we need to resist the temptation to attribute intentions and meanings to events *now* that they did not have at the time they were experienced (see Larson, 2007). Whatever intentions or meanings we attribute arrive to us via the vast space between *then* and *now*.

"The conclusion that follows from this analysis of the workings of memory and story-making is that truth in autoethnography is not a literal truth but a poetic one, not a historical truth but a narrative one. We are striving for honesty, authenticity, clarity, and meaningfulness, interrogating the past to root out its emotional truths. Our truth is a human truth.

"The neurologist Oliver Sacks (2013) could not find any evidence of a mechanism in the brain that could ensure the truth of one's recollections. 'The events of the world,' he wrote, 'are experienced and constructed in a highly subjective way…and differently reinterpreted or re-experienced whenever they are recollected…. Frequently, our only truth is narrative truth, the stories we tell each other, and ourselves—the stories we continually re-categorize and refine' (p. 11)."

"Doesn't that disturb you?" Leon asks.

"Not at all. The way I look at it, we have the real on our side. The self is in a constant state of change over the course of a person's life. Anything we can write about life ought to be understood as conditional, incomplete, and unsettled. What happened to us in the past may be fixed, but our memory of it, and what we can say about it, will keep changing as long as we live.

"This seems like a good time to bring Carolyn into the conversation, since the book she wrote on *Revision* (Ellis, 2009) relates directly to narrative truth as we've been discussing it."

Revision

Carolyn stands. "Thanks, Art. That's a hard act to follow. I'll try to personalize what you've been saying and provide a concrete example. I promise to be brief, since we want to conserve time for an appropriate ending to the workshop.

"In *Revision*, I start with some autoethnographic stories I have written over the last 25 years. I order them chronologically and include the interpretations I had written then about what the stories meant to me. Around these segments, I wrap a framing story about the curve of my life—the intersection of the personal and professional—as I moved from small town rural America, to the more urban North, then Florida, and finally back to the rural southern mountains of North Carolina. Coming full circle, I try to understand and make sense ethically of the life I have lived and the person I have been and have become, my love for family and my grief over family members I have lost, the conflicting values of the communities in which I have lived, and the autoethnographic work I have come to do.

"Within this framing story, I re-present, re-examine, and re-vision the stories I have published by writing new stories into the gaps, including and reacting to voices of other scholars and students whose responses and critiques were evoked by my work. Then I add meta-autoethnographic responses that include current reflections, narrative vignettes, alternative explanations, and critical analyses that serve to fast-forward these stories to the present. Thus I alter the frame in which I wrote the original stories, ask questions I didn't ask then, consider others' responses to the original story, and include vignettes of related experiences that now affect the way I look back upon these experiences.

"My goal was to turn the narrative snapshots I had written in the past into a form akin to a video—the kind of text in motion that Art was talking about—one in which I drag and drop in new experiences and revised interpretations of old storylines, then reorder and restory them. I tack back and forth between now and then, where 'now' keeps evolving, and 'then' moves from denoting the distant past to representing the recent past and several points in time and memory.

"I try to make sense of my experience in as deep and layered a way as I can, following the paths back and forward, providing a story and frame that marks and holds the scenes in place, at least for now, one that moves from beginning to end and circles back to the beginning again.

"My hope is that my revisions move readers to 'contemplate similar ways of accessing [their] own lives' (Birkerts, 2008, p. 22). I want readers to consider how partial, tentative, and incomplete our stories and memories can be; how throughout our lives we constantly revise, reframe, and reinterpret our lives, yet feel a desire to view our life as a continuous and coherent whole. Revision allows us to expand and deepen our understandings of the lives we have led and the culture in which we have lived, offering alternatives to staying stuck in the same old interpretations. We can seize opportunities to compose a story for ourselves that continues to be worth living (Ellis, 2009, pp. 12–13).

"So what is the true story of one's life? How does memory affect the truth of that life? These questions will continue to be a source of concern, controversy, and debate among qualitative researchers. Recognizing the partial and situated truth of any life we represent in words, we try to use our stories to make our readers feel, think, question, consider, and engage with life, ours and their own. We try to do this as mindfully as we are capable, following the practices that Art and I have talked about during this workshop. We write our stories with conviction but pepper them with doubt."

Carolyn and Art take a bow together, signifying the end of the session but not the workshop. When participants' clapping quiets, Carolyn says, "Take one last short break while we rearrange the room for the final act." Wondering what is about to take place, participants hang around watching and talking. Carolyn and Art push back chairs to create space, pull down the projector screen, and turn on their laptop computer. Two newcomers enter the room and greet Carolyn and Art. Participants quickly take seats.

Coda

Restoring Harmony

Carolyn begins, "Remember the consent form in your packet that you signed allowing us to record these sessions?" Participants nod.

"Good. We're grateful for your support and cooperation. Now Art and I want to give something to you in return. We've actually been working on our book for the past year, and about two months ago we invited an artist I know to collaborate with us on a design for the cover. Good news! The cover is finished and the artist, Csaba Osvath, is in the room with us today."

Carolyn directs attention toward Csaba. Then she nods toward Art, who clicks the computer mouse. Immediately, the large screen is saturated in color. The workshop participants gasp at the beauty and intricacy of glistening pieces of glass, and admire the vivid embracing figurines that seem to move outward toward them. In mass, they lean forward, seeking to catch sight of the treasures peeking through the translucent shards. Carolyn waits a moment while participants talk to each other.

"When we found out Csaba and his wife Erica were going to attend the Congress and present a story about the process of designing the cover, we invited them to enact a performative reading of their story for you. We think their performance will provide a fitting close to the workshop.

"It gives me great pleasure to introduce Csaba Osvath and Erica Newport," Carolyn continues. "Csaba is a graduate student in the College of Education at the University of South Florida, pursuing literacy studies with a special focus on qualitative methods and arts based research. I first met Csaba when he audited my autoethnography class. His research explores the epistemological and pedagogical dimensions of art making in literacy education. In his current work, he is creating a mixed media collage technique and an artistic method for knowledge acquisition and production in educational settings. Growing up in Hungary, he studied theology and horticulture prior to undertaking graduate studies and service as an artist and educator in the United States. He secured a doctorate in arts and theology in 2006 and was awarded the Tibor Chikes scholarship. Csaba is a studio artist who works in shadow puppetry, pen and ink drawing, large-scale installations, oil painting, photography, clay sculpting, kilned formed glass, mosaic, and mixed media glass. He has participated in numerous fine art exhibitions nationally and internationally, including those at the Ringling College of Art and Design in Florida and the Buda Castle in Budapest.

"Erica Newport is a doctoral candidate in the College of Journalism and Communications at the University of Florida (UF). She has taught courses in editing, feature writing, and communications, and worked as a writing and editing coach for long-form storytelling at an NPR affiliated media outlet at UF— WUFT, 89.1, and PBS media. She served as a judge for the 2014 Society of American Travel Writers and was invited to write and present short stories from a magical realism perspective at the highly respected Haystack Institute in Deer Isle, Maine. Her current research is focused on race, violence, alienation, and news media. Prior to her graduate studies, she worked as a print and digital journalist and covered issues affecting marginalized groups.

"And now…"

Restoring Harmony
by Csaba Osvath and Erica Newport

Harmony (July, 2004)

"Csaba, would you please put aside your art work while we're having dinner? You haven't stopped since we got home over three hours ago." With a sweeping motion of her hand, my wife Erica gestures for me to move my cutting board, a stack of construction paper, and cutting tools to the basement.

"This is our dinner table; it's for eating," she says, stating the obvious, "and your art materials are all over it. It's a mess. And so is the rest of our house," she says, now glancing behind my chair. "Look, there's paper all over the floor."

Erica is right. I have made a mess. But I also have stumbled, cut-by-cut, upon something fresh and inviting. I have never experienced such a flow of creative expression. For the first time, I am creating paper cutout compositions without deliberate planning, outlining, or sketching. The improvisation is liberating!

"Hold on, just one second," I say, quickly crumbling my last paper cutout figurine and tossing it on the floor. I pull out a new sheet of dark blue construction paper from the pile. Out of the corner of my eye, I see Erica, hands on her hips, head tilted. Her cat eyes practically hiss at me. With one quick and deliberate cut, I release a new figurine from its paperbound existence.

"Here," I exclaim. "What do you think?"

I hold up the cutout for Erica to see. Her earlier irritation begins to dissolve. Relaxing her posture, she stares at the figurine. In a muted voice she says, "I like it." I position the dark blue figure onto

259

a sheet of light blue construction paper, next to a similar bright red figure I had cut out earlier.

"Oh, I see," she says. With one hand, she holds the background paper in place. With the other, she slowly moves the blue figurine closer to the red one until they merge. I feel uneasy about her intervention into my original composition, but I am too excited about the new configuration to object.

"I didn't even outline them!" I say with pride. "No sketches, and no templates; just one uninterrupted cut." I lift the cutting knife to demonstrate my technique. Erica ignores my presentation and looks over the newly arranged configuration.

"Quite good. I think you should title it 'Harmony.'"

"Harmony," I repeat the word, drawing it out. "H-A-R-R-M-O-O-N-E-E. Yes, I like that."

Broken Harmony (August, 2015)

"Here," Erica says. I feel her hand touch my wrist. "You should take another pain pill. It's been four hours."

I experience the coolness of the capsule in my open palm. The touch of Erica's warm fingertips lingers on my hand. She presses a plastic straw to the side of my mouth, which I momentarily reject. When I reach to remove the eye mask from my left eye, her hand brushes my arm. "Just leave it on. It's okay. I'm right here."

Supported by small decorative pillows, I lift myself into a half-sitting posture by turning on to my side, resting on one elbow. I am relieved to no longer be lying face down. I've voluntarily confined myself to live in darkness ever since my emergency eye surgeries to correct a fully detached retina and macula in my right eye two weeks ago. Although I can still see out of my left eye, nausea and headaches fade in and out whenever I try to use it. A nurse informed me these effects were symptomatic of the double vision now affecting my working eye, a result of the surgery on my problematic eye. I use Erica's black sleep mask to keep both eyes covered nearly all the time.

"I want to die!" I utter dramatically. "The pills are messing with my head. They cause strange dreams. Nightmares really,"

Erica dismisses my complaints, pressing me to swallow the medicine. "It's better than living in pain," she says.

"I'm not sure," I answer, but lift the pill to my mouth and swallow it without hesitation. I am aware of the touch of the cold glass on my right hand, as she hands me water.

"Slowly," she warns. "See, I take good care of you."

"Thank you," I answer to assure her.

"You should lie back now and try to rest."

I kick the one remaining blanket off the bed, shoving it toward the two others already on the floor. They provide evidence of my constant wrestling with my body to lie still. "Rest? I haven't rested for weeks."

"I know," Erica says. "But I don't think you want to go through a repeat surgery because you moved too much and the eye couldn't heal properly." She's right. I can't imagine another eye surgery. I couldn't face spending another two weeks face-down on a U-shaped airplane headrest, lying still that long again, unable to turn my head for fear of disturbing the gas bubble holding my retina in place.

"Would you like me to read your e-mails?" Erica asks.

"Sure," I say.

I hear her push in the chair toward the computer and recognize the clicking sounds of the keyboard as she types my password. She takes several deep breaths. The long inhales and exhales as she waits for my inbox to load suggest a weary duty; she hasn't slept much for weeks. Then there is silence. "You have a message from Dr. Ellis."

"Read it to me."

> Hi Csaba, Art and I are writing a book on autoethnography based on workshops we've been doing on autoethnography for the last 20 years. It will likely be called: *Evocative Autoethnography: Writing Lives and Telling Stories.*
>
> Originally I had planned to discuss with you the possibility of using some of your art on the cover, if we could find something we agreed would work. Then you had the eye issue, and I didn't think it a good time to approach you about this. But after thinking about it a while, I thought I'd at least introduce the possibility...

"Do you think I can do this?" I ask after a moment of silence. I take off the eye mask and lift my head to see Erica's expression. But the afternoon sunlight entering the west side of the bedroom blinds my sensitive eyes and my face immediately collapses back onto the head-rest.

"Put your mask back on," Erica reminds. "Honestly, I don't think you can handle taking on such a project, especially in your current state. Do you have an old art piece they might use instead?"

The sun from the window burns the back of my neck. "I'd rather create something new." I pause to think. She's quiet. "I think I'll create something from glass."

Erica exits the room, saying under her breath, "No, absolutely not, your surgeon would never approve. You can't see well enough to work, especially with raw fragments of glass."

Restoring Harmony (September, 2015)

"Dr. Ellis and Dr. Bochner love 'Harmony,' the paper cut-out piece," I tell Erica. "I sent them photos of glass work I have done, and they chose that one. They asked if I could recreate it in glass."

I sense Erica's disappointment, as she answers, "But you lied about your condition. I think you pressured them by suggesting the cover art should be made of glass. You should have let them use 'Harmony' as it was."

She's right, but I relish this opportunity to escape from my stationary existence and return to my work as an artist. I miss the deliberate process of putting tiny glass fragments together until they form a complete image. "Dr. Butler said that I can slowly return to my daily routines, including art making."

"Yes, but didn't you hear him also say that the artistic outcome might be disappointing?" Erica reminds. "You have significant double vision, and you can't even read more than ten minutes at a time." She looks away and adds, "I think it's all about your ego. You could really hurt yourself in the process of creating a new art piece."

I protest by appearing to sleep.

A few days later, I go to my studio, which I had abandoned abruptly in early August. All the projects I was working on before the surgery stare at me, unfinished. The room looks like a forgotten battlefield with decaying corpses. I reach for my glass-cutting tool, but my lack of depth perception causes my hand to miss and it lands on a table two inches from the cutter.

Erica is right. This is about me. But it's not about recreating harmony; it's about restoring harmony—my harmony. Returning to art offers me a chance for restoration.

I know what the creative process requires of me, but I am losing confidence in my abilities. I see the world differently now; I see it through a lens of pain. Swollen, dry, and unable to produce tears, my left eye feels like a foreign object. Each attempt to focus on some manifestation of reality brings me the feeling of needles piercing an open wound. I reach for eye drops for relief.

Feeling overwhelmed, I stare at the printout of the two cutout figures in "Harmony," wishing I still had the original three-dimensional art piece to examine. I try to envision a final product for the book cover: the intricate glass mosaic covering the entire surface; thousands of broken translucent pieces assembled into a whole; all surrounding the two raised and embracing figures in bright red and deep blue.

First, I must rescale the image. "For the cover, I need a larger ratio," I mumble. "This should be easy." I take out a blank sheet of paper the exact size of the planned, new composition.

I adjust the eye patch my doctor referred to as an "eye shield," meant to protect my surgically repaired eye. I hope it will reduce the intensity of my double vision. Since I still cannot see well enough, I put my prescription glasses over the patch. I stare at the photo of "Harmony" for some time, waiting for my vision to adjust and improve. Under the patch, my eye burns from the steady drain of fluid produced by its healing. I place a cotton ball between my glasses and the patch to keep this eye shut, while I struggle to keep the other eye open.

This is horrible. I'm glad no one can see me like this. Then as I look at the small printout of "Harmony," I start to feel nauseous. The image waxes and wanes between blurry and hostile. Holding a pencil rigidly, I draw slowly, enlarging the art for a new ratio. The design is simple, but each time I draw, the figures look different. I fill the wastebasket with my failed attempts. Anxiety churns to panic, then anger. What once seemed an effortless task now feels impossible. Sick and frustrated, I stop.

I leave the studio, lie down on my stomach, and close my eyes. In my mind, I hear Erica's response, "You made a commitment without acknowledging your limitations."

"But at this point, I can't tell them I am unable to do this," I say to myself as I struggle to sleep. At some point in my restlessness, I grasp the amber bottle knowing that the pills inside will soon quell the voice in my head.

The next day, when I go back to my studio, something shifts in me. I realize that I must return to the work as an inexperienced beginner. I place the black and white copy of "Harmony" on my desk, take out my old ruler, and mark the edge of the paper with equal distances to create a grid. Like a child, I learn the basics of replication. I make a similar grid on the scaled paper and begin measuring distances between lines with a ruler, carefully copying the original image, paying close attention to intersecting lines and distances. I move my pencil slowly and accept the guiding straight lines, as though they are crutches or braces for the lame and injured.

Am I regressing? Have I lost basic skills? Do I have to re-learn my craft? Will I regain the effortlessness in drawing that I took for granted? As I work, my double vision gets worse, forcing me to look more closely in order to differentiate the real lines from the illusionary ones—all for the sake of simply duplicating an image.

I hate the process. I hate the lack of progress. I hate the pain of the burning eye, joined by migraines, nausea, and looming depression. I hate needing the aid of the grid lines, being forced to distinguish the visual illusions, and being unable to judge distances on paper and in everything I try to do.

"I am so far from finishing this piece!" I say to Erica, my hope deflated. "Look." I show her the enlarged version of "Harmony." "This took two days of my life." She does not answer. There is nothing she can say to help. "I wasn't ready to do this," I admit.

The following day, I return to the studio, ready to release "Harmony" from its paper bound existence. I use scissors and precision knives to cut out the embracing figures before tracing them onto the foam board, which will give them a three-dimensional quality. What once required a few minutes of work now takes hours. I hold the image close to my face and with trembling hands I slowly cut along the lines, hoping to avoid the illusionary ones. Suddenly my consciousness shifts again. As I hold the first paper figure, now removed from its context for the first time, a sense of relief melts away my days of angst. I am learning new skills and making progress. I send a photo of the images to Drs. Ellis and Bochner, so they can follow my process.

In the glasswork I usually construct, a viewer can look closely through the transparent glass fragments and see a collage of imagery. Thus, the next day, feeling more confident, I ask Drs. Ellis and Bochner to send me photos of images from their daily lives and scenes that move them as they write *Evocative Autoethnography*.

I open my laptop and am happy to see several attachments from Dr. Ellis. I download the photos and drag them to my image browser. Curious, Erica leans over my shoulder. I click through the images one-by-one.

"That one is neat," she says, pointing to two photos of their hands positioned on the computer keyboard.

"Yes, I have to use those," I respond. "This one, as well—the mailbox in front of their home in the mountains. Also look at the photos of highlighted documents on their computer screens with memos and suggestions written on them."

"Oh, wait." Erica leans in for a better look. "They edit each other's work like we do."

I print the photos on light blue paper to complement the bright red and dark blue color scheme of the composition. I print and then play with the fragments of their written work, cutting and pasting. I love this part of the process. The double vision doesn't interfere, so I spend a few hours purposefully placing and securing each picture and written text fragment around the figures on the foam-based artboard's surface. I also read and reflect on the written and visual content of these fragmented pieces, feeling this collaborative process is bringing us all closer. I have the sense that I am making a lasting and uniquely improvised record of our intersecting lives.

The next day, I begin the slow and painstaking process of covering the surface with the glass shards, individually gluing each tiny piece to the surface. Rather than working with unified shapes, I search out the best fitting shard or use tools to reshape the glass, in order to maintain an organic design. In my inventory of broken pieces, I have glass shards from demolished homes, synagogues, and churches, and broken glass fragments handed down from other artists, many who are no longer creating, and some who are no longer alive. I also use hand-made glass that I have created in the kilns of my studio. Handling broken glass cuts my fingers; thus each work mixes with some trace residue of my corporeal life.

This process of working with glass fragments has always been a slow and iterative process. But given my eye condition, it is now harder than I thought it would be. After 30 minutes, my eyes are failing and I have covered only three square inches of the 166-square-inch surface. Panic alternates with cycling thoughts about how to complete this composition. As each cut of glass fills the barren background, the panic comes less frequently and intensely. Hours are lost in this flow to the point where I create through my sense of touch, often closing my eyes to rest. Still, I perceive progress.

It takes nearly 80 hours of work to position all the glass fragments into their places. When I situate the last one, I am overwhelmed by emotion. This routinely happens when I complete a new piece, but this time the feeling has a new, unknown quality. I feel more than satisfaction or relief. I feel at home, safe again, restored. The title "Restoring Harmony" reveals not only its "adaptation" of and origin in "Harmony," but also its role as testimony. Despite continued pain and reduced abilities, I now celebrate within a restored equilibrium. My work has become healing, and through this creative process I have experienced restoration.

One final step remains. Like the celebrant of a religious rite, completing a sacred liturgy, I carefully begin filling the space between glass fragments with colored mortar I have prepared. This process allows me to come into contact with each piece, as I clean and polish its surface. Using a brush, carving tools, and a moist sponge, I slowly remove the excess grout, completing the artwork.

I place "Restoring Harmony" on my photo board to take an image for the publisher. When I look at the screen of my camera, I am aware that the photograph makes my work appear static. But when it is displayed, the glass-covered surface will infinitely interact with and reflect the light present in the surrounding environment. The combination of iridescent, opaque, dichroic, and translucent glass will offer new experiences to each viewer, transforming what is seen from various angles dependent on context and light.

I imagine my art hanging in the home of Carolyn and Art. I imagine them looking at it as the sun streams into their home.

"Restoring Harmony" is no longer merely testimony and proof of my ability to create. "Restoring Harmony" has become a mirror. When I look at it closely, I see my fragmented reflection in the background. I see and recognize myself on the surface of the broken shards of glass, which form fragmented mirrors that reflect my image.

Light particles leave my face and return from the surface of glass, interacting with a healing retina. Restoration is a continuum, which may never reach completion. But accepting, partaking, and being embedded in restoration, I feel fulfilled. My imperfections, pain, and disabilities are part of the whole and they fit in perfectly, as does each piece of glass shard in "Restoring Harmony."

~

Participants clap as Csaba and Erica sit down and Carolyn and Art move to the front of the room. "Thank you, Csaba and Erica," Carolyn says. "Your story provides an exquisite closing to our workshop. You put autoethnography as art and art as autoethnography on display, showing evocative, compassionate, and healing aspects of both." The participants applaud again.

Art clears his throat and the applause dwindles. "Let me tell you why I think the cover fits our book project so perfectly. The cover carries a reminder of the connection between collage, the lives we humans actually live, and the ways in which autoethnography underscores relationality and connection. Donald Kuspit (2010) refers to collage as 'a demonstration of the many becoming the one, with the one never fully resolved because of the many that continue to impinge upon it' (p. 128). As we've indicated throughout the workshop, evocative autoethnography keeps the possibilities of connection between the one and the many in play, highlighting the never finished, continually becoming, qualities of meanings in motion. What we see, think, and feel about what we've lived through continues to evolve rather than resolve."

"I love how the integrated materials of Csaba's art links to the realities of our daily lives—our hands on the keyboard, the mailbox, our desk, words, and texts," Carolyn adds. "He builds an immediate identification, both real and imagined, between his work of art and viewers' lives."

"Yes, the objects he used were ours, but Csaba's collage makes them yours," Art says, pointing to the participants. "As viewers, you can use them to recover the sensations of your own lives.

"Collage also shares a feeling kind of truth with autoethnography," Art continues. "It invites viewers to rearrange the fragmented materials. Those observing participate by giving form to connections they themselves make among and with the materials. The result is a kind of subjective concreteness activated by viewers, which also is what we seek from readers of autoethnography."

Carolyn and Art join hands. "That's our workshop." The participants stand and applaud, then move to speak one-on-one to Art, Carolyn, Csaba, and Erica. Gradually, the room empties.

"Hey, let's get our traditional, post-workshop ice cream cone," Carolyn says to Art. "Erica and Csaba, want to come? It's the best ice cream in town. Our treat." Csaba and Erica nod enthusiastically.

"You're on," says Art, "but we better hurry before the ice cream shop closes."

THE END

"Maternal Connections"[1]
by Carolyn Ellis

With one hand, she holds tightly to the support bar along the wall of the bathroom. I take her other hand gently in mine, wash each finger, noting the smoothness of her skin, the beauty of her long, slender fingers. "My fingernails," she says, "they're dirty." Without speaking, I run my index nail, covered with a washcloth, under each of her nails, systematically snapping out the dirt as I go. It's a good sign that she cares. Until now, she hasn't been that concerned even about urinating in bed.

When I push hard on the soap dispenser, small globs of thick, pink, liquid soap, smelling of perfumed bleach, drop onto the translucent washcloth. I load the white cloth with many squirts, hoping to wash away the lingering smell of feces, urine, perspiration, bile bags, plastic tubes, stale hair oils, and hospital odors.

She extends her arm and I slowly wash from wrist to shoulder, observing the intrusion of the spreading black bruises marking needle points. Her washed hand holds onto my wrist for support now as I unclasp her other hand from the railing. I repeat the process on that side.

"I'm going again," she says, sucking in slowly through open lips and closed teeth, eyebrows raised as though she is asking my permission and apologizing at the same time. I'm glad she is sitting on the toilet. It'll be less of a mess than before.

"That's okay," I respond, "maybe this will be the last time. Hopefully the laxative has run its course."

I hold her hand and touch her shoulder gently as she lets it all go. Then, "I'm sorry about last night," she says. "It seemed like it was every hour. You shouldn't have to do that."

"I didn't mind," I say, remembering my reflex gag reaction the first time her bowels exploded in the night. Only my determination that she not know how much the smell—that rotten, chemical odor—bothered me kept me from adding my regurgitation to the brown liquid I poured into the toilet on her behalf. "I'm glad I was here for you."

"Yeah, the nurses don't come right away," she says. "Even with you here, some ended up on the bed, didn't it?"

"Yes, but now we know better how to do it, get the bedpan under you sooner. It helps when you raise your hips."

"If anybody told me I'd have to be doing this. . ."

". . . you used to do it for me," I interrupt. We laugh like two good friends sharing a memory.

Being careful of the tubes and IVs, I unsnap and remove her soiled gown. She tries to help. I cover the front of her body with a towel, to protect her from cold. "It feels good when you wash my back," she says, and I continue rubbing. When she shivers, I run the washcloth under hot water. I wonder about washing the rest of her body.

Around front, I wash her belly, noting the faded scars of my younger brother's cesarean birth—and shudder at the reminder that he is now dead—and I look closely at the new scars of the gall bladder surgery. Her stomach is puffy, but almost flat now, not rounded as before. The extra skin hangs loosely. Then her legs. Although her skin is dry and flaky, I admire her thin, almost bony, yet still shapely, legs. Our bodies have the same form, I note. Long, slender, and graceful limbs, fatty layers on top of the hips and belly, and a short and thick waist.

I move to her breasts, still large and pendulous. Now they hang to her waist and, as her shoulders curve forward, they rest on her belly, like mine, only lower.

I take one tenderly in my hand, lift it gently from her belly to wash it, noting the rash underneath. "Would you like cream on that?"

"Oh, yes, it's real sore." She holds her breast while I rub in the cream.

Feeling no particular emotion, I observe from a distance. Her body is my body, my body in thirty-six years. So this is what it will look and be like. I see.

I hand her the soaped washcloth. "Can you wash your butt," I ask, "and between your legs?"

"I think so," she replies, taking the washcloth into her left hand as she holds onto the support bar with her right hand to balance that side of herself a few inches above the seat. My pubic hair also will be thin and gray, I think, as I notice hers. Then I walk away, to give her the illusion of privacy.

"Are you ready to get back in bed now?" I ask.

"Yes, I'm worn out."

I extend both arms. The bile bag pinned to her gown threatens to become entangled in our embrace. "Put it around my neck," she cleverly suggests. "It'll be my necklace." I smile, appreciating her humor, which bonds us and makes it easier to refer to the bag. But what a breakdown in boundaries—her bile is on the outside of her body for everyone to see, more personally revealing than the butt that sticks out of the back of her gown!

I hold my arms out straight again. When she grabs on, she and I pull her to a standing position. When she winces in pain, I embrace her around her middle, steadying her for the long journey back to bed, eight feet away. The tubes extending from her chest and abdomen, the bile bag necklace—all are properly positioned. She shuffles her feet in baby steps, all the while holding onto my outstretched arms. She looks into my eyes as I walk backwards, to pick up my cues, when to move forward, when to turn. We are intimately connected. We are totally trusting.

Taking care of her feels natural, as though she is my child. The love and concern flowing between us feels like my mom and I are falling in love. The emotionality continues during the four days and nights I stay with her in the hospital. My life is devoted temporarily to her well-being. She knows it and is grateful. I am grateful for the experience. I do not mind that she is dependent on me. I am engrossed by our feeling, and by the seemingly mundane but, for the moment, only questions that matter. Are you dizzy? In pain? Comfortable? Do you want to be pulled up in bed? Can't you eat one more bite? Do you need to pee? Have gas? Want water? Prefer to sleep now? As I help with these events, I do not question their meaning, as I so often do about most things in my life.

While my mom sleeps, I take my daily walk down the hall to peer at the newborn babies. On the other side of the glass partition, there are three—one boy covered in blue and two girls in pink. I wince at the institutional marking of gender roles and then shrug. I strain to read the identification cards, to have a story about each one: birthday, weight, length, parents' names—not much to go on.

A man stares intently at one of the girls. Knowing the answer, I ask anyway, "Are you the father?" He nods yes and beams. "She has jaundice," he says, "a mild case." I feel his bond to her even through the glass pane. I recognize the connection from the feelings I have for my mother. He leaves and another young man, in his early twenties, arrives. Ignoring the young son pulling on his pants leg for attention, this man stands off to the side, to peer through the glass into an inner room almost out of view. Out of the corner of my eye, I watch and imagine his story. His new baby must be in there. Perhaps he is worried about his newborn, like I am worried about my mother. If he could just get a glimpse, or better yet, do something, he would feel better.

I continue watching, fantasizing that one of the babies is mine, and try to generate what the feeling would be. What would it be like to take the baby home? To bond? The dependence? Experiencing unconditional love for my mother makes me, for the moment, crave to feel it toward and from a child as well. Do I just want someone who will wash me when I'm seventy-nine? What if something is wrong with the baby? What about my career? Travel plans? Yet how can I omit this meaning-giving experience from my life?

When I return, my mom is having her vitals read by a nurse who "usually works in the nursery," my mom announces. "How old is the oldest mother you have had?" I ask nonchalantly, hoping my question is not too transparent.

"Forty-two," the nurse answers.

I must look disappointed, because she adds quickly, "But I have only worked there for eighteen months, I'm sure there have been some older. Yes, I'm sure."

I'd be almost forty-four before my first child could be born, I think, turning back to my mother.

"Groaning from the Soul"[1]
by Carolyn Ellis

Arm in arm, we cautiously yet rhythmically make our way over the uneven cobblestones toward the memorial at Treblinka. To steady Jerry, I grasp his left arm tightly: his daughter-in-law Jo Anna does the same with his right. Three of Jerry's grandchildren and our guide traverse the path ahead of us. Jerry, Jo Anna, and I slowly follow the trail bordered by large egg-shaped stones symbolizing the bob-wired boundaries of the camp. We walk alongside the row of railroad ties carved of concrete representing the path of the old railroad tracks.

Momentarily, I conjure the image of the trains arriving there during the Holocaust and of the peoples' terror as they were herded down the "road to Heaven" to their fates at this death camp—the men shoved to the right and the women and children to the left. "To be showered and deloused," they were told. From the exhibits at the small museum we visited and the history I have read, I know that approximately 800,000 people died at Treblinka, almost all immediately upon arrival. I visualize the crowds getting off at the fake train station, with the fake clock and fake ticket window casting a last ray of hope. How much worse could this be than the long journey in a crowded boxcar with dehydrated and emaciated people defecating and dying during the trip? They soon would find out.

I wonder if Jerry and Jo Anna are thinking similar thoughts as we walk quietly toward the monument. The silence feels overwhelming and a sense of tragedy permeates the air. A slight wind blows and birds chirp, but I quickly block them out, pushing away any semblance of peacefulness that threatens to permeate the edge of this dense forest on a summer day. The atmosphere and the slow, steady pace remind me of the many times I have walked the hill to the burial site in my home town where my mother, father, brother, and aunt are "laid to rest." Oh, how I miss them at this moment. I wonder, is there any "rest" here? I can feel Jerry's tenseness, apprehension, and sadness through my arm linked with his, and I sense—and share—his desire and reluctance to approach the towering monument up ahead. Please may he find here some sense of what he is looking for—be it peace, connection, or release of grief. He may have no idea of what to hope for. I know I don't; I am just glad to be here, with him, on this journey. Though I think of videotaping, my camera hangs by my side. After quickly filming the entryway, I sense it is disrespectful to turn it on, to record this emotional, spiritual, and sacred experience.

After ten minutes, we see ahead the garden of approximately 17,000 multi-shaped and multi-colored stones ranging from the size of a hand to a large tombstone. I take a deep breath and imagine the piles of burning bodies in the crematorium. I imagine the women waiting in line, naked, their heads shaven, holding their babies close to their chests as long as they can, while the men are gassed first, their moans and screams shattering any remnant of hope. Fifteen to twenty minutes is all it took. Did it seem a lifetime or a quick moment to them? Maybe both. I imagine the women and children now herded into the crematorium after the men were shoveled out in heaps on the other side, some still gasping. I imagine the children—the ones who had not already been flung against walls, their brains splattering—tossed in on top of the women who were made to stand with their hands in the air to make room for more. Though I don't fully understand why, I must make myself imagine the horror, though I know, and am glad, that I really cannot.[2]

We talk quietly as we walk, commenting on what we see in front of us. Jerry stops several times to blow his nose. "I feel like I'm finally able to pay my respects," he says, "to come to their grave. If only there was a marker."

"Maybe we can find the Bodzentyn stone," I say, remembering that one hundred and thirty stones are engraved with the names of the towns of the victims. Bodzentyn is the location of the small ghetto from which Jerry's mother and younger sister were taken. Delineating the extermination camp, the symbolic gravestones spread out in a circular formation in front of us as far as the eye can see. I fear I have raised Jerry's hopes in vain. Still it's worth a try. If the stone is here, I'm determined to find it.

As we enter the garden, I begin scanning the jagged stones. Quickly, I see what appears to be Bodzentyn imprinted in large letters on a four foot high stone. Could that be? "Come this way," I say to Jerry. "I think I see Bodzentyn."

"What?" asks Jerry, cupping his ear.

Then, "Stay here a moment," I motion, fearing I am wrong, and not wanting him to make the trek for nothing. I quickly approach the stone, and I see that, yes, Bodzentyn is engraved on its front.

"I've found the Bodzentyn marker," I say to Jerry and Jo Anna when I return.

"Really?" Jerry says. His face lights up for a moment before the tears start to fall. "Where?"

"Over there." Jerry walks fast in the direction I point, and Jo Anna and I rush to hold onto him.

"Bodzentyn, there it is," Jo Anna says, as we approach the marker. She and I support Jerry until he can lean on the tombstone shaped marker. He begins to weep, and we begin to cry quietly as he hangs his head over the stone and touches it reverently. We take turns gently rubbing his back, to let him know we are there, then move away, to give him a sense of privacy. Continuing to weep, Jerry lovingly traces each of the engraved letters with the tips of his fingers. His grandson, a Brother in the Catholic Church, approaches and prays aloud with him. I note the small pebbles that visitors have left on top of the marker, signifying permanence and a reminder to all who arrive that others have been here as well and that we are connected and continue through memory.

Our guide from Warsaw stands apart watching the scene. I think of our drive here and how the guide's commentary was halted when Jerry said his mother and sister had died in Treblinka. The guide turned to

Jerry then and began asking him questions. If he had not identified Jerry as a mourning survivor, he likely would be talking to us now, describing what we are seeing, as though we were tourists. Instead he gives us time to grieve on our own. He acknowledges the sacredness of our being there, that it is an event in need of no words.

From a respectful distance, the guide takes a video of Jerry at the stone. Jo Anna also steps back and snaps a few iPad photos of Jerry. With that, I feel I have permission to record the scene, though I too move away and film Jerry for only a short time. Listening to the video later, I hear weeping and sniffling, and it takes a while to recognize the sounds as mine. Even as I write this, I sigh and feel deep sadness, which I experience as a heaviness in my body, an emptiness in my stomach, and tightness in my chest.

Jerry turns away from the stone and signifies with a nod that he is ready to go. "Finally I have been able to grieve," he says. "Before I didn't have a place to come to, no cemetery, nothing." Jo Anna and I link to his arms again and we wander with no purpose around the cemetery, commenting on the names on the stones. We walk toward the tall monument in the center of the garden. Standing at the site of the former gas chamber, the granite tower is shaped like a tall tombstone with a crack down the middle, and capped by a mushroom shaped block covered with carvings of a Menorah and Jewish symbols. Without a word, we then turn back, forgoing a visit to the pits of mass graves, the stone arch that marks the location of the crematorium, and the labor camp section of Treblinka.

We start the long trek back to the car, along the same railroad tracks that brought Jerry's mother and sister to their deaths. Jerry will say later, "The railroad tracks were the hardest part, as I imagined my mother and sister arriving in the boxcar. The death itself," he will add, "was swift; at least I hope it was. And I hope they already had lost their minds from shock so they did not know what was happening."

When Jerry sighs with relief, I consider turning on the video camera. But that would be intrusive, I think, and might interrupt the solemn and contemplative mood. Besides, I can't point the camera toward him and continue holding his arm. It is most important to be with Jerry, to support and feel with him. I feel honored that he invited me to be part of this experience. It feels irreverent to risk making a spectacle out of his grief. I know now that my decision to forego bringing a film crew on this part of our trip together was the right one.

We walk a ways in silence. Still wanting to have a record of this moment, I think that perhaps Jerry and his family might want one as well. I turn on my palm-size video camera, and continue walking with it pointed toward our feet, to unobtrusively record the sounds of our steps and our words. After a while we begin to talk—about suffering, ongoing genocide, death as a relief from suffering, and Treblinka as a memorial. When Jerry says he wishes he could pray better, Jo Anna replies that prayer is "groaning from the soul—it's not the words that matter."

"When I left Bodzentyn I knew I would never see them again," Jerry says, a moan escaping from deep in his throat. "I feel close to them now being here."

"They must be smiling," I say.

"What?" asks Jerry.

"Your mother and sister. To have you here with your daughter-in-law, your wonderful grandchildren. It signifies that their deaths were not in vain. You survived. *You* survived," I repeat with emphasis on 'you.' "And through you their memories live on."

Jerry nods. Then "Do you hear the birds?" I ask Jerry, suddenly becoming aware of the chirping. He says yes. "Their song is beautiful," I say and he agrees. We walk and listen quietly to the serenade.

—

"Bird on the Wire"[1]
by Arthur Bochner

> Under history, memory and forgetting
> Under memory and forgetting, life
> But writing a life is another story
> Incompletion
> (Paul Ricoeur, 2004)

In 1997, I published a story that focused on an epiphany I experienced after I learned that my father had died while I was attending a national communication convention (Bochner, 1997). When I received the news, two worlds collided within me—the personal and the academic and I was forced to confront the large gulf that divided them. As a child, I had experienced my relationship with my father as traumatizing and destructive. Though both of us may have wanted to settle our differences, somehow we never managed to find each other. One day I awoke to the reality that he had grown old and fragile before I could come to terms with the fierce father of my youth. Now, in the aftermath of his death, I had to accept that any chance to rise above these circumstances was gone. I could never prove to be any better as a son than he had been as a father. We would never have a purifying conversation that I could look back on with a sense of resolution and closure. For a long time, I had imagined I would be by his side when he died, holding or stroking him as he passed—as if a tender, loving touch could magically transform a lifetime of painful experience between a father and his son. But now I had to face that his sudden death had stolen my fantasy of a cathartic and healing ending. Our relationship would live on in my mind, but conversation between us had ended. He was gone; *we* were gone.

Fifteen years later, May 2011, I sit here at my desk, reviewing published papers of mine to put into a volume of my collected work (Bochner, 2014). Re-reading my article, "It's About Time: Narrative and the Divided Self," I feel a sudden urge to reopen the door I had closed when I said that "conversation between us had ended" (Bochner, 1997, p. 420). *Did Dad's death really have to be the exclamation point marking the end of conversation between us?*

I suppose all survivors with "unfinished business" continue to go over and over the blown opportunities they had to set things right. What if, just one time, I had summoned the courage to speak my mind? What if he and I had created an opportunity to have that conversation? What would I have said? How would he have responded? *Could one more conversation together have shaped a different memory of who we were and what we meant to each other?*

I close my eyes and imagine my father entering the room. I see him in the doorway and start to rise from my chair, but he waves at me to stay seated, then he takes the chair beside me. *This is it, Art, the chance you've been waiting for all these years.*

***

Like a bird on the wire,
Like a drunk in an old midnight choir,
I have tried in my way to be free.
(Leonard Cohen, 1969)

I was 43 years old when you died. Now I'm 65, only a year younger than you were when you fell off that ladder and broke your hip. Remember? You called the accident 'the beginning of the end.' No more lettering tractor-trailers, storefronts or billboards. No more hard, strenuous, demanding work to justify your existence—nothing left to smother "the lava of nothingness boiling in your gut" (Henry, 1971, p. 181).

When I look in the mirror, I see your face in mine. I see you staring back at me and I think, *he's always going to be there judging me, telling me I don't measure up* (see Roth, 1996).

For a long time, I thought I could break free from your grip by becoming everything you were not. Every three weeks, you brought Leon, the barber, to the house to shave off all my hair (for a dollar). So I let my hair grow down my back. You hated beards; I grew one. You had a hair-trigger temper, so I prided myself on composure and self-control. You were up at the crack of dawn and asleep after the evening news. I became a night owl and a late-sleeper. You were shy and introverted, didn't want to mix with other people, hated to go out in public. I became a college debater and relished the public spotlight.

Then one day I realized that these choices only tightened the noose around my neck. Acting *against* is just another form of submission and dependence. A person can't change the past merely by opposing it. That's an expression of bad faith (Sartre, 2001), an act of self-deception. If I was ever to break free, to weaken your grip on me, I would have to take responsibility for my own psychic life. Isn't that the meaning of freedom?

What did you say? "You don't understand why it's so important to me to be free of you." *"You turned out fine, Art. You're a distinguished university professor. I'm proud of the person you became."* I tremble when I hear you say that, Dad. My academic achievements have little to do with what went on between us. I won't allow you to take credit for what turned out well and I'm not here to blame you for what went wrong either, with perhaps one exception. A man wants to love his father; I know I did. But your actions made it so difficult and confusing. I can still hear the echo of your words when you beat me with your belt—"it's for your own good." Crap. Humiliation and coercion is never good for a person. You wanted me to obey and respect you. That's what you thought you were teaching me. But that's not what I was learning. You earned my respect in other ways. You worked hard, "like a slave" you used to say, ten hours a day, seven days a week. You were honest to a fault and you put every ounce of energy into your work. There was love in those signs, and they expressed all the beauty, joy, and self-discipline missing from the rest of your life.

But what you created through the pleasure of your work, you destroyed through the sham of your fathering. You were a master of the paint brush and a disaster of a parent. The respect you earned in your work, you destroyed in your home. When you beat me, I learned to hate you. I didn't realize until much later how much rage and resentment I felt. When I was a kid, I wasn't allowed to feel. Remember what you used to say, "Be tough. Don't cry." In other words, renounce your feelings. Later, when I was gone—out on my own—and these feelings broke loose, they overwhelmed me. As far as I was concerned you were a rotten bastard, a bully, and a tyrant. I wanted you out of sight and out of mind. But, of course, that just made you figure larger in my life.

You're probably thinking, "You read too many books, Art. Is that something you read in one of those psychology texts? You never said anything like that to me."

No, Dad, I just left home and didn't come back until it was too late. When we reunited more than fifteen years later, you weren't the father I remembered. Your vigor and energy had disappeared and the sparkle was gone from your eyes; you couldn't hear me unless I raised my voice and your steel, muscular body of 230 odd pounds had softened into a fleshy 160.

I recall thinking, "Who is this man sitting in the corner pretending to be my father? That's not my father. That's a fragile, gentle, frightened old man standing on the edge of oblivion."

Now I had all the time in the world to talk to you—and nothing to say. What good would it have done to tell this father what I felt about the other father? The situation was tragic and sorrowful. Once I had convinced myself I had no right to feel; now that I no longer was denied the power to feel, the pain was palpable, but I had nobody with whom to share it.

I'm not blaming you for getting old and sick. If you were not the same father, neither was I the same son. If I had been "blind to the impress of your bearing" on myself, as Philip Larkin expressed it (see Rorty, 1989, p. 23), at least I was aware of the surrogate fathers—mentors, friends, and lovers—with whom I had co-created a life I had not imagined possible. When I looked at you staring blankly across the room, I knew I was not there to hear you say "forgive me" or to blame you for any lingering trauma I carried from the past. There could be no redemption and no closure, no completion, final resolution, or catharsis. There was nothing to finish, only "a web of relations to be rewoven" (Rorty, 1989, p. 43). Then you died and I was on my own—as I had been for many years—still facing the work of memory and mourning, still feeling the need "to reshape a past which the past never knew" (Rorty, 1989, p. 29), not so much to question my being or yours, but rather to find a way into *ours*."

***

Like a worm on a hook,
Like a knight from some old fashioned book,
It was the shape, the shape of our love that twisted me.
(Leonard Cohen, 1969)

"You made sure I would never depend on you no matter how much I might need to. How often did you tell me the same story over and over again until it burned on my brain?

"My father threw me out when I was sixteen," you said. "He made me quit school in the 10th grade. Told me to go get a job and bring back some money so we could have food to eat."

You made it clear I would be responsible for myself as soon as I graduated high school. "If you want something, go and earn it." That was your mantra.

But I want to be clear about how we parted when I went off to college. I'd like to be able to say I decided to leave the toxic environment of our home because I realized I needed to let go of you. But this was not a choice I made. It was you who let go of me, pushed me away.

Let go of me? That's a laugh. You can't let go of something to which you were never attached. Mom told me several years after you died how angry you were when she told you she was pregnant—with twins no less. "He didn't want any more children. I had to trick him," she said. I felt as if she had stuck a dagger in my heart. I guess I had deluded myself into thinking that when you ran me down, smacked, or beat me with your belt, you were showing that I mattered to you.

When I tell these stories to my partner, Carolyn, she tells me I'm making myself sound like a victim. She's right—up to a point. It's not as if I were some sort of passive prey. I knew how to get under your skin, how to work you into a frenzy, and oh, how badly I wanted you to notice me! If that meant taking a whipping, then I'd take one. But, Dad, you didn't have to bruise me so badly, to relish every opportunity to break my will. What was it, Dad? Did you need to knock against someone to feel alive? Was your spirit that crushed, were your desires so buried beneath the rubble of your own childhood that you couldn't contain the fire burning in your belly?

After hearing mother's account of my birth, I could no longer hold on to the self-serving interpretation that inflicting pain on a child is an act of love. Do you know what it feels like to realize your father didn't see your birth as a blessing? Maybe you're the wrong person to ask.

But I needed a jolt like that to wake me up. After my conversation with mom, I felt as if I no longer had to hide my scars or bury my anger. I had been pushed to the brink of freedom. I had thought that keeping it all inside protected me from danger and harm, but really what I was shielding was my own conscious self-reflection. I had never blamed you for the person I had become. I felt lucky that I hadn't been stigmatized by some label like *hyperactive, co-dependent,* or *A.D.D.* But neither had I allowed myself the opportunity "to give birth to myself," to borrow Harold Bloom's lovely phrase (1973). What I was seeking, Dad, was the kind of freedom Frederick Nietzsche refers to as "the supreme will to power" (Nietzsche, 1968). You enlarge your capacity for assuming responsibility for yourself by engaging in "a constantly continuing and continually broadening process of appropriating your experiences and actions" (Nehamas, 1983, p. 410).

But damn if I didn't see this as another instance of bad faith. Isn't it ironic, Dad, how the one thing I thought you drilled into my skull—to take responsibility for my own choices and actions—was the one thing I had negated by unwittingly becoming a copy of you? Not an exact replica, mind you. I was sufficiently aware of my anger and pain not to take a chance of passing them on to children. Rejecting the option of a life of emotional detachment and obsessive withdrawal, I refused to throw in the towel the way you did. Still, I've had to work mighty hard to resist the impulse to live exclusively in my head and submerge my craving for life in a cave of cerebral reflection. I always wondered what was going through your head when you buried yourself in your work, confining most of your waking life to the four walls of that cold, damp basement shop of yours.

Now you can see the contradictions of lived experience, can't you? For so long I stood proudly in opposition to your *habitas* of physical and emotional being, while all the time slaving away, working hour after hour, day after day, securing a safe dwelling in the sacred spaces of introspective solitude. It took me a long time to realize that safety is not as important as intimacy. Vulnerability always runs the risk of exposing one's self to cruelty, but sheltering one's self from the storms of life, refusing to venture out of the capsule, only ensures that one will never feel the compassion, tenderness, and immanence of real love. This would be death in life. Do you know the passage in the *Song of Songs*, a book of the Hebrew Bible, the one that says "love is as strong as death" (see Ricoeur, 2004)? What makes love so decisive is that everybody dies, but not everybody loves.

***

I saw a beggar leaning on his wooden crutch
He said to me, "You must not ask for so much."
(Leonard Cohen, 1969)

When you died so suddenly in 1988, I was terrified. There was a time when I wished you were dead. But now I felt this huge hole and nothing to fill it. Sure, I knew you were sick, that you'd grown old and fragile. What I didn't realize was the strength of your will—your will to die. I remember pleading with you to stop popping those sleeping pills.

"Dad, quit acting as if you know more than your doctors," I demanded.

"They don't know what I need," you blared back.

"But Dad, it's no good to take all those pills. They have side effects, and they interact with each other. Eventually they're going to kill you."

"You don't know what it feels like not to be able to sleep," you replied. "Is a good night's sleep too much to ask for? I just want a good night's sleep."

"Do the pills ever work?' I asked. "Do you ever get the kind of sleep you want?"

"Yes. Eh, well, no, not exactly. It doesn't matter because I have to get up to pee. And it takes me so long to get started. My bladder feels full, but I can't get started. I wait and wait. And I get so frustrated. Then, when I finally do finish, I have to take more pills to get back to sleep."

"Oh, Dad, I'm so sorry. It's a vicious circle," I said, peeking at your swollen ankles and taking in the appalling contradictions imposed by the competing demands of insomnia and heart disease. When I looked up, our eyes met. I tried to hide the sorrow I felt that you had to go through this and then you whispered ever so softly, "Don't get old, Art. Not if you want to hold onto your dignity." I noticed your eyes were watering. It was the first time you ever openly expressed pain in my presence. Your shame and humiliation were palpable.

I sit here now, all these years later, Dad, wondering whether those words were exuberant. There's a blaze of light and a fog of darkness in that utterance. Was that moment metaphoric? Were you really talking about the humiliation you had suffered as a child, then passed on to me as an adult? Was the hurt so deep, was that why you never talked about it, never even mentioned it?

Some time later, after you died, Mom told me you had started taking Sominex capsules when you were 40 and once they quit working you moved to prescription sleeping pills. What kept you up at night?

You were eleven years old when you arrived at Ellis Island in 1920, penniless and with no English words in your vocabulary. Stigmatized by the Yiddish jargon you spoke, the odd clothing you wore, and the filthy environment in which you dwelled, you internalized deep-seated feelings of inferiority and a social awkwardness you never overcame. I recall the stories you used to tell about how easily you were deceived and tricked by classmates. "Greenhorn, greenhorn," they would tease and make fun of you. You were stigmatized as one of those ignorant, uncouth, and gullible immigrants. Remember that jingle you used to chant, "When I was young and in my prime, I wasn't worth a single dime." I never grasped how literal you were being until I was much older. Riddled in abject poverty, you had to quit school at the age of sixteen and get a job to help feed the seven hungry mouths at home. Then you learned you couldn't tell prospective employers you were a Jew because the big companies like Heinz and Westinghouse wouldn't hire Jews. Time after time, you got fired when you returned to work after calling in sick during the Jewish High Holy Days. It didn't matter that you were the hardest working and most talented sign painter in the company. It must have been heartbreaking to realize that your circumstances would never allow you to fulfill your dream of becoming a real artist. Is it any wonder you were filled with rage?

How does one resist the compulsion to pass down the despair of growing up poor, insecure, and out of place? You endured the Great Depression and anti-Semitism. A poverty of spirit was etched on your body, submerged in your unconscious. So you shut yourself off from outside influences, protected yourself against the risks of exposure, tried to bury your pain. For you, life was a problem and a struggle, not a mystery or adventure.

As a kid, I couldn't understand why you were always in a state of perpetual anxiety, as if you were waiting for the next shoe to drop. When you would throw one of your tantrums, you would remind us again that "you worked like a slave," as if it were all for us, as if there was no pleasure in the work and you didn't desperately need to keep busy in order not to feel the anguish of your unmet needs. I was confused. If work was nothing but coercion and sacrifice, then why was it so important to you? Would it always feel like a form of slavery and coercion or could one love work as much as play? Couldn't work be play?

The truth is you didn't work like a slave. You may have felt like a prisoner, but you weren't a slave. You weren't owned by anyone, bound in servitude, or chained to your workbench. You were more like Sisyphus, the mythological hero of Camus' famous essay (Camus, 1955) on the absurdity of existence. Accepting the confining and strenuous demands of his work, Sisyphus keeps the rock rolling up the hill. Camus says, "One must imagine Sisyphus happy" (1955, p. 123), because he has chosen to take responsibility for his fate; he doesn't give up or give in to the absurdity and disappointment of his plight. The way I see it, Dad, work was the way you rose above the absurd struggles of your life and filled your heart.

But Sisyphus had no other hearts to fill. He was alone on the slope. It was just the rock and him. "His rock is his thing," wrote Camus (p. 123). Moreover, Sisyphus had a passion for life. His tragedy was his consciousness of his plight. Were you conscious of yours?

I remember one of the last times I saw you. You kissed me on the lips and held me tight. Then you whispered in my ear, "Try to see me more often." Driving home, I felt as if I couldn't breathe. First, the rage exploded inside of me and I swore I'd never come to see you again. Then, suddenly my fantasies of revenge dissolved in a pool of tears. It wasn't over; it would never be over. But my body was telling me something. If there was any hope to break the cycle of repetition, it would come, not through rage, but only through an epiphany of sorrow (Miller, 1983).

***

> And a pretty woman leaning in her darkened door
> She cried to me, "Hey, why not ask for more."
> (Leonard Cohen, 1969)

Hettema (2000) claims, "Only forgiveness is able to release a human being from the past, and set someone free to live towards the future." I think he's mistaken.

"You never asked me to forgive you; I never asked you to ask me either. The way I saw it, this was not Hollywood. There would be no happy ending, no kiss and make up. But neither was this tragedy— at least not for me. My work, the labor of a narrative inquiry, is the work of memory, a determination to be faithful to the past even in the absence of any single enduring truth to be discovered (Freeman, 2010). You did bad things and you did good things. You weren't a demon and you weren't heroic. The fact is that you weren't a father to me. You didn't protect me and you weren't really interested in me as a separate and unique person. I was wounded more by your disinterest than by your belt. Now I understand your indifference when it came to my life. I can see that I was not singled out. You were just not interested in life, yours was a kind of death in life. You provided food and shelter, but you were too wounded and damaged to make a home for your children, a dwelling place of love, support, and acknowledgement.

Some readers may say I'm being too hard on you. They may perceive my story as just another rant, another hurt kid refusing to grow up, expressing his rage. If they say this, either I have failed to express what I am after here or they just don't get it. They may simply not understand that memory is both an epistemic project, a seeking after fidelity with what actually took place, and a pragmatic one, a coming to terms with what chance has given us in order to make a self for oneself (Rorty, 1989). The question that drives this inquiry, then, is how to cut the ties that hold one in the grip of the past, a project you, my father, could not have imagined, given the indignities and humiliations you suffered as a child. Recognizing the importance of such a project does not make me better than you; it only suggests that I have been the beneficiary of kinder strangers. My memory work does not seek to discover precisely what caused me to be the self that I am but rather to confront and deal with the contingencies of my past by re-describing them, so I am not condemned to stay in the bubble of my psychic inheritance.

In our culture, a moral priority is given to the victim, but what if one is the victim of a victim? Dad, who was there to meet your demand for reparation? Did you ever get to grieve the loss of the child within you? If you and I had been able to mourn together, to grieve the irreversibility of a past we both regretted, maybe you would no longer have needed to defend your principles and together we could have spun a different web of relations, something jointly constructed that acknowledged our differences and expressed the love we held in reserve (Miller, 1983).

When I started this conversation, I thought I was seeking to break from the past once and for all, and free myself from you, *my* father. But now I see two fathers; you, the father I wanted and never had, the one whose loss I've mourned and come to terms with. But there's another father, a second father inside me trying to break loose, the one I never accepted, never gave a voice. I can see now that the only possibility for reconciling the impress of *my* father is to free the other father within me; the father I could have been; the father I still can be; the father I denied, submerged, and rejected, the one I suppressed in order to stop the cycle of cruelty and pain. By imagining and accepting myself as a father, I make myself available and free to provide a dwelling place of love, nurturing, and acknowledgement for the sons and daughters who may seek connection with me. This is the freedom I choose, the liberty I seek, the freedom to live not against the past but with it.

***

I open my eyes and realize I am alone with my thoughts. *You weren't really here, Dad, were you?* In the background, I hear the satellite radio and instantly recognize the gravelly voice of Leonard Cohen (1969):

> If I, if I have been unkind,
> I hope you can just let it go by.
> If I, if I have been untrue,
> I hope you know, it was never to you.

Notes

Preface

1 In 2014, we had approximately 40 participants in our workshop, representing disciplines of communication, sociology, anthropology, theater, education, music, counseling and adult education, psychology, organizational psychology, art education, sport, special education, continuing education, English, sustainability, medical humanities, counseling and psychotherapy, deaf education, visual arts, and community health. They hailed from several of the more than 60 countries represented at the Congress; for example, many universities in the United States plus Australia, the UK, Brazil, New Zealand, Israel, The Netherlands, South Africa, and Turkey. In 2015, we again had approximately 40 participants, representing disciplines of communication, theatre and performance, psychology, social work, education, curriculum and instruction, education leadership, sociology, criminology, creative arts therapies, art education, creative industries, engineering education, ESL and multicultural education, nursing, humanities and social sciences, and academic administration. Though more than one-half were from the United States, the rest hailed from several other countries, including Belgium, Canada, the UK, Australia, Columbia, and India.

Session 5

1 Portions of this section are excerpted and edited from Ellis, 2007, forthcoming.

2 These boards are called Research Ethics Committees (REC) in the UK, Research Ethics Boards (REB) in Canada, Human Research Ethics Committees (HRECS) in Australia, and Faculty Ethics Committees in South Africa. Nordic Countries and New Zealand also have ethics boards. See Farrimond, 2013; International Compilation of Human Research Protections, Office for Human Research Protections, U.S. Department of Health and Human Services at www.hhs.gov/ohrp/international/intlcompilation/intlcompilation.html. See also, van den Hoonaard, 2011.

3 See chnm.gmu.edu/digitalhistory/links/pdf/chapter6/6.23c.pdf and historynewsnetwork.org/article/160885 for discussions of ongoing debates in oral history and history associations and in the Department of Health and Human Services about these matters.

4 Portions of this section are excerpted and edited from Ellis and Rawicki, 2013; Ellis, forthcoming.

5 Portions of this section call on Ellis and Rawicki, 2013; Ellis, forthcoming.

6 Portions of this section are excerpted and edited from Ellis, forthcoming.

Session 6

1 Portions of this section are excerpted and edited from Ellis, 2004, pp. 194–199.

2 Portions of this paragraph are excerpted and edited from Bochner, 2000, pp. 270–271.

Appendix A

1 Ellis, C. (1996a).

Appendix B

1 Excerpt from Ellis, C. (forthcoming).

2 The information in this section about Treblinka comes from online sites, including "Treblinka Concentration Camp: History and Overview" (www.jewishvirtuallibrary.org/jsource/Holocaust/Treblinka.html#what) and "Symbolic Cemetery at Treblinka" (www.scrapbookpages.com/Poland/Treblinka/Treblinka05.html).

Appendix C

1 An earlier version of this story was published as "Bird on the Wire: Freeing the Father within Me" (Bochner, 2012b).

References

Adams, T. E. (2006). Seeking father: Relationally reframing a troubled love story. *Qualitative Inquiry, 12*(4), 704–723

Adams, T. E. (2008). A review of narrative ethics. *Qualitative Inquiry, 14*, 175–195.

Adams, T. E. (2011). *Narrating the closet: An autoethnography of same-sex attraction*. Walnut Creek, CA: Left Coast Press, Inc.

Adams, T. E., & Holman Jones, S. (2008). Autoethnography is queer. In N. K. Denzin, Y. S. Lincoln, & L. T. Smith (Eds.), *Handbook of critical and indigenous methodologies* (pp. 373–390). Thousand Oaks, CA: Sage.

Adams, T. E., & Holman Jones, S. (2011). Telling stories: Reflexivity, queer theory, and autoethnography. *Cultural Studies ↔ Critical Methodologies, 11*, 108–116.

Adams, T. E., Holman Jones, S., & Ellis, C. (2015). *Autoethnography: Understanding Qualitative Research*. Oxford: Oxford University Press.

Alexander, B. K. (2005). Performance ethnography: The reenacting and inciting of culture. In N. Denzin & Y. Lincoln (Eds.), *The Sage handbook of qualitative research* (3rd. ed., pp. 411–422). Thousand Oaks, CA: Sage.

Alexander, B. K. (2014). Critical autoethnography as intersectional praxis. In R. M. Boylorn & M. P. Orbe (Eds.), *Critical autoethnography: Intersecting cultural identities in everyday life* (pp. 110–122). Walnut Creek, CA: Left Coast Press, Inc.

Alexander, B. K., Moreira, C., & kumar, h. s. (2012). Resisting (resistance) stories: A tri-autoethnographic exploration of father narratives across shades of difference. *Qualitative Inquiry, 18*(2), 121–133.

Allardice, L. (2013). Nobel prizewinner Alice Munro: 'It's a wonderful thing for the short story.' *The Guardian* (December 6). www.theguardian.com/books/2013/dec/06/alice-munro-interview-nobel-prize-short-story-literature

Anderson, L. (2006). Analytic autoethnography. *Journal of Contemporary Ethnography, 35*, 373–395.

Anderson, L. (2011). Time is of the essence: An analytic autoethnography of family, work, and serious leisure. *Symbolic Interaction, 34* (2), 133–157.

Anderson, L., & Glass-Coffin, B. (2013). I learn by going: Autoethnographic modes of inquiry (pp. 57–84). In S. Holman Jones, T. E. Adams, & C. Ellis (Eds.), *Handbook of autoethnography*. Walnut Creek, CA: Left Coast Press, Inc.

Anderson, N. (1934/1961). *The hobo: The sociology of the homeless man.* Chicago: University of Chicago Press.

Andrew, S. (2015). The search for an autoethnographic ethic. Unpublished Thesis, School of Psychology and Public Health, La Trobe University.

Atkinson, P. (1997). Narrative turn or blind alley? *Qualitative Health Research, (7)*3, 325–344.

Austin, D. (1996). The same and different. In C. Ellis & A. Bochner (Eds.), *Composing ethnography: Alternative forms of qualitative writing* (pp. 206–230). Walnut Creek, CA: AltaMira Press.

Bamberg, M. (2006). Stories: Big or small: Why do we care? *Narrative Inquiry, 16*(1), 139–147.

Bartleet, B. L. (2013). Artful and embodied methods, modes of inquiry, and forms of representation. In S. Holman Jones, T. E. Adams, & C. Ellis (Eds.), *Handbook of autoethnography* (pp. 443–464). Walnut Creek, CA: Left Coast Press, Inc.

Bartleet, B. L., & Ellis, C. (Eds.). (2009). *Music autoethnographies: Making autoethnography sing/Making music personal.* Brisbane: Australian Academic Press.

Bateson, G. (1972). *Steps to an ecology of mind: Collected essays in anthropology, psychiatry, evolution, and epistemology.* Chicago: University of Chicago Press.

Bateson, G. (1979). *Mind and nature: A necessary unity.* New York: Hampton Press.

Becker, E. (1968). *The structure of evil: An essay on the unification of the science of man.* New York: George Braziller.

Becker, E. (1971). *The birth and death of meaning.* New York: George Braziller.

Becker, E. (1973). *The denial of death.* New York: The Free Press.

Behar, R. (1996). *The vulnerable observer: Anthropology that breaks your heart.* Boston: Beacon.

Benson, P. (1993). *Anthropology and literature.* Urbana: University of Illinois Press.

Bergum, V., & Dossetor, J. (2005). *Relational ethics: The full meaning of respect*. Hagerstown, MD: University.

Bernstein, R. J. (1983). *Beyond objectivism and relativism: Science, hermeneutics, and praxis*. Philadelphia: University of Pennsylvania Press.

Berry, K. (2013). Spinning autoethnographic reflexivity, cultural critique and negotiating selves. In S. Holman Jones, T. E. Adams, & C. Ellis (Eds.), *Handbook of autoethnography* (pp. 209–227). Walnut Creek, CA: Left Coast Press, Inc.

Berry, K., & Patti, C. (2015). Lost in narration: Applying autoethnography. *Journal of Applied Communication Research, 43*, 263–268.

Billig, M. (2013). *Learn to write badly: How to succeed in the social sciences*. New York: Cambridge University Press.

Birkerts, S. (2008). *The art of time in memoir: Then, again*. St. Paul, MN: Graywolf Press.

Bloom, H. (1973). *The anxiety of influence*. New York: Oxford University Press.

Bochner, A. (1981). Forming warm ideas. In C. Wilder-Mott & J. H. Weakland (Eds.), *Rigor and imagination: Essays from the legacy of Gregory Bateson* (pp. 65–81). New York: Praeger.

Bochner, A. (1994). Perspectives on inquiry II: Theories and stories. In M. L. Knapp & G. R. Miller (Eds.), *Handbook of interpersonal communication* (2nd ed., pp. 21–41). Thousand Oaks, CA: Sage.

Bochner, A. (1997). It's about time: Narrative and the divided self. *Qualitative Inquiry, 3*, 418–438.

Bochner, A. (2000). Criteria against ourselves. *Qualitative Inquiry, 6*, 266–272.

Bochner, A. (2002). Perspectives on inquiry III: The moral of stories. In M. Knapp & G. Miller (Eds.), *Handbook of interpersonal communication* (3rd ed., pp. 73–101). Thousand Oaks, CA: Sage.

Bochner, A. (2007). Notes toward an ethics of memory in autoethnography. In N. Denzin & M. Giardina (Eds.), *Ethical futures in qualitative research: Decolonizing the politics of knowledge* (pp. 197–208). Walnut Creek, CA: Left Coast Press, Inc.

Bochner, A. (2010). Resisting the mystification of narrative inquiry: Unmasking the real conflict between story analysts and storytellers. *Sociology of Health and Illness, 32*, 662–665.

Bochner, A. (2012a). On first-person narrative scholarship: Autoethnography as acts of meaning. *Narrative Inquiry, 22*(1), 155–164.

Bochner, A. (2012b). Bird on the wire: Freeing the father within me. *Qualitative Inquiry, 18*(2), 168–173.

Bochner, A. (2012c). Suffering happiness: On autoethnography's ethical calling. *Qualitative Communication Research, 1*(2), 209–229.

Bochner, A. (2014). *Coming to narrative: A personal history of paradigm change in the human sciences*. Walnut Creek, CA: Left Coast Press, Inc.

Bochner, A. (2015). Nitty-gritties of autoethnography: The heart of the matter. Keynote Address, *Doing Autoethnography Conference*, San Angelo, TX.

Bochner, A., & Ellis, C. (1992). Personal narrative as a social approach to interpersonal communication. *Communication Theory, 2,* 165–172.

Bochner, A., & Ellis, C. (1995). Telling and living: Narrative co-construction and the practices of interpersonal relationships. In W. Leeds-Hurwitz (Ed.), *Communication as social construction: Social approaches to the study of interpersonal interaction* (pp. 201–213). New York: Guilford.

Bochner, A., & Ellis, C. (1996). Talking over ethnography. In C. Ellis & A. Bochner (Eds.), *Composing ethnography: Alternative forms of qualitative writing* (pp. 13–45). Walnut Creek, CA: AltaMira Press.

Bochner, A., & Ellis, C. (2002). *Ethnographically speaking: Autoethnography, literature, aesthetics.* Walnut Creek, CA: AltaMira Press.

Bochner, A., & Ellis, C. (2004). Our writing lives: An introduction to writing and research—personal views. In M. Saarnivaara, E. Vainikkala, & M. van Delft (Eds.), *Writing and research—Personal views* (pp. 7–19), *Publications of the Research Centre for Contemporary Culture,* University of Jyväskylä, Jyväskylä, Finland.

Bochner, A., Ellis, C., & Tillmann-Healy, L. (1997). Relationships as stories. In S. Duck (Ed.), *Handbook of personal relationships* (pp. 307–324), New York: John Wiley.

Bochner, A., & Riggs, N. (2014). Practicing narrative inquiry. In P. Leavy (Ed.), *The Oxford handbook of qualitative research* (pp. 195–222). New York: Oxford University Press.

Bochner, A., & Waugh, J. (1995). Talking-with as a model for writing about: Implications of Rortian pragmatism for communication theory. In L. Langsdorf & A. Smith (Eds.), *Recovering pragmatism's voice: The classical tradition and the philosophy of communication* (pp. 211–233). Albany: State University of New York Press.

Boylorn, R. (2013). *Sweetwater: Black women and narratives of resilience.* New York: Peter Lang.

Boylorn, R., & Orbe, M. (Eds.). (2014). *Critical autoethnography: Intersecting cultural identities in everyday life.* Walnut Creek, CA: Left Coast Press, Inc.

Brill, A. (Ed.). (1938). *The basic writings of Sigmund Freud.* New York: Random House.

Broyard, A. (1992). *Intoxicated by my illness, and other writings on life and death.* New York: Fawcett Columbine.

Bruner, J. (1986). *Actual minds, possible worlds.* Cambridge, MA: Harvard University Press.

Bruner, J. (1987). Life as narrative. *Social Research, 54,* 11–32.

Bruner, J. (1990). *Acts of meaning.* Cambridge, MA: Harvard University Press.

Burke, K. (1974). *The philosophy of literary form: Studies in symbolic action* (3rd ed.). Berkeley: University of California Press.

Butler, J. (1990). *Feminism and the subversion of identity*. New York: Routledge.

Camus, A. (1947). *The plague*. New York: Knopf.

Camus, A. (1955). *The myth of Sisyphus*. New York: Random House.

Carless, D., & Douglas, K. (2009). Songwriting and the creation of knowledge. In B. Bartlett & C. Ellis (Eds.), *Musical autoethnography: Creative explorations of the self through music* (pp. 23–38). Queensland: Australian Academic Press.

Carter, S. (2002). How much subjectivity is needed to understand our lives objectively? *Qualitative Health Research, 12*(9), 1184–1201.

Casey, E. S. (1987). *Remembering: A phenomenological study*. Bloomington: Indiana University Press.

Chang, H. (2008). *Autoethnography as method*. Walnut Creek, CA: Left Coast Press, Inc.

Chang, H., Ngunjiri, F., & Hernandez, K. A. (2012). *Collaborative autoethnography*. Walnut Creek, CA: Left Coast Press, Inc.

Charmaz, K. (2000). Grounded theory: Objectivist and constructivist methods. In N. Denzin & Y. Lincoln (Eds.), *Handbook of qualitative research* (2nd ed., pp. 509–535). Thousand Oaks, CA.: Sage.

Chase, S. (1996). Personal vulnerability and interpretive authority in narrative research. In R. Josselson (Ed.), *Ethics and process in the narrative study of lives* (vol. 4, pp. 45–59). Thousand Oaks, CA: Sage.

Chatham-Carpenter, A. (2010). "Do thyself no harm": Protecting ourselves as autoethnographers. *Journal of Research Practice, 6*(1). jrp.icaap.org/index.php/jrp/article/view/213/183

Chawla, D. (2014). *Home, uprooted: Oral histories of India's partition*. New York: Fordham University Press.

Clifford, J., & Marcus, G. E. (1986). *Writing culture: The poetics and politics of ethnography*. Berkeley: University of California Press.

Cohen, L (1969). *Bird on the wire*. New York: Columbia Records.

Cohen, L. (1992). *Anthem*. Brooklyn, NY: Genius Media Group.

Coles, R. (1989). *The call of stories: Teaching and the moral imagination*. Boston: Houghton Mifflin.

Conquergood, D. (1990). Rethinking ethnography: Cultural politics and rhetorical strategies. Paper presented at the Temple Conference on Discourse Analysis, Temple University.

Couser, G. T. (1997). *Recovering bodies: Illness, disability, and life writing*. Madison: University of Wisconsin Press.

Crawley, S. (2012). Autoethnography as feminist self-interview. In J. F. Gubrium, J. A. Holstein, A. B. Marvasti, & K. D. McKinney (Eds.), *The Sage handbook of interview research: The complexity of the craft* (2nd ed., pp. 143–160). Thousand Oaks, CA: Sage.

Davis, C. S. (2013). *Communicating hope: An ethnography of a children's mental health care team*. Walnut Creek, CA: Left Coast Press, Inc.

Davis, F. (1959). The cabdriver and his fare: Facets of a fleeting relationship. *American Journal of Sociology, 62*, 158–165.

Davis, F. (1994). *Fashion, culture, and identity*. Chicago: University of Chicago Press.

Delbo, C. (1995). *Auschwitz and after* (Reprint Ed.). (Trans. by R. C. Lamont). New Haven, CT: Yale University Press.

Denzin, N. (1997). *Interpretive ethnography: Ethnographic practices for the 21st century*. Thousand Oaks, CA: Sage.

Denzin, N. (2003). *Performance ethnography: Critical pedagogy and the politics of culture*. Thousand Oaks, CA: Sage.

Denzin, N. (2008). *Searching for Yellowstone*. Walnut Creek, CA: Left Coast Press, Inc.

Denzin, N. K. (2014). *Interpretive autoethnography* (2nd ed.). Thousand Oaks, CA: Sage.

Denzin, N. (2015). *Indians in color*. Walnut Creek, CA: Left Coast Press, Inc.

Denzin, N., & Lincoln, Y. S. (Eds.). (2011). *The Sage handbook of qualitative research* (4th ed.). Thousand Oaks, CA: Sage.

Dillard, A. (1989). *The writing life*. New York: Harper Perennial.

Diversi, M., & Moreira, C. (2009). *Betweener talk: Decolonizing knowledge production, pedagogy, and praxis*. Walnut Creek, CA: Left Coast Press, Inc.

Duneier, M. (1999). *Sidewalk*. New York: Farrar, Straus and Giroux.

Durham, A. (2014). *Home with hip hop feminism: Performances in communication and culture*. New York: Peter Lang.

Eakin, P. J. (1985). *Fictions in autobiography: Studies in the art of self-invention*. Princeton, NJ: University of Princeton Press.

Eakin, P. (2008). *Living autobiographically: How we create identity in narrative*. Ithaca, NY: Cornell University Press.

Eastman, S. (2007). *Recovering Paul's mother tongue: Language and theology in Galatians*. Grand Rapids, MI: Eerdmans.

Einwohner, R. (2011). Ethical considerations on the use of archived testimonies in Holocaust research: Beyond the IRB exemption. *Qualitative Sociology, 34*, 415–430.

Ellingson, L. (2009). *Engaging crystallization in qualitative research: An introduction*. Thousand Oaks, CA: Sage.

Ellis, C. (1986). *Fisher folk: Two communities on Chesapeake Bay*. Lexington: University Press of Kentucky.

Ellis, C. (1991a). Sociological introspection and emotional experience. *Symbolic Interaction, 14*, 23–50.

Ellis, C. (1991b). Emotional sociology. *Studies in Symbolic Interaction, 12*, 123–145.

Ellis, C. (1993) 'There are survivors': Telling a story of sudden death. *The Sociological Quarterly, 34*(4), 711–730.

Ellis, C. (1995a). *Final negotiations: A story of love, loss, and chronic illness.* Philadelphia: Temple University Press.

Ellis, C. (1995b). Emotional and ethical quagmires in returning to the field. *Journal of Contemporary Ethnography, 24,* 68–98.

Ellis, C. (1995c) The other side of the fence: Seeing black and white in a small, southern town, *Qualitative Inquiry, 1*(2), 147–167.

Ellis, C. (1995d). Speaking of dying: An ethnographic short story. *Symbolic Interaction, 18,* 73–81.

Ellis, C. (1996a). Maternal connections. In C. Ellis & A. Bochner (Eds.), *Composing ethnography: Alternative forms of qualitative writing* (pp. 240–243). Walnut Creek, CA.: AltaMira Press.

Ellis, C. (1996b). On the demands of truthfulness in writing personal loss narratives. *Journal of Personal and Interpersonal Loss, 1,* 151–177.

Ellis, C. (1997). Evocative autoethnography: Writing emotionally about our lives. In W. G. Tierney & Y. S. Lincoln (Eds.), *Representation and the text: Re-framing the narrative voice* (pp. 116–139) Albany, NY: SUNY Press.

Ellis, C. (1998a). Exploring loss through autoethnographic inquiry: Auto-ethnographic storytelling, co-constructed narrative, and interactive interviewing. In J. Harvey (Ed.), *Perspectives on loss: A sourcebook* (pp. 49-61). Philadelphia: Brunner/Mazel.

Ellis, C. (1998b). I hate my voice: Coming to terms with minor bodily stigmas. *The Sociological Quarterly, 39,* 517–537.

Ellis, C. (1999). He(art)ful autoethnography. *Qualitative Health Research, 9*(5), 653–667.

Ellis, C. (2000a). Creating criteria: An ethnographic short story. *Qualitative Inquiry, 6,* 273–277.

Ellis, C. (2000b). Negotiating terminal illness: Communication, collusion, and coalition in caregiving. In J. Harvey & E. D. Miller (Eds.), *Loss and trauma: General and close relationship perspectives* (pp. 284–304). Philadelphia: Brunner-Routledge.

Ellis, C. (2001). With mother/with child: A true story. *Qualitative Inquiry, 7,* 598–616.

Ellis, C. (2002). Being real: Moving inward toward social change. *Qualitative Studies in Education, 15,* 399–406.

Ellis, C. (2004). *The ethnographic I: A methodological novel about autoeth-nography.* Walnut Creek, CA: AltaMira Press.

Ellis, C. (2007). Telling secrets, revealing lives: Relational ethics in research with intimate others. *Qualitative Inquiry, 13,* 3–29.

Ellis, C. (2009). *Revision: Autoethnographic reflections on life and work.* Walnut Creek, CA: Left Coast Press, Inc.

Ellis, C. (2013) Crossing the rabbit hole: Autoethnographic life review. *Qualitative Inquiry, 19*(1), 35–45.

Ellis, C. (2014a). Seeking my brother's voice: Holding onto long-term grief through photographs, stories, and reflections. In E. Miller (Ed.), *Stories of complicated grief: A critical anthology* (pp. 3–21). Washington, D. C.: National Association of Social Workers Press.

Ellis, C. (2014b). No longer hip: Losing my balance and adapting to what ails me. *Qualitative Research in Sport, Exercise and Health, 6*(1), 1–19.

Ellis, C. (forthcoming). Compassionate research: Interviewing and storytelling from a relational ethics of care. In I. Goodson, M. Andrews, & A. Antikainen (Eds.), *The Routledge international handbook on narrative and life history.* New York: Routledge.

Ellis, C., & Adams, T. E. (2014). The purposes, practices, and principles of autoethnographic research. In P. Leavy (Ed.), *Oxford handbook of qualitative research* (pp. 254–276). New York: Oxford University Press.

Ellis, C., Adams, T. E., & Bochner, A. (2011). Autoethnography: An overview [40 paragraphs]. *Forum Qualitative Sozialforschun /Forum: Qualitative Social Research, 12*(1), ISSN 1438–5627. www.qualitative-research.net/index.php/fqs/article/view/1589

Ellis, C., & Bochner, A. (1992). Telling and performing personal stories: The constraints of choice in abortion. In C. Ellis & M. Flaherty (Eds.), *Investigating subjectivity: Research on lived experience* (pp. 79–101). Thousand Oaks, CA: Sage.

Ellis, C., & Bochner, A. (Eds.). (1996a). *Composing ethnography: Alternative forms of qualitative writing.* Walnut Creek, CA: AltaMira Press.

Ellis, C., & Bochner, A. (Eds.). (1996b). Taking ethnography into the twenty-first century, special issue of *Journal of Contemporary Ethnography* (April), *25* (1), 1–168.

Ellis, C., & Bochner, A. (2000). Autoethnography, personal narrative, reflexivity: Researcher as subject. In N. Denzin & Y. Lincoln (Eds.), *The handbook of qualitative research* (2nd ed., pp. 733–768). Thousand Oaks, CA: Sage.

Ellis, C., & Bochner, A. (2006). Analyzing analytic autoethnography: An autopsy. *Journal of Contemporary Ethnography, 35*(4), 429–449.

Ellis, C., Kiesinger, C., & Tillmann-Healy, L. (1997). Interactive interviewing: Talking about emotional experience. In R. Hertz (Ed.), *Reflexivity and voice.* Thousand Oaks, CA: Sage.

Ellis, C., & Patti, C. (2014). With heart: Compassionate interviewing and storytelling with Holocaust survivors. *Storytelling, Self, Society, 10*(1), 389–414.

Ellis, C., & Rawicki, J. (2013). Collaborative witnessing of survival during the Holocaust: An exemplar of relational autoethnography. *Qualitative Inquiry, 19*(5), 366–380.

Ellis, C., & Rawicki, J. (2015). Collaborative witnessing and sharing authority in conversations with Holocaust survivors. In S. High (Ed.), *Beyond testimony and trauma: Oral history in the aftermath of mass violence* (pp. 170–191). Vancouver: University of British Columbia Press.

Ellis, C., & Weinstein, E. (1986). Jealousy and the social psychology of emotional experience. *Journal of Social and Personal Relationships*, 3(3), 337–357.

Etherington, K. (2007). Ethical research in reflexive relationships. *Qualitative Inquiry*, 13, 599–613.

Fahie, D. (2014). Doing sensitive research sensitively: Ethical and methodological issues in researching workplace bullying. *International Journal of Qualitative Methods*, 13, 19–34. ejournals.library.ualberta.ca/index.php/IJQM/article/view/19018 Farrimond, H. (2013). *Doing ethical research*. London: Palgrave MacMillan.

Faulkner, S. (2014). *Family stories, poetry, and women's work: Knit four, frog one (poems)*. Rotterdam: Sense.

Foster, E. (2007). *Communicating at the end of life: Finding magic in the mundane*. New York: Routledge.

Foucault, M. (1970). *The order of things: An archeology of the human sciences*. New York: Random House.

Foucault, M. (1982). The subject and power. *Critical Inquiry*, 8(4), 777–795.

Franck, D. (1994). *Separation*. New York: Knopf.

Frank, A. (1995). *The wounded storyteller: Body, illness and ethics*. Chicago: University of Chicago Press.

Frank, A. (2004). Ethics in medicine: Ethics as process and practice. *Internal Medicine Journal*, 34, 355–357.

Freeman, M. (1997). Death, narrative integrity, and the radical challenge of self-understanding; A reading of Tolstoy's *Death of Ivan Ilych*. *Aging and Society*, 17, 373–398.

Freeman, M. (2010). *Hindsight: The promise and peril of looking backward*. New York: Oxford University Press.

Freeman, M. (2014). *The priority of the other: Thinking and living beyond the self*. New York: Oxford University Press.

Freud, S. (1968). *The standard edition of the complete psychological works of Sigmund Freud—Volume XIV (1914-1916): On the outline of the psychoanalytic movement, papers on metapsychology and other works*. London: Hogarth Press.

Frisch, M. (1990). *A shared authority: Essays on the craft and meaning of oral and public history*. Albany, NY: SUNY Press.

Gannon, S. (2013). Sketching subjectivities. In S. Holman Jones, T. E. Adams, & C. Ellis (Eds.), *Handbook of autoethnography* (pp. 228–243). Walnut Creek, CA: Left Coast Press, Inc.

Gale, K., Pelias, R. J., & Russell, L. (2012). *How writing touches: An intimate scholarly collaboration*. Cambridge: Cambridge Scholars.

Gale, K., & Wyatt, J. (2009). *Between the two: A nomadic inquiry into collaborative writing and subjectivity*. Cambridge: Cambridge Scholars.

Geertz, C. (1973). *The interpretation of cultures*. New York: Basic Books.

Geertz, C. (1980). Blurred genres: The refiguration of social thought. *The American Scholar, 49*(2), 165–179.

Geertz, C. (1988). *Works and lives: The anthropologist as author.* Palo Alto, CA: Stanford University Press.

Geist-Martin, P., Gates, L., Wiering, L., Kirby, E., Houston, R., Lilly, A., & Moreno, J. (2010). Exemplifying collaborative autoethnographic practice via shared stories of mothering. *Journal of Research Practice, 6* (1). jrp.icaap.org/index.php/jrp/article/viewFile/209/219

Gergen, K. (1973). Social psychology as history. *Journal of Personality and Social Psychology, 26*(2), 309–320.

Gergen, M., & Gergen, K. (2012). *Playing with purpose: Adventures in performative social science.* Walnut Creek, CA: Left Coast Press, Inc.

Gilligan, C. (1988). Remapping the moral domain: New images of self in relationship. In C. Gilligan, J. V. Ward, and J. M. Taylor (Eds.), *Mapping the moral domain: A contribution of women's thinking to psychological theory and education* (pp. 3–21). Cambridge, MA: Harvard University Press.

Gilmour, K., Mason, N., Waters, R., & Wright, R. (1973). Breathe [Recorded by Pink Floyd] On *Dark side of the moon* [Vinyl]. London: Harvest, Capitol.

Gingrich-Philbrook, C. (2005). Autoethnography's family values: Easy access to compulsory experiences. *Text and Performance Quarterly, 25*(4), 297–314.

Giroux, H. (1984). *Ideology, culture, and the process of schooling.* Philadelphia: Temple University Press.

Goffman, A. (2014). *On the run: Fugitive life in an American city.* New York: Farrar, Straus and Giroux.

Goffman, E. (1963). *Behavior in public places: Notes on the social organization of gatherings.* New York: Free Press/MacMillan.

Goffman, E. (1967). *Interaction ritual: Essays on face-to-face behavior.* New York: Anchor.

González-López, G. (2011). Mindful ethics: Comments on informant-centered practices in sociological research. *Qualitative Sociology, 34,* 447–461.

Goodall, H. L. (2005). Narrative inheritance: A nuclear family with toxic secrets. *Qualitative Inquiry, 11,* 492–513.

Gornick, V. (2008). Truth in personal narrative. In D. Lazar (Ed.), *Truth in nonfiction: Essays* (pp. 7–10). Iowa City: University of Iowa Press.

Greenspan, H. (2010). *On listening to Holocaust survivors: Beyond testimony* (2nd ed.). St. Paul, MN: Paragon House.

Guillemin, M., & Gillam, L. (2004). Ethics, reflexivity, and "ethically important moments" in research. *Qualitative Inquiry, 10,* 261–280.

Habermas, J. (McCarthy, T., Trans.) (1985). *The theory of communicative action: Lifeworld and system: A critique of functionalist reason* (Vol. 2). Boston: Beacon Press.

Hacking, I. (1995). *Rewriting the soul: Multiple personality and the sciences of memory.* Princeton, NJ: Princeton University Press.

Hall, S. (1973). Encoding and decoding in the television discourse. CCCS stenciled occasional paper no. 7. Center for Contemporary Cultural Studies: University of Birmingham, UK.

Hampl, P. (1999). *I could tell you stories: Sojourns in the land of memory.* New York: W. W. Norton.

Harrè, R., & Secord, P. F. (1972). *The explanation of social behavior.* Oxford: Blackwell.

Harris, A. (in press). *Video as Method.* Oxford: Oxford University Press.

Harrison, K. (2008). The forest of memory. In D. Lazer (Ed.), *Truth in nonfiction: Essays* (pp. 17–25). Iowa City: University of Iowa Press.

Hart, J. (2012). *Storycraft: The complete guide to writing narrative nonfiction.* Chicago: University of Chicago Press.

Hayano, D. M. (1979). Auto-Ethnography: Paradigms, problems, and prospects. *Human Organization, 38,* 113–120.

Hedtke, L., & Winslade, J. (2004). *Re-membering lives: Conversations with the dying and the bereaved.* Amityville, NY: Baywood.

Heidegger, M. (1962/2008). *Being and time.* (J. Macquarrie & E. Robinson, Trans.). New York: Harper and Brothers.

Heider, K. (1975). What do people do? Dani-autoethnography. *Journal of Anthropological Research, 31,* 3–17.

Held, V. (1995). Introduction. In V. Held (Ed.), *Justice and care: Essential readings in feminist ethics* (pp. 1–3). Boulder, CO: Westview Press.

Henry, J. (1971). *Pathways to madness.* New York: Vintage Books.

Herrmann, A. F. (2007). How did we get this far apart? Disengagement, relational dialectics, and narrative control. *Qualitative Inquiry, 13*(7), 989–1007.

Hettema, T. L. (2000). Ethics and hermeneutics: On forgetting. Paper presented at the Nijmegen Conference of the Society for Literature and Religion: Canons and Religious Identity, the Netherlands.

High, S. (2014). *Oral history at the crossroads.* Vancouver: University of British Columbia Press.

Hodges, N. (2015). The chemical life. *Health Communication, 30*(6), 627–634.

Holman Jones, S. (2011). Lost and found. *Text and Performance Quarterly, 31*(4), 322–341.

Holman Jones, S., & Adams, T. E. (2010). Autoethnography and queer theory: Making possibilities. In N. K. Denzin & M. G. Giardina (Eds.), *Qualitative inquiry and human rights* (pp. 136–157). Walnut Creek, CA: Left Coast Press, Inc.

Holman Jones, S., Adams, T. E., & Ellis, C. (2013). *Handbook of autoethnography.* Walnut Creek, CA: Left Coast Press, Inc.

Hughes, E. C. (1958). *Men and their work.* New York: The Free Press.

Huisman, K. (2008). 'Does this mean you're not going to come visit me anymore?': An inquiry into an ethics of reciprocity and positionality in feminist ethnographic research. *Sociological Inquiry, 78*, 372–396.

Hyde, M. (2010). *Perfection: Coming to terms with being human.* Waco, TX: Baylor University Press.

Jackson, M. (1989). *Paths toward a clearing: Radical empiricism and ethnographic inquiry.* Bloomington: Indiana University Press.

Jackson, M. (1995). *At home in the world.* Durham, NC: Duke University Press.

Jacobs, J. L. (2004). Women, genocide, and memory: The ethics of feminist ethnography in Holocaust research. *Gender and Society, 18*, 223–238.

Jago, B. (2002). Chronicling an academic depression. *Journal of Contemporary Ethnography, 31*(6), 729–757.

Janesick, V. J (2015). *"Stretching" exercises for qualitative researchers* (4th ed.). Thousand Oaks, CA: Sage.

Josselson, R. (1996). On writing other people's lives: Self-analytic reflections of a narrative researcher. In R. Josselson (Ed.), *Ethics and process in the narrative study of lives* (Vol. 4, pp. 60–71). Thousand Oaks, CA: Sage.

Kantrowitz, B., King, P., & Witherspoon, D. (1986). Help for retarded parents. *Newsweek* (23 June), 62.

Kerby, A. P. (1991). *Narrative and the self.* Bloomington: Indiana University Press.

Kiesinger, C. (1998a). From interviewing to story: Writing Abbie's life. *Qualitative Inquiry, 4*, 71–95.

Kiesinger, C. (1998b). Portrait of an anorexic life. In A. Banks & S. Banks (Eds.), *Fiction and social research: By fire or ice* (pp. 115–136). Walnut Creek, CA: AltaMira.

Kiesinger, C. (2002). My father's shoes: The therapeutic value of narrative reframing. In A. Bochner & C. Ellis (Eds.), *Ethnographically speaking: Autoethnography, literature, and aesthetics* (pp. 95–114). Walnut Creek, CA: AltaMira.

Kim, J-H. (2015). *Understanding narrative inquiry.* Thousand Oaks, CA: Sage.

King, S. (2002). *On writing.* New York: Simon and Schuster.

Klass, D., Silverman, D., & Nickman, S. (Eds.). (1996). *Continuing bonds: New understanding of grief.* London: Taylor and Francis.

Knausgaard, K. (2013). *My struggle: Book 2: A man in love* (D. Bartlett, Trans.). New York: Farrar, Straus, & Giroux.

Kuhn, T. (1970). *The structure of scientific revolutions* (2nd ed.). Chicago: University of Chicago Press.

Kuspit, D. (2010). Collage: The organizing principle of art in the age of the relativity of art. In B. J. Craige (Ed.), *Relativism in the arts* (pp. 123–147). Athens: University of Georgia Press.

Lamott, A. (1994). *Bird by bird: Some instructions on writing and life.* New York: Anchor.

Lang, B. (2005). *Post-Holocaust: Interpretation, misinterpretation, and the claims of history.* Bloomington: Indiana University Press.

Larson, T. (2007). *The memoir and the memoirist.* Athens: Ohio University Press.

Laub, D. (1992). Bearing witness or the vicissitudes of listening. In D. Laub & S. Felman (Eds.), *Testimony: Crises of witnessing in literature, psycho-analysis, and history* (pp. 57–76). New York: Routledge.

Leavy, P. (Ed.). (2014). *The Oxford handbook of qualitative research.* New York: Oxford University Press.

Leavy, P. (2015). *Method meets art: Arts-based research practice.* New York: Guilford Press.

Le Guin, U. (1986). The mother tongue. *Bryn Mawr Alumnae Bulletin (Summer),* 3–4.

Le Guin, U. (1989). *Dancing at the edge of the world: Thoughts on words, women, places.* New York: Grove Press.

Lilly, A., & Moreno, J. (2010). Exemplifying collaborative autoethnographic practice via shared stories of mothering. *Journal of Research Practice,* 6(1). jrp.icaap.org/index.php/jrp/article/view/209/187

Lopate, P. (2013). *To show and to tell: The craft of literary nonfiction.* New York: Free Press.

Lorde, A. (1984). *Sister outsider.* Berkeley, CA: Crossing Press.

Lyotard, J-F. (1984). *The postmodern condition: A report on knowledge.* (G. Bennington & B. Massumi, Trans.). Minneapolis: University of Minnesota.

MacIntyre, A. (1984). *After virtue: A study in moral theory.* Notre Dame, IN: University of Notre Dame Press.

Mairs, N. (2008). Trying truth. In D. Lazar (Ed.), *Truth in nonfiction: Essays* (pp. 89–92). Iowa City: University of Iowa Press.

Mann, T. (1947). *Essays of three decades.* New York: Random House.

Manning, J., & Adams, T. E. (2015). Popular culture studies and autoethnography: An essay on method. *The Popular Culture Studies Journal, 3,* 187–222.

Marak, Q. (2015). Writing the 'self': Introducing autoethnography. *Man in India, 95*(1), 1–10.

Marcus, G. E., & Fisher, M. M. J. (1986). *Anthropology as cultural critique: An experimental moment in the human sciences.* Chicago: University of Chicago Press.

McRae, C. (2015). *Performative listening: Hearing others in qualitative research.* New York: Peter Lang.

Medford, K. (2006). Caught with a fake ID: Ethical questions about slippage in autoethnography. *Qualitative Inquiry, 12*(5), 853–864.

Miller, A. (1983). *For your own good: Hidden cruelty in child-rearing and the roots of violence.* New York: Farrar, Straus, Giroux.

Mitchell, W. J. T. (Ed.). (1981). *On narrative.* Chicago: University of Chicago Press.

Myerhoff, B. (1980). *Number our days.* New York: Simon and Schuster.

Myerhoff, B. (2007). Stories as equipment for living. In M. Kaminsky & M. Weiss (Eds.), *Stories as equipment for living: Last talks and tales of Barbara Myerhoff* (pp. 17–27). Ann Arbor: University of Michigan Press.

Nabokov, V. (1989). *Speak, memory: An autobiography revisited.* New York: Random House.

Nehamas, A. (1983). How one becomes what one is. *Philosophical Review, 92,* 385–417.

Nietzsche, F. (1968). *The will to power.* (W. Kaufmann & R. J. Hollingdale, Trans.). New York: Vintage Books.

Noddings, N. (2002). *Starting at home: Caring and social policy.* Berkeley: University of California Press.

Norris, J., Sawyer, R. D., & Lund, D. (2012). *Duoethnography: Dialogic methods for social, health, and educational research.* Walnut Creek, CA: Left Coast Press, Inc.

Oral History Review, The. (2003). Special issue on "Sharing Authority." *30*(1).

Parks, R. E. (with R. D. McKenzie & E. Burgess). (1925). *The city: Suggestions for the study of human nature in the urban environment.* Chicago: University of Chicago Press.

Parks, R. E. (1950). *Race and Culture.* Glencoe, IL: The Free Press.

Patti, C. (2013). Compassionate storytelling with Holocaust survivors: Cultivating dialogue at the end of an era. Unpublished dissertation, University of South Florida, Tampa.

Patti, C. J. (2015). Sharing "a big kettle of soup": Compassionate listening with a Holocaust survivor. In S. High (Ed.), *Beyond testimony and trauma: Oral history in the aftermath of mass violence* (pp. 192–211). Vancouver: University of British Columbia Press.

Paxton, B. (2015). Feeling at home with grief: An ethnography of continuing bonds and re-membering the deceased. Unpublished dissertation, University of South Florida, Tampa.

Pelias, R. (1999). *Writing performance: Poeticizing the researcher's body.* Carbondale: Southern Illinois University Press.

Pelias, R. (2002). For father and son: An ethnodrama with no catharsis. In A. Bochner & C. Ellis (Eds.), *Ethnographically speaking: Autoethnography, literature, and aesthetics* (pp. 35–43). Walnut Creek, CA.: AltaMira Press.

Pelias, R. (2004). *A methodology of the heart: Evoking academic and daily life.* Walnut Creek, CA: AltaMira Press.

Pelias, R. (2011). *Leaning: A poetics of personal relations*. Walnut Creek, CA: Left Coast Press, Inc.

Pelias, R. (forthcoming). *If the truth be told: Accounts in literary forms*. Rotterdam: Sense.

Pensoneau-Conway, S. L., Bolen, D. M., Toyosaki, S., Rudick, C. K., & Bolen, E. K. (2014). Self, relationship, positionality, and politics: A community autoethnographic inquiry into collaborative writing. *Cultural Studies ↔ Critical Methodologies, 14*, 312–323.

Phillips, A. (2013). *Missing out: In praise of the unlived life*. New York: Farrar, Straus and Giroux.

Pinquart, M., & Sörensen, S. (2003). Associations of stressors and uplifts of caregiving with caregiver burden and depressive mood: A meta-analysis. *The Journals of Gerontology Series B: Psychological Sciences and Social Sciences, 58*(2), 112–128.

Polkinghorne, D. (1988). *Narrative knowing and the human sciences*. Albany: State University of New York Press.

Polkinghorne, D. (1995). Narrative configuration in qualitative analysis. In J. A. Hatch & R. Wisniewski (Eds.), *Life history and narrative* (pp. 5–23). Washington, D.C.: Falmer.

Poulos, C. N. (2008). Narrative conscience and the autoethnographic adventure: Probing memories, secrets, shadows, and possibilities. *Qualitative Inquiry, 14*, 46–66.

Qualitative Inquiry. (2000). Special partial issue on assessing alternative modes of qualitative and ethnographic research: How do we judge? Who judges? (June), *6*(2).

Rabinow, P., & Sullivan, W. M. (Eds.). (1987). *Interpretive social science: A second look*. Berkeley: University of California Press.

Rahman, Md. A. (2008). Some trends in the praxis of participatory action research. In P. Reason & H. Bradbury (Eds.), *The Sage handbook of action research* (pp. 49–62). London: Sage.

(Rambo) Ronai, C. (1995). Multiple reflections of child sex abuse: An argument for a layered account. *Journal of Contemporary Ethnography, 23*, 395–426.

(Rambo) Ronai, C. (1996). My mother is mentally retarded. In In C. Ellis & A. Bochner (Eds.), *Composing ethnography: Alternative forms of qualitative writing* (pp. 109–131). Walnut Creek, CA: AltaMira Press.

Rambo, C. (2015). Strange accounts: Applying for the department chair position and writing threats and secrets "in play." *Journal of Contemporary Ethnography*.

Reed-Danahay, D. E. (Ed.). (1997). *Auto/ethnography: Rewriting the self and the social*. New York: Berg.

Rennels, T. (2015). "You better redneckognize": White working-class people and reality television. Unpublished doctoral dissertation, University of South Florida, Tampa.

Richardson, L. (1994a). Writing: A method of inquiry. In N. Denzin & Y. Lincoln (Eds.), *Handbook of qualitative research* (pp. 516–529). Thousand Oaks, CA: Sage.

Richardson, L. (1994b). Nine poems: Marriage and the family. *Journal of Contemporary Ethnography, 23,* 3–14.

Richardson, L. (1999). Feathers in our CAP. *Journal of Contemporary Ethnography, 28*(6), 660–668.

Richardson, L. (2000). Writing: A method of inquiry. In N. K. Denzin & Y. S. Lincoln (Eds.), *Handbook of qualitative research* (2nd ed., pp. 923–948). Thousand Oaks, CA: Sage.

Ricoeur, P. (1980). Narrative time. *Critical inquiry, 7,* 169–190.

Ricoeur, P. (1992). *Oneself as another.* Chicago: University of Chicago Press.

Ricoeur, P. (2004). *Memory, history, forgetting.* (K. Blamey & D. Pellauer, Trans.). Chicago: University of Chicago Press.

Riessman, C. K. (1993). *Narrative analysis.* Thousand Oaks, CA: Sage.

Roberts, G. (2015). Into the mystic: Bereaved parents, love and spontaneous creativity. Unpublished doctoral dissertation, Deakin University, Melbourne, Australia.

Rodriquez, R. (1983). *Hunger of memory: The education of Richard Rodriguez.* New York: Bantam.

Rorty, R. (1982). *Consequences of pragmatism (Essays: 1972–1980).* Minneapolis: University of Minnesota Press.

Rorty, R. (1989). *Contingency, irony, and solidarity.* Cambridge: Cambridge University Press.

Rorty, R. (1990). *Objectivity, relativism, and truth: Philosophical Papers.* (Vol. 1). Cambridge: Cambridge University Press.

Rorty, R. (1991). *Essays on Heidegger and others: Philosophical papers* (Vol. 2). Cambridge: Cambridge University Press.

Rosaldo, R. (1989). *Culture and truth: The remaking of social analysis.* Boston: Beacon Press.

Rose, D. (1990). *Living the ethnographic life.* Thousand Oaks, CA: Sage.

Rosenau, P. (1991). *Post-modernism and the social sciences: Insights, inroads, and intrusions.* Princeton, NJ: Princeton University Press.

Rosenwald, G. C. (1992). Conclusion: Reflections on narrative understanding. In G. C. Rosenwald & R. L. Ochberg (Eds.), *Storied lives: The cultural politics of self-understanding* (pp. 265–289). New Haven, CT: Yale University Press.

Roth, P. (1996). *Patrimony: A true story.* New York: Vintage Books.

Rough, B. (2007). Writing lost stories: When bones are all we have. *Iron Horse Literary Review, 8*(2), 64–72.

Rubin, A., & Greenspan, H. (2006). *Reflections: Auschwitz, memory, and a life recreated.* St. Paul, MN: Paragon Press.

Sacks, O. (2013). Speak, memory. *New York Review of Books* (February 21), www.nybooks.com/articles/2013/02/21/speak-memory/

Sandstrom, D. (2014). My life as a writer: Interview with P. Roth. *New York Times Sunday Book Review* (March 2), www.nytimes.com/2014/03/16/books/review/my-life-as-a-writer.html

Sartre, J.-P. (2001). *Being and nothingness: A phenomenological essay on ontology.* New York: Kensington.

Sawyer, R., & Norris, J. (2004). Null and hidden curricula of sexual orientation: A dialogue on the *curreres* of the absent presence and the present absence. In L. Coia, M. Birch, N. J. Brooks, E. Heilman, S. Mayer, A. Mountain, & P. Pritchard (Eds.), *Democratic responses in an era of standardization* (pp. 139–159). Troy, NY: Educator's International.

Scott-Hoy, K., & Ellis, C. (2008). Wording pictures: Discovering heartful autoethnography. In J. G. Knowles & A. Cole (Eds.), *Handbook of the arts in qualitative research* (pp. 127–140). Thousand Oaks, CA: Sage.

Sheftel, A., & Zembrzycki, S. (2013). *Oral history off the record.* New York: Palgrave Macmillan.

Shields, D. (2013). *How literature saved my life.* New York: Vintage.

Sikes, P. (Ed.). (2013). *Autoethnography: Four volume set.* Thousand Oaks, CA: Sage.

Singer, M. (2013). On convention. In M. Singer & N. Walker (Eds.), *Bending genre: Essays on creative nonfiction* (pp. 141–149). New York: Bloomsbury.

Singer, M., & Walker, N. (Eds.). (2013). *Bending genre: Essays on creative nonfiction.* New York: Bloomsbury.

Smith, R. (1997). *The Norton history of the human sciences.* New York: W. W. Norton.

Speedy, J. (2015). *Staring at the park: A poetic autoethnographic inquiry.* Walnut Creek, CA: Left Coast Press, Inc.

Speedy, J., & Wyatt, J. (2014). *Collaborative writing as inquiry.* Newcastle upon Tyne, UK: Cambridge Scholars.

Spry, T. (2001). Performing autoethnography: An embodied methodological praxis. *Qualitative Inquiry, 7*(6), 706–732.

Spry, T. (2011). *Body, paper, stage: Writing and performing autoethnography.* Walnut Creek, CA: Left Coast Press, Inc.

Stévance, S., & Lacasse, S. (2013). Les enjeux de la recherche-création en musique. Institution, définition, formation. Quèbec: Presses de l'Université Laval [English version forthcoming from Ashgate, 2016].

Stone, L. (Ed.). (1997). *Close to the bone: Memoirs of hurt, rage and desire.* New York: Grove Press.

Stroebe, M., van Son, M., Stroebe, W., Kleber, R., Schut, H., & van den Bout, J. (2000). On the classification and diagnosis of pathological grief. *Clinical Psychology Review, 20* (1), 57–75.

Strunk, W., & White, E. B. (1979). *The elements of style* (3rd ed.). New York: Macmillan.

Swim, S., St. George, S. A., & Wulff, D. P. (2001). Process ethics: A collaborative partnership. *Journal of Systemic Therapies, 20,* 14–24.

Tamas, S. (2009). Writing and righting trauma: Troubling the autoethnographic voice. *Forum Qualitative Sozialforschung/Forum: Qualitative Social Research, 10*(1), www.qualitative-research.net/index.php/fqs/article/view/1211/2641

Tamas, S. (2013). Who's there? A week subject. In S. Holman Jones, T. E. Adams, & C. Ellis (Eds.), *Handbook of autoethnography* (pp. 186–201). Walnut Creek, CA: Left Coast Press, Inc.

Taylor, C. (1977). Interpretation and the sciences of man. *The Review of Metaphysics, 25*(1), 3–51.

Taylor, C. (1985). *Human agency and language: Philosophical papers 1.* New York: Cambridge University Press.

Taylor, C. (1989). *Sources of the self: The making of modern identity.* New York: Cambridge University Press.

Tedlock, B. (1991). From participant observation to the observation of participation: The emergence of narrative ethnography. *Journal of Anthropological Research, 41,* 69–94.

Tedlock, B. (2000). Ethnography and ethnographic representation. In N. Denzin & Y. Lincoln (Eds.), *Handbook of qualitative research* (2nd ed., pp. 455–486). Thousand Oaks, CA: Sage.

Tillmann, L. M. (Producer and Director). (2014). *Weight problem: Cultural narratives of fat and "obesity."* Orlando, FL: Cinema Serves Justice Films.

Tillmann, L. M. (Producer and Director). (2015). *Off the menu: Challenging the politics and economics of body and food.* Orlando, FL: Cinema Serves Justice Films.

Tillmann-Healy, L. (2001). *Between gay and straight: Understanding friendship across sexual orientation.* Walnut Creek, CA: AltaMira Press.

Tillmann-Healy, L. (2003). Friendship as method. *Qualitative Inquiry, 9,* 729–749.

Tillmann-Healy, L. (2009). Body and bulimia revisited: Reflections on 'A secret life.' *Journal of Applied Communication Research, 37*(1), 98–112.

Tilley-Lubbs, G. A. (2011). 4/16: Public tragedy collides with personal trauma. *Qualitative Inquiry, 17*(2), 144–147.

Tilley-Lubbs, G. A. & Bènard Calva, S. (Eds.). (forthcoming). *Retelling our stories: Critical autoethnographic narratives.* Rotterdam: Sense.

Tolich, M. (2004). Internal confidentiality: When confidentiality assurances fail relational informants. *Qualitative Sociology, 27,* 101–106.

Tolich, M. (Ed.). (2015). *Qualitative ethics in practice.* Walnut Creek, CA: Left Coast Press, Inc.

Tompkins, J. (1987). Me and my shadow. *New Literary History, 19*(1), 169–178.

Toyosaki, S., Pensoneau-Conway, S. L., Wendt, N. A., & Leathers, K. (2009). Community autoethnography: Compiling the personal and resituating whiteness. *Cultural Studies ↔ Critical Methodologies, 9*, 56–83.

Tracy, S. J. (2004). The construction of correctional officers: Layers of emotionality behind bars. *Qualitative Inquiry, 10*(4), 509–533.

Tullis J. (2014). Self and others: Ethics in autoethnographic research. In S. Holman Jones, T. E. Adams, & C. Ellis (Eds.). *Handbook of autoethnography* (pp. 244–261). Walnut Creek, CA: Left Coast Press, Inc.

Turner, V. (1967). *The forest of symbols: Aspects of Ndembu ritual.* Ithaca, NY: Cornell University Press

Turner, V. (1974). *Dramas, fields and metaphors: Symbolic action in human society.* Ithaca, NY: Cornell University Press.

Van den Hoonaard, W. C. (Ed.). (2002). *Walking the tightrope: Ethical issues for qualitative researchers.* Toronto: University of Toronto Press.

Van den Hoonaard, W. C. (Ed.). (2011). *The seduction of ethics: Transforming the social sciences.* Toronto: University of Toronto Press.

Van Maanen, J. (1988). *Tales of the field.* Chicago: University of Chicago Press.

White, H. (1980). The value of narrativity in the representation of reality. *Critical Inquiry, 7*, 5–27.

White, J. (forthcoming). *Permission: The international interdisciplinary impact of Laurel Richardson's work.* Rotterdam: Sense.

White, M., & Epston, D. (1990). *Narrative means to therapeutic ends.* New York: W. W. Norton.

Woolf, V. (1929). *A room of one's own.* New York: Harcourt, Brace.

Yalom, I. (1991). *Love's executioner.* New York: Penguin.

Yalom, I., & Elkin, G. (1991). *Everyday gets a little closer: A twice-told therapy.* New York: Basic Books.

Zimbardo, P. G., & Duncan, N. (2012). *The demise of guys: Why boys are struggling and what we can do about it.* Seattle, WA: Amazon Digital Services.

Zinsser, W. (2001). *On writing well: The classic guide to writing nonfiction.* New York: HarperCollins.

Zola, I. (1982). Tell me, tell me. In I. Zola (Ed.), *Ordinary lives: Voices of disability and disease* (pp. 208–216). Cambridge, MA: Applewood Books.

Index

About the Authors

Arthur P. Bochner is Distinguished University Professor of Communication at the University of South Florida and one of the leading figures in autoethnography and personal narrative. His most recent book, *Coming to Narrative*, won best book awards from both the National Communication Association (NCA) Ethnography Division and the International Congress for Qualitative Inquiry. Bochner has received career achievement awards for his teaching and research from the Southern Communication Association and the Eastern Communication Association as well as Ohio University's Elizabeth Andersch Award. He is coauthor of *Understanding Family Communication*, coeditor with Carolyn Ellis of two influential edited volumes on interpretive ethnography—*Composing Ethnography* and *Ethnographically Speaking*—and coedits the "Writing Lives" book series. He has authored over 100 refereed articles, stories, and book chapters on personal relationships, personal narrative, autoethnography, qualitative methods, and the philosophy of communication. Bochner served as president of the National Communication Association in 2008, was elected an NCA Distinguished Scholar, and was honored with the career Legacy Award from the NCA Ethnography Division in 2014.

Carolyn Ellis is Distinguished University Professor of Communication and Sociology at the University of South Florida and one of the leading figures in autoethnography. She was honored with the 2012 Lifetime Achievement Award in Qualitative Inquiry from the International Congress for Qualitative Inquiry (ICQI) and with the career Legacy Award from the National Communication Association (NCA) Ethnography Division in 2013. In 2014, the NCA awarded Ellis and Arthur Bochner the Charles H. Woolbert Research Award for their 2000 chapter, "Autoethnography, Personal Narrative, Reflexivity: Researcher as Subject," which has stood the test of time. In 2015, she was honored with the title of NCA Distinguished Scholar. Her book *The Ethnographic I: A Methodological Novel about Autoethnography* is the foundational work on autoethnographic methods. *Revision: Autoethnographic Reflections on Life and Work* (2008) received both the Cooley Award of the Society for the Study of Symbolic Interaction and the outstanding book award from the ICQI. Equally well known are her groundbreaking autoethnographic studies, for example, *Final Negotiations: A Story of Love, Loss, and Chronic Illness.* She also has coauthored two books on autoethnography with Tony E. Adams and Stacy Holman Jones. Her current work involves compassionate interviewing and storytelling with survivors of the Holocaust.

Lightning Source UK Ltd.
Milton Keynes UK
UKHW022137260321
381070UK00004B/88